IT'S A GREAT LIFE
IF YOU DON'T WEAKEN

FAMILY, FAITH, AND 48 YEARS ON TELEVISION

DAVE LOPEZ

Cassie Abby Hallie Elaine Henry, Inc.

LONG BEACH, CA

Disclaimer: This book reflects the author's recollections of his personal and professional experiences over the span of several decades. No names have been changed, no characters have been invented, and no events have been fabricated. The author includes accurate dialogue to the best of his ability to recall the details of his individual conversations.

Published by:
Cassie Abby Hallie Elaine Henry, Inc.
LONG BEACH, CA

ISBN-13: 978-0-578-37010-1 (print) / 978-0-578-37011-8 (ebook)

Edited by Carol Killman Rosenberg
www.carolkillmanrosenberg.com

Cover and interior by Gary A. Rosenberg
www.thebookcouple.com

Cover photo by Su E Tan, courtesy of CBS

Photos in Chapters 9, 10, 11, 13, 14, 16, and 17 courtesy of CBS.

Photo in Chapter 15 courtesy of Todd Bigelow.

Photo in Chapter 19 courtesy of Southern California News Group/The Orange County Register.

Printed in the United States of America

THE BEST DAY OF MY LIFE

Gregory M. Lousig-Nont, PhD

Today, when I awoke, I suddenly realized that this was the best day of my life. Ever.

There were times when I wondered if I would make it to today . . . but I did.

I'm going to celebrate what an unbelievable life I've had so far: the accomplishments, the many blessings and, yes, even the hardships and heartbreaks—because they have served to make me stronger.

I will go through this day with my head held high and with a happy heart. I will revel at God's seemingly simple gifts—the morning dew, the sun, the clouds, the trees, the flowers, the birds. Today, none of those miraculous creations will escape my notice.

Today I will share my excitement for life with other people. I'll make someone smile. I'll go out of my way to perform an unexpected act of kindness for someone I don't even know. Today I will give a sincere compliment to someone who seems down. I'll tell a child just how special he is, and I'll tell someone I love just how deeply I care for her and how much she means to me.

Today is the day I quit worrying about what I don't have and start becoming more grateful for all the wonderful things God has already given me. I will remember that worry is a waste of precious time and energy, because my faith in God and His Divine Plan ensures everything will be just fine.

Tonight before I go to bed, I will go outside and raise my eyes to the heavens. I'll stand in awe at the beauty of the stars and the moon, and I will praise God for these magnificent treasures.

As I lay my head down on the pillow, I will thank the Almighty God for the best day of my life. And I will slip into the sleep of a contented child, knowing that tomorrow is going to be the best day of my life, ever!

—Gregory M. Lousig-Nont, PhD,
in *Chicken Soup for the Cancer Survivor's Soul*

It's a great life if you don't weaken.
—AL LOPEZ

*I was born in Tijuana, and I learned
to shine shoes at a very young age.*

*I tell people that sometimes, but I'm just kidding.
Of course, it wasn't really like that . . .*

Contents

FOREWORD

AS A TELEVISION REPORTER FOR 48 YEARS on the Channel 2 CBS outlet in Los Angeles, Dave Lopez became as hallowed a part of the Southern California landscape as the Dodgers, sunshine, earthquakes, race riots, surfing, landslides, infamous murders, congested freeways, movie stars, Lakers, hillside fires, and crooked public officials.

Mr. Lopez became sort of a TV weathervane, as his presence on the screen so often would be an indicator of a major event unfolding from serial killers being captured to O.J.'s famous voyage up the 405 to massive out-of-control, house-burning conflagrations to raging civic eruptions to so many tragic and poignant and uplifting and bizarre tales that to relate them all would entail an *Encyclopedia Britannica*-like endeavor.

But, remarkably, Dave Lopez has done just that in his riveting autobiography, *It's a Great Life if You Don't Weaken,* that kept me immersed from the moment I started reading it to its conclusion in a book I found so absorbing that it inspired me afterward to plead with Mr. Lopez to write a sequel.

Now I've never been a person who engages in hyperbolic praise—I have gained a lengthy list of detractors through the years for my less than favorable assessments of their work—and I have read countless memoirs across the decades.

Some were quite good, others quite boringly banal, but none engulfed me like this one in which Mr. Lopez skillfully threads three narratives throughout the nearly 290 pages.

One is on his close-knit family of five brothers and two sisters and his conflicted relationship with his stern father and adoration of his mother, another on his long first marriage that produced two children and ended so sadly and then the unexpected pleasure of a second marriage, and, of course, another recounting some of his most memorable reporting assignments that includes a frightening five-day stay in Mogadishu, in the East African country of Somalia in 1991, when the country was in the midst of a raging civil war and his playing an impact in bringing down Orange County Sheriff Mike Carona and his testifying at the trial of the Freeway Killer William Bonin and so many other similarly intriguing vignettes.

Mr. Lopez relates his anecdotes in prose not embroidered with excessive adjectives and polysyllabic words, and his language flows seamlessly with a wryness, irony, and humor that aptly keeps your attention. No straying in this entertaining yarn.

Dave Lopez gained a well-deserved reputation—he earned an impressive nine Emmys—for being a master storyteller in his TV appearances and he has translated this innate knack throughout his book.

He idolized his father, Al Lopez, an immigrant from Mexico who became a professional fighter, who worked hard and through guile and perseverance started a successful upholstery business in the small enclave of South Gate, who broached no dissent from his kids and kept everyone in line with an intimidating resoluteness.

Dave Lopez's father took his son to the first Super Bowl game on January 15, 1967, between the Green Bay Packers and Kansas Chiefs at the Memorial Coliseum, and also to the South Gate Arena and Olympic Auditorium to watch fights and to long-gone Wrigley Field at 42nd and Avalon in LA to watch Pacific Coast League games featuring the hometown Angels and to the Coliseum to watch the Rams.

It isn't surprising that Dave Lopez gravitated towards athletics and that he became a sportswriter while at South Gate High School penning articles for the *Huntington Park Signal.*

Mr. Lopez would go on to college at Cal State LA, and, in a maddening series of consequential occurrences, soon would hook on with Channel 9 in LA before departing for a San Diego station, from where he would be lured back to LA in 1977 by Channel 2.

There he would remain until he retired on June 30, 2020, and one of the many pleasures in this book were his insights on the inner workings of TV news and the turmoil endemic to it and the constant turnover of personnel in the wake of the latest Nielsen Ratings.

Dave Lopez worked for 20 news directors during his career, or as Mr. Lopez himself says, survived 20 news directors, as he somehow escaped the dark fate of so many of his cohorts who were ushered out the door.

But, in retrospect, it's a rare development that's not so startling, for from his beginnings in TV he faced obstacles that conspired against the longevity that he would attain.

In those long-ago days, Hispanics weren't exactly plentiful on LA TV newscasts—Henry Alfaro and Tony Valdez were among the very few—yet Dave Lopez not only endured for almost a half century but gained a well-respected reputation among colleagues and viewers for his laudatory work.

Mr. Lopez has become a trailblazer, a groundbreaker in his profession who has written a glowing book that perfectly encapsulates his life and its joys and sorrows and immense achievements.

—Doug Krikorian
Sportswriter, sports talk show host, and author of
*Between the Bylines: The Life, Love and Loss of Los Angeles's
Most Colorful Sports Journalist*

INTRODUCTION

YOU HAVE TO KNOW WHEN to leave the party, and my timing when I retired in 2020 after forty-eight years as a reporter could not have been better. I received a steady paycheck every Thursday starting in 1972 until the day I officially left my longtime home at Channel 2. That's simply unheard of in this industry. Even more surprising was my sheer staying power. News is a brutal business where reporters come and go, but I outlasted twenty news directors without once being fired, suspended, or relocated to nowheresville. Though once or twice I was sorely tempted, I never stomped off the job or threw in the towel. None of the usual fates that befall reporters ever happened to me. I was lucky. I had fun. No . . . I had a ball!

This is partly the story of a life spent chasing the stories and reporting the news, but I have no desire to rehash in great detail the many thousands of events I covered. Born and raised in Los Angeles, I was on the scene for every major story in my hometown for close to five decades. Earthquakes, fires, floods. Elections, politicians, school boards. The Hillside Strangler, the Freeway Killer, the O.J. Simpson circus. And the true passion of my life: sports. Five Dodgers World Series. The Rams. The Kings. UCLA basketball. And, of course, what I became best known for: countless human-interest stories—regular people caught up in funny, tragic, or otherwise extraordinary events.

Way back when I started on this journey, there were very few, if any, Hispanic reporters on the air. Even today, there is no network anchor with a Hispanic face or surname leading national English-language nightly newscasts. Not even right here at home, where Hispanic people make up half the Los Angeles population. In some ways, I blazed a trail, but this is God's honest truth: I never even gave it a thought. I was not naive enough to believe I lived in an unprejudiced world, but I never let it slow me down. It's not at all remarkable that I overcame any prejudice, but I do believe I was particularly well prepared to face whatever the world threw at me due to my upbringing.

That's what this book is really about. The families who shaped me . . . the family I grew up in; the family my late wife, Elaine, and I raised together; and the family I enjoy today with my grandchildren and current wife, Diandra. The story of the Lopez family is a truly American story, and I credit my families with giving me everything I needed to go after all my dreams. When I look back on my life, I feel like Lou Gehrig, Iron Man of the New York Yankees, the day he gave his moving goodbye speech to the game he loved. I truly consider myself the luckiest man on the face of the earth.

My very first job was writing up sports for the *Huntington Park Daily Signal* in high school. Back in those days, every time you finished a story, you wrote the number 30 in the middle of the typewritten page and circled it. That was official newsroom procedure: the number 30 signaled that the story was done, no more changes or editing to come. The final copy with its "30" was then submitted to the desk. We had no fax machines back then, much less the internet.

I decided to officially retire on June 30, 2020, because that date represented the perfect cap to a career that was so fully complete, there couldn't be one more elaboration or punctuation mark added to it. Now, I am ready to mark a big 30 on these recollections and hand them over to you, my readers.

Thank you for allowing me to share so many stories.

CHAPTER ONE

SO MANY QUESTIONS

I SPENT HALF A CENTURY CHASING DOWN STORIES and reporting them to the best of my ability. One of the biggest regrets of my life is that I never pressed my father harder about his own story. So ironic; I was a reporter, and I always carried the necessary equipment with me. If only I had sat him down, pulled out my tape recorder and video camera, and made him talk. I would have said, "Dad, tell me about when you were growing up . . . what was it like when you were a kid?" But I didn't. Life was busy. I always meant to do it, someday . . . and now it's too late.

THERE ARE SO MANY HOLES, so much my five brothers, two sisters, and I will never understand. The facts I do know came piecemeal, gathered bit by bit over the years, usually while driving with Dad in his old blue work truck on the way to a job. Like all Americans, the story of the Lopez family begins somewhere else. For me, a first-generation kid, all this history is not so long ago and faraway. But the picture is hazy; so many of the "whys" will remain a mystery.

My paternal grandfather, a gentleman named David Santini and my namesake, was a prominent Italian architect. He used to travel to Mexico City to design and oversee construction on buildings. He lived in the city off and on for long periods while his projects were active. When he was in his early fifties, he began an affair with a local Mexican woman named Paula, only eighteen years old, my paternal grandmother. Along came a son they named Antelmo—Memo, for short—my dad, born in 1926. For several years, the family enjoyed a good life. Unfortunately, Signore Santini had a bit of a drinking problem. When my dad was three years old, the architect was drunk at a worksite, fell off his own building, and died from his injuries. That was the end of what had been a comfortable life in Mexico City and a swift decline for Mom and son.

With Signore Santini gone, there was no longer any money coming in. Whether my young grandmother was grief-stricken and simply couldn't cope or felt too overwhelmed handling a child on her own with no money is unclear. My dad never elaborated on his mother's reasoning on such a life-altering decision: she gave up her son. Dad was soon named a ward of the court and lived in a series of foster homes throughout Mexico City for the next five or six years, till he was eight or nine.

In one of the few stories he ever recounted about his childhood, Dad said he remembered staying with a family who lived in a second-story apartment. "I can see it so clearly," he told me. "Me standing there watching a bunch of kids down below playing jacks in the courtyard. I was on the balcony, alone, just watching through the bars. They didn't want me to play. So I pissed on them." Perhaps it's needless to say, but he was immediately kicked out of that place and shuffled on to the next. This went on for five long years. It became well known in the system that Memo was trouble.

Memo's mother had a distant cousin named Santos Ybarra, who was anxious to leave Mexico and live in America, where he already worked. Santos and his wife, Socorro, lived close to the border. Every Monday, Santos met his group of fellow fruit pickers at the assigned place in a border town and crossed into Texas as part of the Bracero (manual laborer) program. While in Texas during the week, the men lived in a rough camp. It was hard labor, but they were paid in American dollars.

Santos was a bit of a wild card. He loved to drink, loved the women, and particularly loved to smoke pot . . . but he got caught. He appeared in front of an American judge and received a warning. Then he got busted a second time. The judge was really angry. This time he said, "If I ever see you again in my court for marijuana, after six months in a Texas jail, you will be deported so far into Mexico you'll never see the light of day." None of this boded well for someone who wanted to move permanently to the United States.

That night, one of his fellow workers told Santos, "Hey, I can file your finger pads so that you have different fingerprints. I'm also really good at copying signatures and forging documents. I can give you an entirely different name and identity."

Santos took the guy up on this offer and was rechristened *Santos Lopez* on his new "official" papers. Immigration was easier as a family unit. Santos needed a child, while Santos's cousin needed someone to care for Memo. Adoption pending, the new Lopez family of three crossed the border and settled in Alamogordo, New Mexico.

Life was not smooth at first. Immigration regularly raided

Dad's local grammar school on their rounds. Dad was literally chased through the schoolyard by officials and deported back to Mexico several times. With Santos's help, Dad kept coming back. Finally, the adoption became official, and the family was left alone. The little family moved to East Los Angeles and settled there. Santos worked on the railroad . . . more backbreaking labor, hammering huge spikes into the ground all day long.

Socorro was a tough woman, very hard with a cold nature and stern manner. She was not the easiest person to warm up to. She took a job at a commercial laundry, the kind you see in old movies, with huge overhead presses. It was hot and exhausting labor, but she made good money. Socorro was nothing if not a hardworking woman—and she did have a soft side.

Shortly after their arrival in California, Dad came down with a mild case of polio. There was very little the doctor could do, but he advised rubbing Dad's legs with a special ointment. Day after day, Socorro spent hours massaging Dad's legs. "That woman was so dedicated to making me well," Dad recalled fondly. He considered Santos and Socorro his true mom and dad. They raised him, which was not an easy task. (I would eventually come to know Santos and Socorro as my grandparents.)

Dad was a tough street kid who was always in a scrap. He graduated from John Adams Junior High in LA. At the age of seventeen, he lied about his age and became a boxer, fighting under the name of Al Santini. Dad wound up graduating from Roosevelt High . . . but, for a period of time, he was a student at Jefferson High, one of the oldest high schools in the Downtown LA area. Knowing Dad, he probably got kicked out and was forced to change schools, but who knows.

What is certain is that one fall morning he was still a student at Jefferson, standing in a long line outside the nurse's office. The school was giving every student some sort of inoculation. Dad tapped the pretty girl standing in front of him on the shoulder and said, "Don't worry . . . if you fall, I'll catch you." And that's how my mom and dad met.

My mother, Matilda, known to all as Tilly, was the second-youngest child of ten living in Mexico. Her father died suddenly of a heart attack when she was only three and a half. Her baby sister was two. At that time, her oldest brother, who was already studying in the United States, was twenty-one. Whatever Tilly's father did for a living, he made sure his family was well provided for. When he died, he left my grandmother a $20,000 life insurance policy. In 1929, that was a small fortune—enough to start a new life in a new country.

As a very old woman, my mother could still remember boarding the train and looking out the window as it chugged down the tracks into Union Station. The large family settled in East LA. The house was on 32nd and Avalon—the heart of current-day South Central. My grandmother never held an official job in Los Angeles, though she took in ironing and did sewing and embroidery jobs for people in the neighborhood. She still had a houseful of kids to raise. The three eldest were on their own, but there were seven to go. My grandmother never learned to speak English. She died in 1976 knowing only one English phrase: *Goddammit.*

The kids all attended Jefferson High, though admittedly, my mom was never much of a student. Her older sister Carmen was the real brain. Had she been alive today, she would undoubtedly have become the CEO of a large company. But Carmen had to drop out of school in the tenth grade to go to work and help support the family. She worked in a seamstress shop, the trade most of the family members took up. My mom tried it after leaving school but never liked it and instead took an office job at a trade school. Memo was her on-again, off-again but persistent boyfriend. They were madly in love, but courtship was not always smooth. Given Dad's hot temper, this does not surprise me.

At one point, they were on the outs, but Dad went by her house to see her anyway. My mom's older sister had a very teasing, hot-and-cold friendship with my dad. She greeted him that night at the door.

"So, where's Mati?" (That was Dad's pet name for Mom.)

"She had a date."

"With who?"

"I don't know . . . just some guy . . ."

My dad was furious. Mom's sister smiled, enjoying her little prank. But this was serious business to my father. Back in those days, guns and knives weren't common weapons. It was brass knuckles and chains, and Dad had both. He was going to do some serious damage to this date. So around 10 pm, my mother came downstairs for a glass of water. She had never gone anywhere that night; she'd been in her room the whole time. Through the window, she saw Dad's car and waved to him. He motioned her to come outside.

"What are you doing here?" she asked.

"Where is he? *Who* is he?"

"What are you talking about, Memo?"

"The guy, the one your sister said you went out with tonight. Tell me where he is."

"Memo, I didn't go out with anybody. Calm down, stop this. I don't know what you're talking about . . ."

It took a while, but she managed to convince him. She was always the only person who could soothe my dad. The photo she had of the two of them that she'd torn to pieces was carefully mended with tape and the romance was back on. I smile every time I look at that patched-together picture. They were just kids.

In 1944, World War II was reaching its zenith, and the country was desperate for fighting men. Dad was working after school and nights at a gas station on Seventh and Alameda. The draft board was grabbing young men right out of high school and putting them in the service. A large part of Dad's job involved gassing up huge tanker trailers that delivered crucial supplies for the war effort across the state and entire nation. So his boss wrote a letter to the draft board, saying that Dad was a critical employee and was needed at the station to keep the war effort moving. The government didn't immediately take him; he graduated from high school in June 1944. From there, it was straight into Army boot camp.

At basic training at Fort Bliss, Texas, Dad found himself with buzzed hair and a new uniform. He was one confused new guy in this diverse group of young men from all over the country beginning the arduous process of forming a cohesive fighting unit.

At the crack of dawn one morning, the sergeant came into the barracks. "Listen up!" he barked. "Garcia, Sanchez, Lopez, Hernandez, Rodriguez! Get up, be outside and on the bus in ten minutes." The sergeant turned on his heel and exited.

Dad jumped out of bed, showered, put on his uniform, and raced for the bus, having no idea where he was headed. The bus took the small group to the courthouse at Fort Bliss.

Dad stood up in front of the judge, who asked, "Who's the president of the United States?"

"Roosevelt," Dad responded.

The other four guys gave the same answer.

"Congratulations," said the judge and banged his gavel. "You're now all United States citizens." It was official. Al Lopez was an American.

For someone who did not take kindly to rules and regulations, Dad thrived in the Army. He soon found himself on a massive troopship headed to the Philippines. Dad got into a lively craps game onboard and won $4,000, a huge pot of money. He knew he was going to need protection with that much cash, so he paid a guy to watch over him and act as his bodyguard. He got beat up anyway and was handily relieved of his winnings. He always swore it was the bodyguard who did the dirty deed.

At the time Dad was drafted, the war was at a turning point. Truman had been told by the generals, "This is what we have to do: invade Japan. You're going to need two million troops for this operation."

Truman supposedly asked, "How many casualties?"

"We estimate about fifty percent survival rate."

Truman was shocked. "What are you talking about? We're going to lose *a million men* doing this? There's no other way?"

At some point someone high up mentioned, "Well, we have this bomb called Manhattan Project, but that's extreme . . ."

President Truman would go on to drop the bomb on Hiroshima and then Nagasaki, ending World War II and sparing my dad from invading the Japanese mainland. Which is why Dad told me more than once, "Harry Truman was the greatest president that ever lived, David. If it wasn't for Truman, I most likely wouldn't be here."

It is hard for me to picture my dad taking orders, but he must have taken them just fine and given plenty too, as he was a sergeant when he came home from the service. He and my mother married on April 19, 1947, and the newlyweds moved into a small house on Soto Street in East LA. It was one of two tiny houses on a large, barren lot. Santos and Socorro lived behind them in the other house. I was Mom and Dad's first child, born on February 10, 1948, and named for my Italian grandfather, the architect. When I got older, I used to tease Mom about the timing of my birth: "Whew . . . you guys made it just in time!"

Dad was employed as a sheet metal worker when my parents first got married. One day he reached over, and the deadly sharp blade just missed cutting off his hand at the wrist. The automatic safety latch had stopped its fall in the nick of time. It was way too close. "That's it. I'm not working here anymore," he told the foreman and quit on the spot. He decided he was going to be a hairdresser. Imagining Dad surrounded by ladies all day long, my mom said, "Oh no, you're not. You can forget that idea."

So, on a whim—and with the help of the GI Bill—Dad enrolled in an upholstery school after seeing an ad for trades open to veterans. He completed the course and showed a real knack for it. Dad was a true craftsman. He could design and make furniture from scratch and reupholster the oldest, most beat-up chair or couch and make it fresh and beautiful again. He took a job at Pacific Furniture on Avalon Boulevard and quickly became their master upholsterer.

One night, relaxing at home, Dad suddenly became ill. The family rushed him to the hospital, Mom carrying me in her arms. Diagnosis: An appendicitis attack, immediate surgery required. Aside from the pain, Dad was freaking out; he didn't know how he would pay for this. Socorro rose from her hard hospital chair in the waiting room and said, "I will take care of this." She walked home, lifted up her mattress, pulled out a wad of bills, and returned to the hospital while my dad was being operated on. She paid the bill in cash.

Socorro was completely devoted to me as her grandchild. She often told my mom, "You're going to have a bunch of kids. I can't have any. So give me David; I'll raise him." Of course, my mom said no, loudly and immediately, but that didn't stop Socorro. She made this offer to my mother every single day for the entire time we lived there. The offers redoubled once my little sister Susie came along . . . and then my brother Danny. Mom held firm that she appreciated all the help but did indeed intend to keep me.

I attended Breed Street, the local elementary school less than a block away. I used to just walk around the corner every morning. I didn't speak English very well because I spent a lot of time with both my grandmothers. My mother only spoke Spanish to her mother and mother-in-law, so that was mostly what I heard. Santos didn't speak much English either. My parents were perfectly fluent in English but spoke Spanish frequently at home. I was pretty confused about what language I was supposed to think in and speak.

I was sent to a special class in kindergarten to learn to speak better English and work on my stutter. The doctor told my parents that my mind was so confused over which language to speak that, as the words tried to emerge, I hesitated and stuttered. By first grade, I had begun speaking predominantly in English and never had an issue with stuttering again, but I was never again able to speak Spanish fluently. This was a shame because I couldn't communicate with my grandparents the way I wanted to.

I could pretty much understand what the adults were saying in Spanish, or at least enough to get the story. When they realized that we kids could pick up enough to follow the gist of a conversation they wanted to keep private, my parents switched to their own version of Spanish pig Latin. Other than that, they used English right along with us. However, we always knew when there was trouble. Boy, you better watch out if Mom's speaking Spanish . . . she's really mad.

As mentioned, Socorro kept bugging my mother about letting me come to live with them. She would not let up, and Mom started pushing my dad to move farther away. The Lopez family bought a house in South Gate in 1955. Mom had just delivered her fourth child, another son. Dad bought our new house for $7,100—his mortgage payment was $73.16 a month. Located at 9929 Pinehurst Avenue, the house was a two-bedroom, one-and-a-half bath with a spacious backyard. It suited our family of five just fine.

Old home movies, recorded in color, show a big family barbecue we held for my brother's christening party. This was for Little Jimmy, the latest arrival. A few months later came the annual Christmas celebration, with a huge, elaborately decorated tree and six or seven presents for each kid stacked up under it. Watching the films decades later, a sister-in-law jokingly remarked, "A color movie camera at home, back then, in the fifties! And I have never seen so many presents. I think your dad must have been in the Mexican mafia!"

Dad made an honest living, and we never went without. There was always plenty of food on the table. Mom raised the kids and was my father's partner in every way; it helped that she was a master at making things stretch. I never once in my life overheard my parents worrying about money, complaining about bills, or fretting that they couldn't afford something. We kids always showed up on the first day of school wearing brand-new clothes and shoes. We didn't take fancy vacations, but we'd always go somewhere every year.

I remember the thrill of going to Disneyland for the first time. I recall driving up the winding coast road to San Francisco; we stopped along the way to pick up my grandmother for the big trip. My dad was by far her favorite son-in-law. We went camping in the mountains. My dad coached our athletic teams. In short, it was a wonderful life for this growing family. The war was over, the economy was booming, and Southern California was a paradise. The future was wide open.

"Good luck follows us everywhere!" Dad said.

For many, many years, it did.

CHAPTER TWO

WILT ONLY SCORED 99 MORE POINTS THAN YOU TONIGHT

RIGHT FROM THE START, I was an inquisitive kid. I was endlessly curious, always fascinated with people and what they were talking about and all that was happening in the great big world outside of South Gate. I vividly recall the 1956 presidential election: Eisenhower against Adlai Stevenson. There was a photo in the paper of Stevenson sitting cross-legged, showing a big hole in the bottom of his shoe. The caption read: HE CAMPAIGNED SO HARD, HE WORE HIS SHOES OUT GOING PERSONALLY DOOR-TO-DOOR IN COUNTLESS PRECINCTS SEEKING VOTES.

Back in the 1950s, the powers that be at the *Los Angeles Times* believed their publication was too sophisticated to appeal to a minority audience. I felt the same way right back at them as a kid, even though I would later greatly admire Jim Murray, the *Times's* star sportswriter—even after he cracked that our beloved local UCLA coach, John Wooden, was so square he was divisible by four. My parents were loyal *Herald Express* readers.

Mom spent a good part of her days in the kitchen, preparing and cleaning up after meals for the always-growing family. She generally wore a housedress; she didn't follow the new fashion of pedal pushers. She was busy and on her feet all day and night . . . except for a few precious minutes after breakfast. Family came first, but after we were all taken care of, fed, and packed off to another day at school or work, she loved to relax with her coffee and sweet roll. She sat at the table in the rare peace and quiet for a quick read of the paper every morning.

I got my first job as a *Herald* newspaper delivery boy. I loved to read the headlines and stories . . . sometimes I'd get so caught up in reading an article I'd be late delivering my papers. I was captivated by the Profumo sex scandal in faraway England that made headlines for weeks, a very mysterious affair to my grade-school mind. The *Herald Express* was like a tabloid, the people's paper—this was their kind of story. Mine too. I had a burning desire to tell stories. From the time I was in the fifth grade, I knew that I was going to work as a journalist in some way. This tied in nicely with my other passion in life . . . sports.

∞

Dad loved boxing; he still worked out at the Main Street Gym, at the top of Angel's Flight downtown. He had a deluxe old-fashioned radio in his shop, which he explained, "cost me two black eyes and a bloody nose!" In his younger years, he used to appear in the preliminary rounds at the South Gate Arena—never the main event. The most he ever fought was a six-rounder. On Friday nights, the boxing match judges would award one fighter a special prize. One night Dad won Boxer of the Night and took home that radio. It played for decades.

Dad had only lost one fight, ever. Sometime before he married my mom, he was fighting out of town, in Bakersfield, and his opponent kept hitting below the belt and on the breaks. Dad complained loudly to the ref, who continued to ignore these violations. Finally, Dad snapped. As he told the story: "I'm in a clinch. And I just bit the guy's ear, as hard as I could, until it bled." He got disqualified and was summarily escorted out of the ring and hall. That was it. It was around that time Mom told him no more . . . she was not going to marry a fighter. Professional boxing was over.

Still, he kept up his routine. I used to sit quietly in the corner of the noisy gym and watch him hit the bags. Dad wasn't a big man, but he was muscular and in great shape. One night, we were sitting at the dinner table with piles of uneaten spinach on every plate. (None of us kids liked spinach—in fact, we hated it.) "You don't like your spinach, huh? I'll show you what it does," Dad said and took a bite. Then just like Popeye, he flexed his arm. He was wearing his usual T-shirt, the old-fashioned sleeveless kind made famous by Marlon Brando. All of a sudden, this huge bicep popped up from one of his skinny, little arms. Our eyes nearly bugged out of our heads.

Friday night fights were a tradition—brought to you by Gillette, super blue blades, with Don Dunphy giving the blow-by-blow. How Dad loved the fights. When someone he admired was boxing, he could barely contain himself. One night, one of his favorites won a hard-fought battle. Dad leaped to his feet, grabbed a living room chair, and marched around triumphantly, holding the chair over his head and cheering. Mom ran in crying, "Antelmo, Antelmo, put that down!" We kids didn't bat an eye. . . . Dad did get passionate about sports.

Dad and I also shared a love of America's favorite pastime—baseball. It had been quite an upsetting development when the Brooklyn Dodgers moved to LA in 1958, when I was ten years old. I didn't know much about them; the minor-league Los Angeles Angels were our hometown team. When the Dodgers arrived, they played at the Coliseum. Dad and I always sat behind the short left-field screen. One day, two guys sitting in the stands with us were having a fierce argument and really going at it. The point of contention was whether Willie Mays had ever hit into a double play—ever, in his career. One guy insisted he had; his seatmate insisted he hadn't. As they stood up and prepared to come to blows, Willie Mays hit into a double play. The argument ended abruptly.

The first year in their new home, the Dodgers were terrible, but in their second year, they made it all the way to the World Series. I was sitting right there next to my dad watching them live in the playoff game against the Milwaukee Braves. Gil Hodges scored, and they won the game. The legendary announcer Vin Scully intoned: "Gil Hodges scores . . . we go to Chicago!" We were on our way to the Windy City, the White Sox, and a historic World Series win. Great memories!

The Dodgers televised only eleven of their games each season, the ones they played in San Francisco. I used to make a scorecard by hand, sit in front of the television, and follow every minute. I was a devoted fan, just like my dad. When Dad took us to games at the stadium, I would look up at the press box and envision myself doing a story. At home, I used to call a play-by-play of the games on TV. If we couldn't go in person, we listened to many games on Dad's radio. Vin Scully, master storyteller of the game, Chick Hearn, and those unforgettable turns of phrase—their timeless voices will live forever in my memory.

My love for sports burned bright from my earliest days. The best times I had as a kid was going to live sporting events. Old Wrigley Field, on 42nd and Avalon—when I drive by that neighborhood today, I still get a lump in my throat thinking of all the wonderful moments I shared with my dad and brothers. Wrigley Field was built just like the original Wrigley Field in Chicago, and the Angels were the Cubs' farm team. Every Sunday they played a doubleheader. The first game was always seven innings. We would sit in the bleachers, just below the big scoreboard in right field.

My dad had developed a system whereby we could sneak down and enjoy the show from better seats. Around the third or fourth inning of the second game, when it was clear no one would be showing up, my brother and I would follow him down to the pricey section and enjoy the finale. Steve Bilko, Casey Wise, Gene Mauch, Carlos Bernier, Dick Stuart . . . blue skies, hot dogs and popcorn, the home team . . . these were magical afternoons.

Then there was football. The Rams had a program where you could buy one adult ticket—cost: three dollars and fifty cents—and with that one paid admission, you were allowed to bring five kids along. They called it Free Football for Kids. We used to go almost every Sunday to see the Rams. Sometimes we'd arrive early and visit the museum at Exposition Park. The Rams weren't great, but we attended faithfully. As we got older, I would take a friend and my brother would take a friend, and my dad would bring a kid from one of the teams he was coaching. My mom used to drop us off at the Coliseum where we'd all meet up. I remember sitting next to my dad the day the Rams played the 49ers. There were 103,000 people there that day!

Speaking of big games . . .

When the game ended, we would leave the Coliseum and walk down the railroad tracks to my maternal grandma's house, three or four miles away. It was a straight shot down the tracks on Jefferson. My mom would meet us there, and we'd all eat a hearty dinner. My grandmother loved to smoke but never actually inhaled, never even put her mouth on the filter. She simply liked to hold a lit cigarette in her hand. The ash would get long, longer, longer, longer . . . until it finally fell off. One afternoon, I was sitting in the kitchen watching her cook. The ash tipped off and fell into the beans. She just mixed it in without missing a beat. When I told my mother, she told me not to worry. The ash simply added a bit more flavor.

And my true love: basketball. The Lakers moved to LA in 1960 and played in the old LA Memorial Sports Arena. One day, Dad and I were out on a call, going somewhere to do an estimate on an upholstery job. "Hey, the Lakers are playing tonight," the customer mentioned as we were leaving. In those days—a much different, easier time—you could just drive right up to the Sports Arena and buy a couple of tickets at the window. So we stopped by to catch the game: The Lakers versus the St. Louis Hawks.

We loved to root for the UCLA basketball team. Crosstown rivals UCLA and USC used to play at a place called the Pan-Pacific Auditorium, where the Television City now stands. The venue was old and dilapidated even then; it was widely known as the B.O. gym because it stunk so badly. All the local high school tournaments were played there. As a little kid, I was utterly entranced by it all. Basketball was my game, and I was pretty good. I wasn't tall, but I was determined.

Dad coached many of our teams . . . and he was tough. No favors for his own kids. The night of February 10, 1959, my eleventh birthday, we had a game, playing a team that wasn't much of a challenge. I was a star on my own team, and I knew it. (Player of the year in grammar school and all that.) I planned to score twenty points that night. There wasn't a doubt in my mind that I would do it. After all, it was my birthday. I got out there and scored zero points and fouled out in the second quarter. Mr. Hotshot . . . not!

As we drove home that night, I was in a mighty sulk. I asked my dad, "Why didn't you take me out after I got my fourth foul?"

"Not my problem," Dad said unconcernedly. That was Coach Dad all right.

Our new house had a big backyard with plenty of room to play and roughhouse. But the best part of living where we did was our easy access to South Gate Park. One block down and across the street lay ninety-eight acres of paradise—a golf course, basketball courts, baseball diamonds, and soccer fields. We kids spent most of our time there, playing one sport or another. Fourth of July was a huge community party and my favorite holiday. I always played in the all-star game, followed by picnics, bands, and a huge fireworks display.

Dad was big in the South Gate Junior Athletic Association, which sponsored numerous kids' teams, complete with uniforms and support from local businesses. There were teams from all the local church leagues as well: Seventh-day Adventist, Lutheran, LDS, Episcopal, Brethren . . . kids everywhere. One day a pastor from the Brethren Church, a chubby little guy, came over to my dad and said, "Hey, Al, your teams always listen to you; they're very disciplined. Will you come over and chew my kids out? I need them to pay attention and behave."

Dad was a strict coach . . . but he always loved a prank or practical joke.

We were playing a game of football under clouds of fog. We shouldn't have even been there on such a gloomy, overcast winter night. From the sidelines, onlookers could barely make out the players on the field. The game wasn't going well, and Dad got frustrated. When one of the players came off the field, Dad said to him, "Hey, I need your jersey. Take it off." The kid obediently took it off and handed it over. Dad threw the jersey over his head and said, "Don't say anything." Then he raced onto the field, right into a huddle. Just like a player, though of course he wasn't. Both teams started buzzing . . . "Hey, *Mr. Lopez* is in the game!"

They hiked the ball to my dad, he ran with it, and the players on the other side tackled him mercilessly. They just piled on, literally jumping up and down on him. The ref called a fifteen-yard penalty for unnecessary roughness. The coach on the other side was absolutely screaming. "How can you call unnecessary roughness . . . That's the goddamn coach out there!"

Dad emerged from the pile of kids all bruised and banged up, with a huge smile on his face. At the end of the year, the Association gave him a trophy, which I still have. Probably intended to be a theater award, the trophy was shaped as the comedy/tragedy masks: one with a smile, the other with a frown.

The presenter said, "This was Al Lopez before he went into the huddle and after he came out."

Dad always found the time to coach our teams. He rose very early and came home every afternoon by four, in time to take us to the park and practice. Dad was doing quite well working at Pacific Furniture. In fact, because he was paid by the job, he was making *too* good a living. He became so proficient that the store owner eventually came to him to protest: "We can't have this arrangement anymore. This is costing us way too much money." Dad took this to mean he was being punished for being too good and efficient.

In 1960, when I was twelve years old, child number six was on the way. I overheard my parents talking late at night. Dad was saying, "I've got to do it now, Mati. It's now or never." My parents had a grand total of $400 in the bank. Dad took half their money—200 bucks—and rented a small industrial building on the corner of Tweedy and Atlantic, within walking distance of our house. He called it Al's Upholstery Shop. He was now his own boss, and this was a one-man show. Dad did it all: He sewed, he did the estimates, he bought the fabric, and he delivered the finished pieces. Instead of going to Riviera, you could call Al.

When it came to business, no one could turn on the charm like my dad. As one of his customers once said admiringly, "He could sell a freezer to an Eskimo in Nome, Alaska, in the middle of winter."

Dad had flair. When he delivered a sofa, he would go inside and set it up, arranging everything just so in the customer's living room. Just before he left, he would run out to the truck and return with a specially sewed piece of fabric to cover the back of the sofa, along with custom covers for the arms to prevent wear and tear. He'd always thank the customer and hand these extras over, saying, "No charge, I appreciate your business." The ladies loved that.

"Everyone likes something for free," Dad said, even though these "extras" were built into the price. He loved to wheel and deal, but it was backed up by hard work and plenty of it. Dad made a go of the new venture. For a year or so, things were humming along smoothly, but the space wasn't ideal for an upholstery shop. It didn't have a large rolling door, for one thing, which made the operation tough. Had I not become a reporter, I most certainly could have become a professional furniture mover. I wrestled hundreds of pieces of bulky furniture through tiny spaces over the years.

One day, Dad got a call from a man whose name was Ray Lopez. He owned an upholstery shop in South Gate called

Garfield Upholstery. Ray asked my dad, "So, you've been in business how long now?"

"About eighteen months."

"You doing OK?"

"Doing fine, still feeding my family."

"So, listen, Al," Ray Lopez said, "I'm going to make you an offer. I have a son who can't stay out of trouble. If I don't get my family out of here, he's going to wind up in prison. I need a new start. What I'm proposing is, I'll sell my business to you. I'll give you a good price. I've been in business for six years; I have an established clientele. I'm starting to have repeat customers coming in. What do you think?"

Dad took over Garfield Upholstery and its existing customer base. He decided to keep the name, as it was well known in the neighborhood, but he relocated to a rental space on California Street. Dad's furniture was dynamite. He had the magic touch. From my earliest childhood, he tried to teach me the art of upholstery, but the few times I tried, I damn near sewed my fingers together. I had zero talent and zero interest, but there was no question that I had to work for him. I was pretty much relegated to stripping off the old fabric at the beginning of a job and moving heavy couches.

On our drives to Dodger Stadium on weekends, Dad would drive through the heart of Skid Row, block after block of misery downtown. He'd say, "You can live like that, if you don't go to college. If you don't study, work hard, get a good job, that's how you're going to wind up." It was the same thing when we drove through Chavez Ravine, well before Dodger Stadium was built; at that time, it was just a ramshackle neighborhood full of dilapidated houses. "See that? This is the kind of house you could have. Don't want to go to college and get a good-paying job? Fine, you can live right here."

We would sit in the back seat with big eyes, looking at each other uneasily. We didn't want to live there.

"The only way you'll make a good living is if you find something you like. In fact, you should love what you do. Don't go to work every day begrudging the time, hating what you do," Dad told me many times. "Find something you're good at that a lot of people aren't. That's how you make money. Do something others can't do. I can make furniture; not everyone has that skill. Whatever you decide to do, be the best at it."

The date was March 2, 1962. I was fourteen years old and still the best player on my school basketball team. However, I was nothing if not realistic. I realized early on that I was not destined to be an outstanding athlete. I had the love for the game and the desire and the will . . . but I was not another Muggsy Bogues. Not too many five-foot-nine basketball stars out there . . . college ball did not lie in my future. However, I was one of those lucky guys who always knew what I wanted to do for a living. I was going to work as a journalist—somehow, some way. My dream was to be a sports announcer.

I had known from the time I was in grade school that being a reporter was my destiny. And once I made up my mind to do something, I did it. Even Dad used to tell me, "You're just a kid, and you act like you're twenty-five." There was some truth to that. I had plenty of friends, plenty of fun, but I was not a kid to fool around. I did not ever waste time, ever, with so many goals to chase. Everything I did had a purpose.

On this night, my purpose was to score a lot of points. From the first opening seconds of a big playoff game, our rivals at St. Aloysius focused all their defensive efforts on me. I could not get my hands on the ball. I didn't get even one shot off. I couldn't move without two or three guys crowding me. Their plan was devastatingly effective; I managed to score one point that night—from a free throw. Our team won the game, but I didn't care. Selfishly, I was only furious at being thwarted.

That night, Dad and I drove home from Loyola High in his work truck. I was quiet, absolutely fuming. He looked at me and said, "What's the matter . . . your team won."

"I didn't score any points today!" I complained. "Well, I mean yeah, I got one lousy point. I don't care who won. I can't believe I didn't score more points!"

Long pause. Then Dad said, "Hey, don't feel so bad. I wouldn't even worry about it. Wilt Chamberlain only scored ninety-nine more points than you did tonight." So he had, that very night, in one of basketball's all-time great victories in Hershey, Pennsylvania.

Fortunately, I redeemed myself several days later. In the final championship game, I hit a basket at the buzzer, and we won the game. The crowd went wild. I felt a little like Wilt Chamberlain!

Dad's business continued to thrive. On Memorial Day 1964, he took a huge step: he moved into his very own space. He hated to leave California Street and his kindly landlord, but a huge brick building, an abandoned auto shop, had come on the market, and it was perfect for his needs. Decades of accumulated car oil and grease covered the floors; we kids scraped away endlessly but eventually got the job done, just in time for move-in and a grand opening party. The new address for GARFIELD UPHOLSTERY was 4570 Firestone Boulevard . . . where it would stand for four decades.

Dad kept his business small, as he was very much a one-man show. He certainly could have grown bigger through the years, but he never wanted to. He had one employee, Ben, an upholsterer who worked for him for ages. Of course, there was also family. All my brothers gave working for Dad a shot—it wasn't like we had a choice.

My grandfather Santos was always around; my dad would find something for him to do. Santos had huge, powerful hands from working on the railroad all those years. Dad taught him how to tie springs tightly and carefully, and he became quite proficient. I never knew the wild and wooly Santos from back in the early days. To me, Santos was always a sweet older man, impassive Mexican Indian face under a hat and big mustache—just the nicest, gentlest grandfather. We called him Tata; Dad just called him Jefe, meaning boss. There were two people in this world who could tell my dad what to do: Santos and my mother. Otherwise, my dad did whatever the hell he wanted to do.

The shop was generally a happy place with the radio going and lots of laughter and joking. We learned so much about small business and salesmanship dealing with every kind of customer at the shop. The sheer variety of characters who would walk in off the street to inquire about upholstering or furniture restoration was fascinating. We watched Dad negotiate in awe. His business motto was "Courtesy, Reliability, Satisfaction." But every now and then somebody would come into the shop who rubbed him the wrong way. Dad would get pissed and throw the guy out of his shop: "Get outta here, I don't want your damn business!"

My brothers and I would be working in the back, and we'd peek out to see the insulted person leave, speechless, and then watch as their car sped away. We'd return to the back room, look at each other, and intone, "Courtesy, reliability, satisfaction . . ." and crack up. Good times.

Garfield Upholstery remained in business for forty-four years, a fixture in the neighborhood.

CHAPTER THREE

Mom Is a Saint

My dad was the man . . . and I worshiped him. Dad was the enforcer, the provider, the fixer, the authority. He was the undisputed head of the household. But it was my mom who really held it all together—she was truly the rock of our family. Without my mother backing him, my dad could not have become the success he was. She was behind him—or next to him—every step of the way with unwavering love and encouragement.

Mom took charge of the family. Dad never had to worry about his kids not being well cared for or eating good healthy meals. Homework, clothes, and cooking were all taken care of. Boy, did my mom ever work hard . . . no days off. As sure as the sun came up, she was always there, reliable cleaning lady/short order cook/nurse/driver/fixer of problems big and small. An actual Saint Matilda existed . . . she was the patron saint of large families, something I did not know until after my mom passed. The namesake could not have been more fitting.

We were blessed to have such a warm and nurturing presence around us—because, make no mistake, Dad was a handful. The truth is that he could scare the shit out of people with his volcanic temper. When Dad got mad, people would scatter. He could be absolutely wonderful one minute, laughing and joking, on top of the world. Two minutes later, you couldn't even talk to him. "Don't bother me, go on, get outta here!" he'd yell with a swift kick to the behind if we didn't move fast enough. These moods came without warning out of nowhere.

One afternoon, we were all sitting in the car, packed up to go somewhere. Dad had one thing to say about excursions. If any of us kids bitched and moaned, he'd say, "Get in the car. We're all going, and we're all going to have a good time, whether you want to or not."

For whatever reason that day, Dad decided he was going to sweep the front walk real quick before we took off. Something he saw displeased him, as he suddenly threw the broom at the house. He flung it as hard as he could, right through one of the front glass windowpanes. We were shocked.

My mother said, "Al, what are you doing?"

"It's my goddamn house. If I want to break a window, I'll break a window." He waved off her protests as he got behind the wheel. "Ahhh, I'll fix it when we get back."

"Al, we can't just drive off and leave the house like that!"

But we did. And he did fix it . . . after we got home.

Dad was not all work and no play; he was a fun-loving man. Apart from his devotion to sports, he read the daily papers and novels. He loved movies starring John Garfield and James Cagney, tough guys. Both my parents loved to dance. Every Sunday, they would go out with my uncle Charlie and his wife, Nena. I did not inherit this skill; I had two left feet. But could my parents ever dance! Back in the big band era, anywhere there was music, they could be found—at church functions, mostly. Fun Al was always ready for a party. He could charm the birds out of the trees. Unfortunately, his shadow side was always there, ready to erupt.

It was a different time; people—men in particular—would not have dreamed they needed help for such anger issues. I strongly suspect Dad had bipolar disorder, though he would have scoffed at such a label. The question is how much was genetic and how much was due to his chaotic upbringing. Those formative years of his childhood, between the ages of three and nine, being abandoned, unwanted, and shuffled around, had done serious damage. We all suffered for it.

Dad and I were in a stadium parking lot one day getting ready to leave a sporting event. A harried woman was nearby, screaming at her young son in Spanish and dragging him roughly by the arm. She was clearly overwhelmed. Dad walked up to her and said quietly in Spanish, "We don't do that in this country. I am an immigration officer, and if you do this again, I will take that kid away from you." He did not like to see any child mistreated. A loving family meant everything to him.

Our dad wanted a big family, and he sure got it. We stuck together. Fighting among the kids was not allowed; it upset Dad like nothing else when we battled. He'd say, "I was all by myself growing up. I didn't have any brothers or sisters! You all are lucky to have each other, and you will get along. You have to love each other!" Dad simply would not tolerate any disagreement within the family. That wasn't always easy . . . there were a lot of us!

I was the first and oldest son, followed by Susie. Then, in rapid succession: Danny; anniversary baby Jimmy, born on Mom and Dad's eighth anniversary in 1955; Victor; Albert; Terry, whose birthday was easy to remember because she was born on the day Sandy Koufax and the Dodgers swept the Yankees in the fourth game of the 1963 World Series; and Tony, the baby. As Mom's sister Carmen used to say, "Too bad they didn't have birth control pills back then, Tilly. You popped out kids like they were popcorn!"

We had two family traditions whenever a new baby was born. My dad would handcraft a rocking chair for the new baby, and my grandma, Mom's mom, would come to the house and take care of us while our own mom was in the hospital. In those days, after giving birth, women stayed in the hospital for three or four days. We loved having Grandma at our house. The language barrier was tricky, but we enjoyed having her around. Still, she would get everything so confused. Our lives were topsy-turvy as we couldn't find our underwear because she'd put it in a different drawer . . . the boys' T-shirts would be all mixed in with the girls' . . .

When my brother Victor was born, Grandma was once again in charge. Grandma packing lunch often meant a surprise in my lunch bag, but not always the good kind. My mother once told her, "The kids love egg salad sandwiches," and it's true, I did. One day during that visit, I was a bit anxious, wondering what I'd get for lunch. When I opened up my sandwich, there was a cooked egg patty stuck between two pieces of bread. Not egg salad, just egg . . . but she tried.

A few months later, Mom and baby Victor were doing well. My mother had to go somewhere, and Grandma came to babysit.

"Listen, he shouldn't be hungry," Mom said. "But if he is, feed him. I'm leaving a bottle in the refrigerator."

As soon as she left, Victor went crazy—red-faced, squalling at the top of his lungs. My grandmother frantically walked with him, then rocked him, trying to soothe him. He would not calm down, and Grandma was frantic.

"Grandma," I said, "feed him!"

My grandmother was a very big-breasted woman. She was so flustered that she simply yanked one boob out of her dress. It just flopped out, and she put my brother to her nipple. My brother's entire curly head simply disappeared—vanished in that massive boob. He stopped crying all right . . . I don't think he could breathe.

I was very close to five of my seven siblings growing up . . . the final two were much younger; it was almost child-raising in shifts. Much was expected of me . . . of us all. "I don't care if you don't have a pot to piss in or a window to throw it out," Dad told us. "You go somewhere, you're going to look good. You're going to be the best-dressed kids there. You gotta be sharp. You're going to have nice clean clothes, shoes shined." I had my own shoeshine kit as a kid. And you better believe I could practically see my reflection in my shiny shoes. Dad taught me how to do it right.

Such attention to detail was something the nuns at church appreciated. Mom and Dad weren't regular churchgoers. Getting up every Sunday morning and taking us all to church was not their regular habit, but they did insist that we kids attend. Sometimes they'd get a little lax about enforcing this rule, and we would skip Sunday services, but we always felt bad when we did. Catholic guilt was built into our education.

Dad was doing well at his own business . . . well enough to send us to private school. Starting in the fourth grade, I attended parochial school, St. Emydius in Lynwood. Tuition was due on the first day of the month. My mom would tuck the cash into an envelope, and I'd carefully put it in my uniform pocket. I'd go to the principal's office where the secretary collected the cash and marked my account as paid. Tuition was $12 a month. As the family grew and three and four Lopez children were there at the same time, they gave us a family discount.

The lessons from those days stuck with me for a lifetime. Before one of the biggest days on the calendar, the nuns always reminded us: "Remember, boys and girls, tomorrow is Good Friday. If you eat meat tomorrow, it will make Jesus bleed more on the cross." That one really got me. Another classic from Sister Mary Shawn was, "You know, God has a tape recorder and it's rolling all the time. Even if you don't actually say the words, your thoughts are recorded, and He knows them." My buddy Michael and I looked at each across the classroom in horror. Simultaneously, we mouthed, "We're screwed!"

I tried hard to be good. The values at home were crystal clear: Study and work hard. Do your best and make your mark. Always stand up for yourself; don't let anyone push you around. Be thankful for the many blessings you enjoy. What goes around comes around, so always do good. Help others. Love your family.

I also took my faith seriously; I even served as an altar boy. Sometimes, after we performed the Mass, a half-empty bottle of wine the priest used for communion might get overlooked. I was the designated grab-the-bottle guy. I used to snatch the bottle, hide it under my cassock, change, and then sneak out and meet my fellow altar boys behind the church. In my later years, I would attend hundreds of business functions serving the finest vintage wines and champagnes. To this day, the most delicious wine I've ever had were those few sips from a shared bottle, standing in the sunshine with my friends, joking and laughing. I will never taste anything finer.

∞

As our family grew, so did the house. New bedrooms and baths were added every couple of years. We lived in a constant state of construction. Dad didn't do anything by the book . . . he ignored the legalities. "I don't need a goddamn permit; who's gonna come inspect me? I'll do what I want to my own house," was his attitude.

Our big yard started to shrink as the house expanded. If we weren't in school or the park, my brothers and I were in the back, playing ball. Naturally our ball often landed in the yard of our grouchy neighbor, Frank. He was the classic mean old neighborhood guy telling kids to get off his lawn all the time. When we ventured onto his porch and knocked to ask for the return of our ball, he'd open the door and snarl, "Get outta here!" Then he'd slam the door in our faces.

My father grew tired of replacing lost balls. "Listen, David. You know what? The next time that happens, just yell over the fence to him as soon as he comes out. Ask him, 'Hey, why do you want to keep all our balls? You play ball with your wife?'"

Next time the ball landed in the neighboring yard and I saw Frank coming to get it, I yelled out, barely understanding the words. Frank immediately came over to see my father. In seconds, they were nose to nose, shouting. I don't know what the hell happened, but suddenly Frank turned away and returned to his own house. Next thing we knew, a couple dozen balls were flying over the fence. Baseballs, softballs, volleyballs, footballs . . . some we hadn't seen for years and long forgotten. Soon all of them lay in a heap in our yard as our neighbor's back door slammed loudly. There was no telling what my dad had said. We shrugged and kept playing as the light faded.

You could say Dad made his presence known in the neighborhood. One day, Dad and I were driving home from a job estimate when he saw a car he recognized. "Hold on!" he said and made a huge illegal U-turn to follow it. I was sliding all around; there were no seat belts back then. Dad pulled right up alongside the car and started motioning. I vaguely recognized the driver, a man named Fred who was also involved in the Parks Association. He looked surprised, then irritated as Dad started forcing his car over.

As we approached the park, the man pulled in. We followed close behind. Fred parked, got out of his car, and stood there. Dad slammed the truck into park and said, "Stay here."

Dad started right up as he walked toward the car. "Hey, come here. I got to talk to you." He got right up in his face. "I heard what you said about me, and it's bullshit. I keep hearing it. I'm going to kick the crap out of you right here and now. I am going to kick your ass. Get on your knees, right now!"

Fred got right down on his knees, saying, "I'm sorry. I'll never do it again, never." He was terrified.

My dad said, "You better not, I am telling you, I will kick your ass if I ever hear another word about this, ever again." Dad stomped back to the truck while Fred continued to apologize. He got in, slammed the door, and looked over at me, where I sat utterly still. "Don't tell your mother." And home we went.

That was outside. But inside . . . inside was Mom's domain, where it was warm and welcoming and something good was always bubbling on the stove. The house was immaculate—Mom was a strict housekeeper—but she managed to find time to chat. She could always be found in the kitchen, stirring a pot while holding a baby and a toddler grabbed at her legs. The phone had a long curly cord so she could move around freely.

How she loved to gossip. She'd be on the phone with somebody, saying . . . "You can't tell anybody about this, anybody, you understand? Yadadadada," as she passed on some family story or bit of movie-star gossip. Then she'd hang up and immediately dial someone else. "Lucy, listen . . . I want to tell you what happened, but you can't tell anyone, promise?" and she'd repeat the same story. This could go on all day . . . Mom was too much.

But she was never too busy to look at an injury, to console us, to referee a fight, to check homework—whatever she could do for us. Mainly she liked to feed us. Oh, my mother could cook; I still dream about her cooking. Mom could produce the spectacular dishes, seemingly out of thin air. A houseful of boys bursting into the house unannounced, ravenous after a long practice, didn't bother her a bit. She loved it, in fact. In just a few minutes, there would be a fresh, hot meal on the table for all. Every plate had at least three separate dishes, always, as rice and beans were a staple. I must have been a teenager before I realized that every meal eaten by every family in Los Angeles did not necessarily include rice and beans.

My mom was never happier than on holidays, where she reigned supreme. It wasn't unusual for her to host thirty people. Thanksgiving was always a feast. Full of delicious aromas, the house would be packed and tables extended, groaning under platters of steaming dishes. Kids would be running around everywhere, and adults would be sitting in the living room and outside in the backyard, where Dad would sip his favorite Hennessey.

On New Year's Eve, the family gathered for Mom's special white menudo (without chili) per the custom in Grandma's native region of Mexico. But the Christmas holidays are what I remember best. My grandmother had been born on Christmas Eve, so this was a meaningful family holiday on top of a holy night. All ten of my grandmother's children would gather at her home—after church, of course—with their own growing families for Tilly's famous tamales. There were dozens and dozens of cousins present as the years passed; it was a noisy, raucous party.

Gift-giving was a ritual. My grandmother sat in the place of honor on an overstuffed chair, daughter Grace next to her, with

pad and pen in hand. My grandma disdained wrapped gifts—
she only wanted money . . . for her old age, she used to say. So,
all she got was a huge stack of cards. She'd open each one and
immediately shake it to see what bill fell out. Then check the
card: who gave and how much? Who contributed what was a
big deal and was duly noted down by Grace. Minimum contri-
bution was twenty bucks, which back then was a lot of money.
If you didn't give at least twenty bucks, you got roundly booed
by the entire room. Cheapskate!

One year, however, there was an exception to the gift rule.
Dad had done some work for a man, restoring his furniture.
The customer mentioned that he was a portrait painter. He had,
in fact, painted Ronald Reagan's official portrait as governor.
Dad asked for a special favor . . . a small custom portrait of my
grandmother based on some of her photos. They reached an
agreement, and the result was simply gorgeous, a true work of
art. Dad carefully wrapped it inside a cushion and handed it to
my grandmother when the cards were done. When she reached
inside the cushion and pulled out this gift, she was speechless. It
hung proudly on her walls for years.

When my own mother passed, this long-ago gift was the
only thing I wanted from the house . . . the small oil painting
of my grandmother. It hangs in the place of honor in my own
home today, a happy reminder of those many wonderful Christ-
mases, with my mother at the very heart of every gathering.

Mom used to drop us off at school some days. This was
always hit or miss . . . as Mom would generally get lost or be
late. If one of my brothers or I called for a pickup . . . "Football
practice is over, Mom . . ." she would always say, "OK, *mijito*,
start walking. See you soon." Whoever was walking would generally run into her on our own street as she would have been
delayed leaving and then got lost on the way. We could be at the
park around the corner, and she'd get lost.

When I got a ride to school, I used to always give Mom a quick kiss before I got out of the car. When I was in the sixth grade, a couple of guys saw this one morning and tormented me for the rest of the day with loud smoochie noises. The next time she dropped me off, I leaned over and kissed her on the hand resting on the seat between us, so no one could see.

"What's this?" she asked, surprised.

I thought about that for the rest of the day and made up my mind. "If I want to kiss my own mom in public, I will!" And I went back to my regular habit, teasing be damned. I would always be Mom's *mijito*.

My dad reupholstered a front room set for an artist in exchange for this beautiful portrait of my grandmother. It hangs in my house today.

CHAPTER FOUR

BLESS THIS BOOK!

I WAS MOVING UP TOO . . . into high school at St. Pius the X, a large Catholic school in Downey. There were probably 300 kids in my class, fewer than twenty of them of Mexican or Hispanic heritage. In all my years of schooling, I never felt like I was different because I wasn't white. Maybe I was just too busy to notice any prejudice, but I truly never felt it. Mom and Dad never made a big deal about our heritage, so I didn't either. We were just another family in South Gate.

The sixties in California were supposedly about free love and dope everywhere . . . not at my house. I never took even one puff on a marijuana joint. This wasn't because I was afraid of the cops or authority figures. My old man would kill me, straight up. I didn't give a damn about the law; Dad was another story. I never was one to party excessively; I was busy working much of the time—if not at the shop, at my future profession. Pius didn't have a school newspaper, so when I was a freshman, I started one with the help of a wonderful instructor, Father Alvarez. The paper came out once a week. I did it all: I wrote the copy, edited it, and printed it. It was a hit.

The *South Gate Press* was our neighborhood paper, which was published twice a week, every Thursday and Sunday. Its offices were over by the public school, South Gate High. One summer day I was in the park and saw Joe, one of the administrators.

"Hear you have a school paper now," he said. "You know, I have to cover park events for the *South Gate Press*, but I really don't like doing it. Not much good at it, to tell you the truth. How 'bout you take over?"

I was more than willing. I headed over to the *Press* office the next day, walked in the front door, and introduced myself. "Joe wants me to take over writing the columns about park activities, so here I am." The staffer asked me for some work samples; I had brought a couple copies of the school paper. They were deemed satisfactory, and I was soon hired.

This was my first official journalism job: I started in the summer of 1964. I covered all the different events at South Gate Park; my pay was ten cents per column inch. When my stories appeared in the paper, I would literally take a ruler, measure the inches, and charge accordingly. The headline didn't count; pay started from the byline down. When the fall came around, I also started writing about the events at my high school.

I had some money coming in and some savings. I wanted a car, badly, and Dad and I did some looking. A lot of looking . . . for months. We found several prospects. Dad held my cash, $500, in his care for safekeeping. I was starting to worry we weren't going to find anything I liked that I could also afford. I woke up on the morning of my sixteenth birthday to see a small blue two-door Ford I'd driven and liked sitting at the curb. Dad had made that deal happen, though the price had been a bit out of my reach.

"HAPPY 16TH BIRTHDAY, DAVE" read the sign propped on the dashboard. I could not have been more elated. How I loved that car. It sure made me popular around the neighborhood, being one of the few kids with his own car. I was always the driver for my group of friends.

One night, we all went to a party where there was plenty of alcohol served. As usual, I didn't touch a drop. There were a few bottles left in a six-pack of malt liquor that one of my friends wanted to bring home with him. When I dropped him off last that night, I noticed he had forgotten and left the bottles in the back seat. No big deal. I pulled away, but immediately felt uneasy. Some sixth sense made me halt at the corner. I parked the car, grabbed the bottles out of the back seat, and set them carefully on the sidewalk. Then I jumped back in and drove toward home.

Not a half-mile later, I got pulled over. The officer came up to the window, looked at my license and registration, said something about how it was pretty close to midnight, blah, blah, blah. "Got anything to drink in the car?" he asked me.

I said, "No, officer."

He shined his light around the inside of the car, front and back seats, and then sent me on my way. My nerves were shot. I could not even bear to think about what would have happened if those bottles had been there. . . . Dad probably would have enrolled me in the Army. He would have driven me to the enlistment station himself, at six in the morning. The Lopez kids were straight arrows. We never got in trouble because we knew what the old man would do. The wrath of Dad was something no one wanted to face.

A few years later, one of my younger brothers would not be so lucky. My mother kept an immaculate house; she was constantly cleaning and straightening. One day, she was sorting the boys' dresser drawers and stuffed way in the back, behind the rolls of socks, was a small bag of marijuana. My brother was just going through a phase: teenager, long hair, a little rebellious. My mother called my dad at the shop. "Memo, come here. I found something in the boys' drawer. I think I know what it is, but I need you to take a look."

Dad immediately came home, and my mom handed over the small plastic bag. Dad looked at it and then said to my mom, "Where is he now?"

"In class, Memo. He'll be home in an hour."

My dad took a seat in the living room and waited. The moment my brother walked through the front door, Dad confronted one very surprised son. Let me just say, there were consequences. The rest of us tiptoed around for weeks after that and never forgot it. The mighty wrath of Dad had come down, and that teenage rebellion was over in a flash.

I got a call one day in June 1965 from man named Willis Arrington, who was the sports editor of the *Huntington Park Daily Signal*. He said, "I've seen your stuff; I'd like to hire you as a stringer." In newspaper jargon, that meant freelancer.

I said, "Great!"

I got a big raise . . . to 25 cents per column inch. This was an enormous boost and a big step up. I really felt like I was in the big leagues now. Soon enough, I started covering local high school sports in our area. I went to school and then attended whatever game was on that Friday night. I had a list of different events Willis asked me to cover, and I managed to get it all done. I was always busy, out of the house doing something. I was never one of those teenagers who wanted to sit home and do nothing. My mother used to say to me, "Why don't you just relax?" Simple: I was not a relaxed kind of guy. Never would be.

Still, I had a good time at Pius. I loved sports—I wasn't a star, but I played on all the teams. I had lots of friends. Since I was a kid delivering papers and deciphering headlines, I had always been interested in politics; I decided to give it a try myself at the end of my sophomore year. I ran for class president for my junior year and won, which really whetted my appetite for the whole process. I had all kinds of ideas to implement . . . one of which had already come to fruition. Pius now even offered an official journalism class.

Toward the end of junior year, I was cruising. It was time to consider senior year. I decided I was going to run for student body president, a major office. Only one problem: a classmate named John—a big, popular football player—was going to run against me. He would be tough to beat. So I approached him and said, "Listen, I have an idea of how we could make things work out for both of us. Why don't you run for senior class president, and I'll run for student body president? And then next year, we can work together and really get a lot accomplished."

I had learned a thing or two from Dad about making a deal. My plan worked like a charm.

My fourth period junior year was homeroom, which was basically just a free study hall period under the supervision of Father Woodman. I was involved in so many school activities:

the paper, junior class activities, and sports events. I hated to waste this free period when there was so much I had to get done, so every now and again, I'd just check in, then leave. Some days I'd just I'd skip fourth period entirely. I certainly wasn't breaking any big rules, like cutting class or smoking or something; I was just pursuing school-related activities, but Father Woodman didn't like it one bit.

The next day in class, he would always say to me sternly, "Mr. Lopez, you must be present for this entire period. Every day."

I always answered, "Well, I'm doing this, I'm doing that," politely trying to explain where I had been and why it was important that I finished my school-related tasks promptly.

Another teacher, Frank Karl, took great offense one day when I left study hall early to do something. In my mind, I was not wasting time; I was maximizing it. I was hardly a rebel, but these minor infractions were adding up. One day, I must have been having a rough day. When Father Woodman reproached me, I snapped, "You're making such a big deal out of nothing! You know I'm working on all sorts of school activities. I am getting things done, doing what I should be doing!" This sort of remark, at Catholic school in 1965, was absolutely unacceptable. You did not speak to a priest that way in those days.

A day or so later, the entire student body was at a rally at the football field celebrating the upcoming end of the school year. Suddenly, passed down the bleacher row, came a note with my name on it from one of the teachers saying, "Please report to Father Parnassus's office, immediately."

Father Parnassus was the principal. I wasn't worried. Why would I be? I was a good kid, the class president, a solid student, and on every sports team. This was all so minor.

When I reported to the office, the secretary ushered me in, and Father Parnassus said to her, "Close the door," as she left. She did so.

I was surprised to see Father Walsh there too; he was the vice principal at Pius. Father Parnassus got right down to business. "Mr. Lopez, we are suspending you from school for two weeks."

I was shocked. "What for?" I asked.

"Let's just call it insubordination. You are not following school rules."

I just stood there, hardly able to speak. To me, this was a bolt from the blue. I just couldn't believe it.

"I want you go directly to your locker and get all your books and go home."

Now I was angry. "Should I bring my religion books too, Father Parnassus?"

He was puzzled. "Yes, of course. Why would you ask me that?"

The words just burst out of me: "Because I want you to bless it before I shove it up your ass!"

Well, that did it. They got my father on the line immediately at his shop. "We are suspending your son David for insubordination. We need you to come here so we can talk about this matter. Also, we are not allowing him to drive his car home."

I was told to wait outside the office for my father to arrive. I collected my textbooks, religion included, and waited at the big glass front doors. Dad had taught us all to stand up for ourselves. I was not afraid of cops. I was not afraid of the principal. I was very afraid of my father. But where else had I gotten this attitude? I ran a silent defense in my head. It's not like I was some troublemaker! If there were rules, I followed them. But give me a legitimate reason for not allowing some minor deviation from one of the hundreds of petty regulations I had unthinkingly obeyed without question for the past ten years.

I was furious at being treated like such a child, so subservient. Class president, student body president next year . . . suspended for the last two weeks of the year. I fought down panic. Was I seventeen years old and finished?

Along came Dad, barreling up to the front of the school in his truck. He pulled a big U-turn in front of the building, tires screeching, and parked. As he strode into the school, he saw me waiting inside the main doors. He stopped.

"I'm out," I said simply.

"Wait here," he ordered.

Dad headed into the principal's office, the door closed behind him, and then all I could hear was a bunch of yelling. No surprise, the meeting got quite heated, quite fast. "Take your collar off," my dad told Father Walsh.

"Why would I do that?" he asked.

"Because I am not going to hit a priest, so take that collar off so I can knock the crap out of you."

Apparently, there was some discussion as to whether the cops needed to be called. Fortunately, they were not. Dad came out and said, "Let's go."

He got in his truck, I got in my car, and I followed him home to face the music.

On this day, Dad really took me by surprise. He didn't jump all over me. He was angry, but he laughed when I told him what I had said to Father Parnassus. I didn't get a whack with the belt or even grounded. Dad just said, "Look, David, you have to learn to control your temper."

I nodded reluctantly.

"Anyway," he continued, "you know you're not going back to that school." I knew that all right. "But what are we going to do?"

Memorial Day weekend was coming up, and Dad said, "Well, we have a family trip this weekend to El Paso. Why don't you give it a few days and think about your options?"

Regarding the trip to El Paso, somewhere along the way, Dad had managed to track down his birth mother. He had a half-brother in Mexico City, who he met with several times. Through this half-brother, he met his half-sister, Goya. She lived with her family in El Paso, and we considered them family. This trip would have been the perfect opportunity to learn more about Dad's childhood and his birth mother, who would live and die without my ever having met her. But I was a teenager with a great deal on my mind. I did a lot of pondering and planning.

As we made the long drive home from El Paso, Dad said, "So, what are you thinking?"

"Well, Dad, I mean, I have to finish high school. For the rest of my junior year, I could go to South Gate," the public school near our house. I knew plenty of guys from the park and our neighborhood who were students there. My father had done furniture work for many of the families in that school. Dad even knew some of the administrators, which made things much easier when I called to explain my situation. Not easy to transfer for the last three weeks of eleventh grade, but I did it. South Gate allowed me to finish my junior year there.

My mother accompanied me to the school to officially enroll me. She was already shaken by my dismissal from parochial school; she did not want her kids in public school. They were too rough, for one thing. It had been an effective threat, for years. When we acted out, she would tell us, "If you don't behave, I'm going to send you all to South Gate Junior High!"

We would all say, "NO! Don't do that!" and straighten right up.

Mainly, she thought public school allowed the students too much freedom. Sure enough, as we were walking up a flight of stairs, we spotted two students hiding in the stairwell, making out like crazy. The boy's hands wandered all over the equally eager girl. My mom was horrified. Poor Mom, she just wanted what was best for me; she was sure this was not it.

For three weeks, I took whatever classes had room to seat me. I managed to finish the year and get promoted on to senior status. Pius eventually sent over all my grades—modified grades, all marked lower than what I had truly earned. Chemistry, for example . . . I was a solid B student, but the report card read D. In every one of my classes, I had been similarly marked down. Of course, I wanted to fight it, but it just wasn't worth the battle. I threw up my hands and moved on.

My summer plans weren't changed; I worked as usual in Dad's shop and had all the work I could handle from the *Huntington Park Daily Signal.* I saw many of my new classmates at the park and planned to make the best of things. I wasn't devastated by this curveball, at all. I was fine with turning the page. School was only till I could get out there in the real world and find work as a journalist.

It was only much later in life that it would occur to me how momentous this event really was. I switched from one local school to another for my last year of high school—not a big deal in the grand scheme of things. But had I remained at Pius as planned, I would have missed out on one of the best things of my life. A few miles away, a pretty blond girl was also planning her own senior year at South Gate. This girl would fulfill my destiny.

CHAPTER FIVE

WHO IS THIS BLONDE?

I LIKED GIRLS JUST FINE, but I was never one of those guys who went crazy chasing them, like a couple of my friends. Some of this was my single-minded focus: sports teams, planning my future as a journalist, and working most of the hours I wasn't in school. I didn't have much spare time. I'd taken some girls out on dates, attended all the school dances, had a few crushes here and there, but I had never had a serious long-term steady girl-friend. At South Gate, I already knew some of the girls because I had played on teams with their brothers and just from growing up in the same neighborhood, but my final year of high school I didn't date much. As always, I was looking ahead.

Senior year somewhere new was not a difficult transition. I jumped into student life at South Gate High. I couldn't play sports because of a transfer rule, but I joined the basketball team and worked out with them, went to games, and did the whole routine. I just never played an official game. When spring rolled around, I joined the baseball team under the same conditions. I wasn't that great at baseball, anyway; I would have ridden the bench in any case. It all worked out fine.

The unexpected bonus was South Gate's terrific journalism program, headed by Ms. Tellez. She taught me so much about putting a newspaper together. I immediately joined the staff as sports editor of the school paper, the *Rambler*. I wrote a column called "Dave's Inside Track"—the title "borrowed" from a guy named Sid Ziff, who used to write for the old *L.A. Mirror* and later the *LA Times*. Could that guy ever tell a sports story! Technically, borrowing his title was plagiarism, and in today's world, he could probably sue me, but my column was a hit. Eventually I was named editor-in-chief. Things moved right along in my new school—I barely missed a beat.

Just to shake things up a bit, I signed up for a German class after years of Spanish. I decided to try another language my first semester. This is where I first encountered Elaine Ekberg. She was a classic All-American girl: blond hair, blue eyes, sweet face. The best thing about Elaine is that she was friendly to everyone, always waving, always smiling. Elaine had it all: she was a cheerleader, popular, a straight-A student, and a member of all kinds of clubs. I liked her immediately, but she was way out of my league. She had a boyfriend and plenty of wannabe boyfriends waiting in line. It never once occurred to me that she would pay any attention to me.

Second semester, I ran into her again, this time in a

physiology class with Mr. Scoles. One day, she came breezing into class and asked me, "Did you do your homework?"

"Yeah, I did."

"Oh, can I borrow it? You see, I had a date with Bob Barubi last night and came home so late, I didn't have time to get it done . . . it was a special occasion—"

"Sure," I interrupted, not at all interested in hearing the details of her date and handed it over. "Here you go."

Elaine handed my paper back to me after she finished copying, and we all turned in our assignments to Mr. Scoles at the end of the period. The next day we got our grades back. I got a B, which surprised me. I had been counting on an A.

At the end of class, I walked over to Elaine and asked, "Hey, how did you do on that homework?"

"Got an A," she said, showing me. *Very well done*, said the handwritten note next to her big red A.

"Wait a minute," I said. "You copied my work, right?"

"Yes," she said.

"Well then, how come you got an A and I got a B?"

Elaine was the picture of innocence. "I don't know, but I copied your answers, exactly. Thank you again, Dave! Okay, I have to run!" With a big smile, she headed out the door surrounded by a bunch of girlfriends.

The minor matter was over, as far as she was concerned. I should have just let it go, but that would never be my way. I approached our teacher, a short guy with big glasses. "Mr. Scoles, I don't want to speak out of turn here, but Miss Ekberg borrowed my homework, and you gave her an A, while I got a B for the exact same answers. I don't understand."

Mr. Scoles drew himself up to his full height and said, "Mr. Lopez, I am pretty sure it was the other way around. I know Miss Ekberg very well and her study habits. They are exceptional. I think you're the one who copied from her. That's why I gave you the lower grade."

As I looked at him with my mouth literally falling open, he admonished me sternly, "Don't do this again."

What could I do? I moved on. The end of the year was fast approaching.

A few weeks later, I saw Elaine walking on campus during a break. She was known for her sunny personality; this day, she looked uncharacteristically drawn and nervous. I walked up to her and said, "How are you doing today, Elaine? Is everything all right?"

I learned that her mother, Elinor, who was not well, was having major surgery that day; Elaine was distracted and worried. We sat to talk for a few minutes and had a nice little casual conversation. "Please don't worry, Elaine. I will say an extra prayer for your mother," I told her as I stood up to leave. She smiled for the first time. I didn't think much more of it . . . until a few days later.

In typical high school style, one of Elaine's good girlfriends, Brenda Abbott, sidled up to me in the hallway between classes. "So, Dave . . . what do you think about Elaine?"

Caught completely off guard, I said, "Oh, she's fine, nice girl. Very pretty."

"Well . . . " Brenda drew it out. "She kind of likes you. If you asked her out, I'm sure she'd go." She gave me a meaningful look and walked away.

Okay then! Of course, I had already asked another girl to go to prom and to join me at grad night the week following. These were two separate year-end celebrations where I'd need a date, so I'd asked Cathy, one of my sister's friends from Pius. She came from a big Italian family that lived over on Alexander Street. A bit younger than me, she was over at our house all the time, and I'd known her forever. She had grown into a really good-looking girl, but that no longer mattered. Elaine was my dream date, and she and I began talking all the time.

When I confided in my mother about this situation, she

quickly laid down the law: "Dave, you are still going to take Cathy. You cannot break the date, that would not be right, and I am not going to let you do it. Besides"—here came the clincher—"I know that she's already bought her dress. You *are* taking her."

Actually, Elaine knew someone at the local dress shop where all the girls shopped and told me that Cathy and her mother had been there, looking for a prom dress. She had tried on a few but left empty-handed. So, I knew that Cathy actually *hadn't* bought a dress . . . but this was all a lot of girlie stuff and the details of what was a major drama have faded. My mother was friends with Cathy's mother, a date was a date, and that was that. Long story short, I took Cathy to the prom, and Elaine went with her own date.

There was so much excitement for my high school graduation. I was the oldest and first in the family to graduate! There was a huge turnout from my family, minus someone important. Mom missed my high school graduation because she was giving birth to my youngest baby brother. Forever after I would tease Tony that I'd never forgive him for disrupting my big day. By that time, my mom had had it. She was thirty-nine years old when Tony was born, and it was a difficult birth with complications.

My dad still wanted more kids . . . he was hoping for an even dozen. Impatient as always, on a visit to the hospital he asked their doctor, who had delivered all of us kids, "Well, how soon can you fix her up so we can have another child?"

Dr. Earnshaw turned to my father and said, "You carry and deliver one, if you want another so badly. This is the last baby for Tilly."

We weren't halfway through grad night celebration when Cathy asked to be taken home. She had gotten wise in the week since prom; it was clear my heart was not at all in this date. She—and everybody else—could easily see the looks Elaine and

I were giving each other. Feeling sheepish, I dropped her off early and met up with Elaine for breakfast. We had so much fun together; we talked so easily. As the sun came up, we planned our first official date.

On June 11, 1966, I picked Elaine up at her house and met her parents. I then took her to a local place called Shady Acres for a game of miniature golf. I purposely let her beat me on the last hole by one stroke, though she insisted she had won fair and square for the rest of her life. Then we went to a place to get hamburgers, right off the Long Beach Freeway. Talking about our childhoods, we discovered we had both attended the same elementary school, Tweedy. But I had left in fourth grade to attend St. Emydius, the same year she arrived from a private school. We had just missed each other.

Elaine laughed as she reminisced about grammar school days. "Remember how the boys used to chase the girls during recess? If they caught us, they got to kiss us," Elaine said. "Dave?" She looked right at me with her big blue eyes. "I let them catch me."

I was a goner—hook, line, and sinker. I would never be far from Elaine's side again.

Elaine was a smart girl with a bright future. Her father was a longtime bottler at Hamm's Brewery. Each year, the company awarded two college scholarships to the son and daughter of an employee. This national award gave the winners a 100 percent free ride to any school that had accepted them. Elaine had flown to San Francisco for her personal interview in a hand-sewn dress at the beginning of our senior year . . . and she won. She had a stack of acceptance letters from a bunch of schools, but Elaine chose UC Santa Barbara—a beautiful campus a hundred miles away, and she would still be close enough to come home on weekends. A math whiz, she planned to study engineering. Her long-term goal was to teach.

I too had my own plans. It was a given that my dad's plan had always included me someday coming in to take over the business. I could run the business side, but there was no getting around the fact that I was simply not a master craftsman. I could take orders, call on customers, manage the vendors and paperwork, and do some odds and ends in the shop. But if I was going to be in charge, I would still need a master upholsterer. That aside, the real issue was that I wanted to be a reporter.

The *Daily Signal* had offered me a full-time job as a summer replacement. It took days for me to work up the nerve to approach Dad, but I finally did it. "Look, Dad, I've been offered a full-time job at the paper, and I'm going to take it."

He was quiet and sullen. No explosion. Just a "Well, good luck then."

I could see his anger and disappointment, but he had told us over and over our whole lives: "I don't care if you pick up trash for a living, as long as you're the best trash guy out there! If you wanna dig ditches, great, but you better be a goddamn great digger!"

There wasn't much he could say; I was on fire to tell stories. I was trying like hell to become the best reporter ever.

In the end, Dad was supportive. After all, I had five brothers. Also, it's not as if I was excused from work at the shop. I already had two jobs: my regular hours at the newspaper and the time I spent covering stories. On Saturdays, I was done at the paper by noon and then I'd hotfoot it over to the shop to help with deliveries and whatever else needed doing that day. Then . . . if I didn't have to cover an event . . . it was date night with my new girlfriend. We were quickly becoming inseparable.

The first time Elaine came over to my house for dinner, my kid brother Albert was suffering from scarlet fever. He was confined to his room, sitting in bed, dolefully picking off dead skin and dropping it onto a pile on the floor. That was her first glimpse of my sibling. What a first impression. There were some funny moments that summer as Elaine adjusted from a quiet house where she was an only child to mine . . . with seven other kids, the baby only weeks old.

That first time she had dinner with all of us was controlled chaos. That night Mom served corn on the cob. At our house, we didn't serve separate pats of butter; we just rolled our corncobs on top of a hard stick of chilled butter, leaving a groove in it. Elaine said politely to my mom, "Tilly, this is so nice. Wherever did you ever find butter shaped like this, just for corn?"

A couple weeks later, Elaine was visiting and wandered into the kitchen. She wasn't there two minutes before she raced out to find me. "David, I went into the kitchen and saw a boiling pot. I lifted the lid and saw a whole dead chicken inside . . . everything!"

"Yes, that's how my mom makes it," I explained. "From scratch."

She had never seen an entire raw chicken in the local grocery store. She was a trooper, Elaine—and the sweetest girl ever.

Things got serious fast. My curfew was midnight, no matter that I had graduated and had a full-time job. One night I lingered saying good night to Elaine, and I got in at ten minutes after twelve. I opened the front door as quietly as I could. My bedroom was far back at the end of a long hallway; I had to pass my parents' room on my left to get there. I came inside, took my shoes off, closed and locked the front door, and quietly tiptoed down the hallway. I got past Mom and Dad's door and down to my own my bedroom.

Out of nowhere, Dad's voice boomed in the quiet house. "Hey, you know what time it is?!"

I was so startled I dropped my shoes, making a loud clatter on the wood floor. We didn't discuss it the next morning. No need to say more. I was never late again.

Elaine's parents had Midwestern roots. Her mom had grown up with every advantage in a small town outside Chicago; she attended a posh secretarial school and became a top executive assistant. Elinor made excellent money; in today's society, she would have become a corporate CEO. She was stern and efficient; Elaine definitely toed the line. Not quite like growing up under my dad's iron thumb, but Elaine understood strict parents.

I hit it off with her father right away. Glen had grown up in a dirt-poor farming family in Nebraska with eight other kids; they really had it tough during the Depression. He had been a bottler at Hamm's for decades, just a solid working-class guy. Salt of the earth. Glen loved sports, and we got along famously.

Elinor was a bit tougher. She had that stereotypical strict Germanic demeanor and brooked no nonsense. She was a formidable woman. On top of that, she suffered from several health issues, much of them stemming from high blood pressure. This was still a mysterious malady and difficult to treat in the sixties. The operation Elaine had been so worried about had been a full hysterectomy, which was a very serious surgical procedure at that time.

When it became obvious that Elaine and I were head over heels, Elaine's mom drove over to my father's shop one day. She walked inside and approached my dad. "Mr. Lopez," she said, "I have big plans for my daughter. She has won a full scholarship. She is going to UCSB this fall, and she will graduate from college. I don't want your son interfering with her schooling or career that will follow."

"Well," Dad said, "I feel the same way. I also do not want your daughter interfering in my son's future plans or career. So we agree."

The parents were indeed all in agreement. After setting the ground rules, they got along quite well. Elaine spent lots of time at our house; I was happy to spend time at hers.

In those days, dating was much different; we used to go out with her folks for dinner all the time. On weekends, her parents enjoyed driving out to Rose Hills Memorial Park in Whittier; one of the largest cemeteries in the country, with its famous Pageant of Roses Garden. They loved to stroll the grounds, take in the views, and see the various roses. I thought it was a slightly odd activity: to visit a cemetery on weekends to look at flowers. But they simply loved it; they had their family plot there. I shrugged my shoulders. Hey, if that's what they wanted to do on a Sunday afternoon, it was fine by me.

The summer flew by. Soon enough, it was time for Elaine to enroll for her freshman year; I went with her parents to help her settle in. Parting was hard on us both, but there would be phone calls and letters, and she really wasn't too far away. It was time to turn my attention to my own career—get out there and see what I was made of.

I walked into the house one afternoon to find Dad, sitting on the couch, with several large pillows clutched on his lap. This was unusual, to say the least. Dad was always at the shop. I headed into the kitchen. "What's going on, Mom? What's Dad doing home?"

"I made him go get the clip," she whispered, making a scissors motion.

Poor Dad, sitting on the couch like a lost little puppy dog. With six sons and two daughters, the Lopez family would finally stop growing . . . just as I was heading out to find my own way.

CHAPTER SIX

NIXON SAVES THE DAY

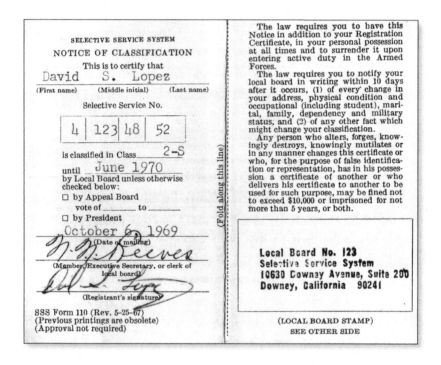

SELECTIVE SERVICE SYSTEM

NOTICE OF CLASSIFICATION

This is to certify that

David   S.   Lopez

(First name)   (Middle initial)   (Last name)

Selective Service No.

| 4 | 123 | 48 | 52 |

is classified in Class_____ 2-S

until ___ June 1970
by Local Board unless otherwise
checked below:

☐ by Appeal Board

vote of _____ to _____

☐ by President

October 6, 1969
(Date of mailing)

(Member, Executive Secretary, or clerk of
local board)

(Registrant's signature)

SSS Form 110 (Rev. 5-25-67)
(Previous printings are obsolete)
(Approval not required)

The law requires you to have this
Notice in addition to your Registration
Certificate, in your personal possession
at all times and to surrender it upon
entering active duty in the Armed
Forces.

The law requires you to notify your
local board in writing within 10 days
after it occurs, (1) of every change in
your address, physical condition and
occupational (including student), mari-
tal, family, dependency and military
status, and (2) of any other fact which
might change your classification.

Any person who alters, forges, knowingly destroys, knowingly mutilates or
in any manner changes this certificate or
who, for the purpose of false identifica-
tion or representation, has in his possession a certificate of another or who
delivers his certificate to another to be
used for such purpose, may be fined not
to exceed $10,000 or imprisoned for not
more than 5 years, or both.

(Fold along this line)

Local Board No. 123
Selective Service System
10630 Downey Avenue, Suite 200
Downey, California   90241

(LOCAL BOARD STAMP)
SEE OTHER SIDE

IT WAS QUITE A TIME to go out into the world to cover stories
. . . I had been in a happy bubble of home, school, and work,
covering local stories—mostly sports. And falling in love! But
the country was raging. In 1966, nearly 200,000 American troops
were in Vietnam. General William Westmoreland was *Time* magazine's Man of the Year. "The Ballad of the Green Berets" was
the number-one hit on the radio. Much more ominously for me,
the Selective Service (draft board) announced some changes to
their policies. Immediate conscription of high school graduates

was virtually a certainty . . . though deferments for full-time students remained in place.

I had zero desire to go to college; I was already doing the job I loved. But I realized that being a full-time student was the only way to avoid getting drafted. I did apply to the University of Southern California (USC), but my grades weren't quite good enough to qualify for a scholarship. I had seven younger siblings; no way was I going to USC without a lot of financial assistance. That dream ended fast, so I enrolled in East LA Junior College. It cost six dollars and fifty cents per semester, and the total for my used textbooks came to about fifty bucks. I was required to take thirty units per year to maintain my deferment.

My typical day started early. I was at my desk at the paper by 7 am. I would get off around 3 or 3:15 pm and head home, where my mom had something hot and delicious waiting for me to eat. Then I'd take off to school from 4 until 10 pm, four nights a week. Saturday was workday at the shop, of course, and I was also the trashman. Every Thursday night, I'd head over to the shop after class and clean up the entire place. It took a good few hours to get everything spick and span and in Dad's preferred order. I'd take out the huge piles of trash last thing, lock the door, and head home, where I fell into bed, exhausted. I was a busy guy.

I loved my job at the *Huntington Park Daily Signal*. My boss at the paper, Cliff Gewecke, had another gig working for the *Christian Science Monitor*; he also wrote lots of pieces for *Sport* magazine (now defunct, like so many great old papers and magazines). He concentrated more on those pursuits than on our little town newspaper, so I got to cover all the Dodger and Angels games, which was hardly work at all. Best of all, I covered the Rams, who were thriving under Coach George Allen. To top it all off: I made $68 a week! As Dad would say, "Well, pin a rose on your nose!" I had a new red Camaro and was quite the newspaper guy, racing around town at top speed to get the stories. That car was my baby!

One day my boss said, "Hey, USC has signed a running back from San Francisco City College. Supposed to be a real hotshot. He goes by his initials . . . O.J. I'm going to go interview him for *SPORT* and the *Monitor*. Want to tag along?"

Of course I did. We headed to a small apartment off Adams Boulevard where we met Orenthal James Simpson and his wife, Marguerite. His wife was sweet; their baby girl, Arnelle, was adorable. O.J. himself was charming and personable, polite and humble. He hadn't even played his first game for USC yet, but there was a buzz going. He was going to do big things.

Sam Skinner, another reporter I used to see around, told me more about this guy. "He's a phenom. He'll be the greatest thing to ever happen to USC; he's going to put them on the map. You've never seen anything like this guy."

I was in the press box for the *Signal*, covering the classic USC/UCLA game in 1967. Both teams were undefeated. USC was number one; UCLA was number two. The game was at the Coliseum, packed with devoted fans of both hometown schools. Everything was on the line. USC was trailing 20–14 as time was running out. O.J. took a pitch from the quarterback; USC called the play "57 Blast." O.J. made the most incredible run for a touchdown, and USC won the game.

Back in the days before cable, every household had a television set with an antenna. The channel lineup was simple: 2, 4, 5, 7, 9, 11, and 13. That was it. In January 1967, CBS and NBC were feuding about who got to air the very first Super Bowl game—Kansas City vs. Green Bay—from the Coliseum; the upshot was the NFL ruled that they could both broadcast it, but it would be blacked out in the Los Angeles market. Viewers would have to drive to Bakersfield to try to pick up the broadcast or rig up a coat hanger antenna to try to catch the signal at home. The

Herald Examiner published a helpful article complete with diagrams about how to accomplish this.

The game was scheduled to start at 1:05 local time on Sunday afternoon. At 11 am, Dad and I were up on the roof. I sat next to him, directing him from the page torn out of the paper while he fiddled with a coat hanger and various tools. Our neighbor, Al Holt, a butcher who lived two doors down, strolled by. "Hey, what are you guys doing up there on the roof? What are you trying to do?"

"Oh, trying to rig this antenna, so we can get this game to come in . . ."

Al nodded. "Oh, that's right. There's a football game today at the Coliseum. Well, you know," he said, reaching into his pocket. "Look here, I happen to have a couple of tickets for that very game. You two interested in going?"

Holy crap! We hurriedly climbed down the ladder. My dad examined the two $12 tickets—an astronomical price at the time but truly priceless to us. Al explained that the owner of the market where he worked knew I was a big football fan. When he was given two tickets from his top salesman, he passed them on to Al, saying, "Hey, you know that neighbor kid of yours, the sports-crazy one—think he'd like to go to the Super Bowl?"

"So, what do you say?" Al said on our sidewalk. We looked at him in disbelief. "Courtesy of Al Carrasco and The Shopping Basket. Go have a great time!"

We scrambled to get ready. Dad actually put on a suit jacket—not a tie, but a suit jacket. We were all surprised; he never got dressed up to go to a game. For this momentous occasion, he did. Dad and got I in the car and took off for the Coliseum. The game wasn't completely sold out—there were 67,000 fans there that day. We sat on the Kansas City side. Too bad, as I was a huge Green Bay Packers fan. I had to be really quiet and hold myself back the entire game. Dad and I saw the very first Super Bowl game . . . together. Green Bay won, 35 to 10!

Cliff Gewecke, God rest his soul, was a terrific mentor. He was superb writer but also a great teacher. Under his tutelage, I really learned how to write. At college, I was majoring in journalism, of course, with its required curriculum. I used to look at the class titles and shake my head: *How to Write a Headline, How to Lay Out the Page.* I didn't really need to learn this; I was doing it every day. Writing for newspapers taught me so much about the nuts and bolts of telling a story. But the main requirement for any writer was to get out there and talk to people. There was no internet or video conferencing; print reporters went to the scene and then returned to the office to type up and turn in the piece.

One night, when Elaine was home for the weekend, I parked near the office to finish up a column. I raced inside, got it done, and called Elaine to tell her I was on my way. We had a date that night. Not half an hour after I'd entered, I walked back outside. There was no car.

"Wait a minute, I know I parked my car right here!" I started running up and down the street. "Where's my car?!"

I hadn't even owned it for a year. My gorgeous red Camaro, with the competition stripe down the middle of the hood, four on the floor and bucket seats . . . gone forever. It was found a couple of days later downtown, gutted and stripped, up on four cardboard boxes. The thieves had taken an expensive trench coat from the back seat and used it as their rag. Coat and car were beyond salvaging. Now, if I wanted to get anywhere, including to see Elaine, I needed to replace my beloved Camaro—and eventually did, with a little Volkswagen.

When we were apart, I missed Elaine—all the time. I took off to visit her in Santa Barbara every weekend I could. Her first year away, I called her all the time . . . till the bill came in. My long-distance calls came to about fifty bucks, a truly outrageous

I LOVE you ELAINE,
IN FOUR years you
will be MRS. LOPEZ

DEC. 4th

Hello SweetheART,

I just got back from the RAM game. they
won 23-3 AND it was A pretty good game. Honey
All through the game I was thinking of you. Only
NINE MORE DAYS Honey — then it will be the 15th.
I'll be talking to you in about three hours
AND I can't wait. I sure miss you DARling, I
LoVE you very much.

IT's RAINING AgAIN AND A NEW storm is
suppose to be coming by tonight — my DAD is
coming. Really Honey, I kind of miss the old
grouch. All the kids ARE saying that VACATION
is over. When my DAD is home they all
jump, when he's not, they just Mess Around.

IT RAINED A little today At the game
AND I forgot my white hat — DARN it! LARRY
says I look like WALTER WINCHell with it
on. FRANKly, I think it looks good on ME.
WAIT till you see it, I know you'll love
it.

I'm in the back room now AND LARRY AND
Susie Are back here. They are playing hand-ball
AND it is sure noisey. My sister has a big
mouth. LARRY's grandma is in the hospital.
She has CANCER AND LARRY doesn't know what
he is going to do if she DIES. HE is staying
by himself now AND the poor guy is broke. My
MOM told him he could EAT over here whenever
(I LOVE you)

When Elaine left for college, she and I started
writing letters several times a week.
I still have them to this day.

he wants to. He told me he went to the M.P.
parade last night but he doesn't remember it. One
beer and he gets stoned out of his mind.

After I saw the UCLA game last night
I saw this real good army movie. That ended
about 11 o'clock. I was going to deliver (mail)
your letter then but my mom told me to
stay home. I went to bed and didn't wake
up until 10:30. Honey, I dreamed of you all
night. I pretended you were my pillow and I
held you so close to me. I love you so
much darling.

I left for the game at **NOON** and
that was my exciting day. Sweetheart, I
wanted so much to see you today. This morning
my mom said it was shocking to see ~~you~~ me at
the breakfast table. Honey, you make a better
breakfast — I have to give you some
confidence. In four years you should be a
good cook — at least you better be! I love
you, I love you, I love you so much Honey.

That stupid window still won't go
up. My car got all wet before and it's
raining hard right now. I'm fixing it tomorrow
for sure or else I'll drown. Honey, H.P.
won yesterday, 14-13. It was raining too hard
so I didn't go to the game but I heard
(I love you)

about it. They were losing, 13-8 and Otis
Colvin scored on a 60 yard run for H.P. with
5 seconds left to play. If only S.G. would
have beaten them I know we (S.G.) could
have gone all the way. H.P. sure is lucky.
   Well Sweetheart, I hope you aren't
getting nervous. Don't worry about your finals.
I know you will pass them. Honey, are your
head-aches gone? I sure hope so. Sweetheart
you are smart and I know you'll pass. Just
study hard, relax, and don't worry. I love
you Darling, the 15th is almost here. Four
years is almost here. I love you Sweetheart,
I love you very much, and I will love you
forever.

                    your lover + future husband
                         Dave
       P.S. Honey, my moustache is
          coming along real fine —

I LOVE YOU HONEY

DAVE López
9929 Pinehurst Ave.
South Gate, California

       Miss Elaine Ehberg
       Tropicana Gardens Box 132
       6585 El Colegio Road
       Goleta, California 93017

sum at the time, and Dad put his foot down. I remember the night I called Elaine once again . . . to say that we were not going to be able to speak to each other nearly as much. Dad refused to run up that kind of a tab, ever again. So Elaine and I started writing letters, several times a week. I still have them to this day.

I would have never been able to get through college while working full time without some serious motivation, and the draft definitely provided that. The thought of losing my deferment kept me going through long days and weeks. My second year, I was required to take economics—four units; we met once a week from 6 to 10 pm every Wednesday night. The class was excruciatingly boring; the subject matter didn't engage me in the slightest. During a really busy month at the paper, I missed a couple of classes. Twice that month I didn't go; I was just too exhausted. I couldn't just sit there for four hours. Then I came to my senses and put my nose back to the grindstone.

Too late . . . I got a letter in the mail from the draft board telling me to report for my pre-induction physical. Did that ever get my full attention! When I showed up, I protested that I was a full-time student. They, in turn, explained to me that I was not taking enough courses to be classified as full time and pulled out a transcript to prove it to me. Sure enough, the economics class wasn't listed.

If the "conflict" had been hot before, it was now a five-alarm fire. By spring of 1968, more than 800 American planes had been shot down, their pilots dead or missing, while thousands more suffered in POW camps. Public sentiment had turned against the war, yet President Johnson had approved 500,000 troops on the ground. If you weren't in college and had a Z in your last name, you were getting drafted; that was simple fact. Take a look at the Vietnam Memorial Wall and check the names sometime . . . the Latino community made heavy sacrifices.

I had to fix this. I drove to the college and camped in the hallway until I was allowed to see the dean. He was pleasant but no-nonsense. "Mr. Lopez, I dropped you from your economics class."

I protested, "Well, you didn't even tell me."

"Well, you didn't show up for two out of three weeks," he replied. "Of course, I dropped you. I don't need to explain that to you."

I explained my situation, and he relented a bit. "Well, I'll reinstate you in that economics class. And I'll write a letter to the draft board explaining that I did so, but that's all I can do. And you can't miss any more classes."

Of course I said, "Fine, absolutely."

The dean gave me the letter on the spot. I immediately raced back to the draft board the next morning, showed the officer my letter, and got it officially stamped. I kept my deferment. "But . . ." the officer said as I was turning to leave, beyond relieved, "you still need to take the physical, since you're here."

I walked a bit further downtown and entered a building directly across the street from the old *Herald Examiner* building on Broadway. I took my place at the end of a long, long line. There must have been about 150 guys, just standing there, all of us between the ages of eighteen and twenty, all scared, following the yellow line into who knew what. The tests involved four hours of getting poked and prodded and answering all kinds of questions. At the end, an officer said to the assembled group, "All right, you'll be notified when you'll be drafted." All except for the guy directly in front of me. He had some sort of condition in his legs, his veins or something, and flunked the physical. The doctor stamped his paper in red right then and there: FAIL. I'll never forget him . . . talk about lucky to flunk.

On the way out, an officer handed each of us a coupon. We

could take it to a stand around the corner and get a free hot dog and Coke on Uncle Sam.

I had been so very lucky. Dad had thrived in the Army; in fact, he loved military life. To me, the idea was utterly frightening. I lived to question authority. I tried to imagine being nearly ten thousand miles away, in hostile enemy territory, being told "March . . . take that hill!" Why the hell would I want to do that? I didn't care about any hill. My answer would be, "You take it!"

While I am grateful for the guys who could follow orders and made the ultimate sacrifice, I just wasn't cut out for that life, and for the moment, I had escaped. You better believe I showed up alert and ready for my economics class from that point forward.

Elaine and I were very much in love . . . but we both had big dreams. Hers was to earn her degree and become a teacher. I wanted to fulfill my career as a journalist and hopefully, someday, become a television reporter. For more than three years, I drove up to Santa Barbara two or three times a month. I'd fill up the tank of my little Volkswagen for two bucks and take off. Elaine and I always had a marvelous time together. And being so close to her parents, she came home frequently as well. The time we spent together was always magical.

Except the one time I found out Elaine had gone on a date. She'd attended a concert with a guy named Bruce. A band she loved was playing, and she went with him to see the concert at his college. They were just friends, she only wanted to see the show, but I lost it. I burned with rage. Elaine had given me a little ceramic doll, an ornament sort of keepsake. When I hung up after hearing about this "date," I grabbed that doll and threw it against the wall as hard as I could. It shattered into a hundred pieces. My little brother Danny saw me. He was shocked. "Wow,

Dave, you threw that really hard," he said, half admiring, half scared. But this was a minor kerfuffle. We knew we'd get married . . . someday. That was just a given.

Elaine was no slouch in terms of her own ambitions and drive. She graduated from UCSB in three and a half years and then immediately enrolled in an accelerated program at LA State College (later called Cal State LA) to get her teaching credential. She and a close friend, Fran, both enrolled under the tutelage of a great professor, Mr. Green. Being the superstar she was, Elaine earned her teaching credential in less than a year. She was awarded a special plaque—a teaching credential for life in the state of California, signed by Ronald Reagan, our governor at the time.

As always, I was looking for ways to advance faster. More efficiently. To keep working at the trade I loved. After graduating from East LA in two years, I immediately enrolled at LA State College. I had the grades, all my units were accepted, and everything was good. Except that, once again, there were a lot of courses I didn't really need; they were simply redundant. I was working full time, getting paid, and earning a raise every year.

I figured out what I needed: a course on plagiarism—a course about journalistic ethics. Those I definitely needed to attend. I loved my new school: the very first time I went to LA State, they had a tiny television broadcast set up. I jumped in front of that camera every chance I got. I was forever practicing, standing in front of a mirror with a hairbrush in my hand, to comment on what was going on around me in a "broadcast." I "announced" every time I was alone in the car. I wanted to be on camera, someday. For the moment, I concentrated on print.

The rest, not so much. I made an appointment with the head of the journalism department and showed him some of my work. I said, "I've been doing this work now, full time, for three years. Tell you what, is there any way I could just monitor some of these classes; show up once a week, and have the teacher give me the assignments I need, which I will complete. I don't need an A; I will accept a C."

I wasn't shooting for grad school or advanced degrees. My adviser agreed, and my schedule lightened up. I suddenly had a bit more breathing room. I spent all the extra time working at the newspaper—and, finally, planning a wedding!

Four years had flown by. When, at the beginning of 1970, I was told during registration, "You're going to graduate this term!" I was surprised. *How had that happened?*

Elaine and I began making plans for a traditional June wedding. Just one cloud on the horizon . . . I would, of course, lose my student deferment upon graduation. This was a big problem; some of my buddies floated the idea of enlisting in the Merchant Marines. By joining the Merchant Marines, the chances of going to Vietnam were slimmer, and we certainly wouldn't be carrying a gun on the front lines. If we got drafted into the Army or the Marine Corps? Straight to the front lines.

Enrolling in the Merchant Marines was a six-year commitment. We would serve on active duty for six months and then return home. There was compulsory service once a year, and anytime over the next five and a half years, we could be called up to serve full time. Still, it seemed like the safest bet. When I told Dad about it, he exploded. "No! You're not going to volunteer for shit! You don't volunteer for anything in the military. The worst thing you can ever do is volunteer. You don't put your hand up. You don't step forward. You don't volunteer for crap. You're not going, you're not doing it."

I could have signed up, I was over eighteen, but I still feared the wrath of Dad more than any authority. Three of my buddies went ahead without me and enlisted.

And then, and then, like a miracle . . . President Nixon stepped in and instituted a lottery system for the draft. All those American males eligible for the draft were put onto a list. Then every birthday of the year was put into a big fishbowl, and dates were drawn out one by one. If your birthdate was pulled out on the first draw, you were number one in line for the draft—and so on down the line. The first year the lottery was instituted, they stopped at #182 before meeting their quota. My number was 185. I literally fell to my knees in church. I lit candles and said, "Thank you, Lord. Thank you, from the bottom of my heart." In an echo of Dad, I would forever after swear that Nixon was the best president ever. His lottery saved my future and possibly my life.

My three friends who volunteered for the Merchant Marines all got draft numbers in the high three hundreds . . . but it was too late. They had already enlisted. Only one wound up actually serving overseas, and it was not in the raging hotspot of Vietnam; they all survived unscathed as they did their duty. It was the other guys I saw coming home that broke my heart. Guys from the neighborhood, guys I had played with in the park, guys who been my classmates and fellow altar boys. When they returned from combat in Vietnam, they were not the same young men I had known all my life. Some of the wounds were obvious: missing limbs, limps, scars. Some were less visible. Still, a light had gone out in all their eyes. It was a terrible, terrible war, and it was sheer blind luck that I missed it.

This was such a tumultuous time in the country's history. The nation was utterly divided on this ongoing conflict—protests, draft card burning, riots, and emigrations to Canada. We would not see the likes of it again for another fifty years.

∞

Elaine's family, the Ekbergs, were faithful Lutherans. I knew from the start if Elaine and I were going to stay together, I would have to give in on religion. I would have to switch churches and attend Lutheran services and agree to raise our children in that faith. I was happy to do so, and I liked their church fine, though sometimes I would go to Mass on Saturday afternoon and then attend services with her family on Sunday morning. My faith was important to me, no matter where I prayed.

There was no question where the wedding would be held: South Gate Redeemer Lutheran Church on Liberty Boulevard, Elaine's longtime place of worship. We spared no expense. It was a large wedding with 250 guests. My immediate family, of course, made up a big contingent! We had a band, a caterer, and a reception at a country club in Downey. The catering alone came to $3.25 a head . . . but that was fine. I was feeling flush . . . I had $7,000 saved up in the bank, a steady job I loved at the *Huntington Park Signal*, and a nice little apartment lined up for us in Long Beach. But all that really mattered was that I was marrying the only girl for me.

The wedding was all that we hoped for. The church was packed with my enormous family plus all the bride's Nebraska relatives, who had flown in for the occasion. Elaine was a radiant bride in a gorgeous gown. I was resplendent in a bespoke suit from a downtown tailor. My brothers could not resist one last joke. They got ahold of my shiny dress shoes and wrote HELP and ME on the soles. Every time I knelt during the ceremony, the message flashed out to the packed church. I never did find out which one was responsible; they refused to own up. I have my suspicions.

My youngest brother Tony was now four; he served as the ring bearer. I had rented him a tiny tuxedo, and the guy at the shop warned me, "You must bring this back cleaned, pressed, and in good condition . . . otherwise, you buy it." Tony was warned, several times, to be careful that day.

Elaine and I followed the custom of not speaking to each other on the big day before the ceremony. At our reception, Tony immediately went outside to the putting green and frolicked, standing on his head and doing flips and handstands as delighted guests threw money at him. I watched through the glass window as he ripped a huge hole in his pants and came up beaming. Just then my new wife came rushing up to me. "Dave! I got offered a job at Patrick Henry Elementary!" Her dream job, in a dream location: Long Beach. It was the perfect place for Elaine, who loved kids. This was the cherry on top of the happiest day . . . though I did have to buy Tony's tuxedo.

We took a two-and-a-half-week honeymoon . . . the first vacation I'd had in years. We headed east, to visit Washington, D.C., Philadelphia, Boston, and even Montreal. Then we returned to our brand-new apartment and our jobs. I was twenty-two years old, Elaine was twenty-one, and we were headed off into the adult world.

CHAPTER SEVEN

THE GREATEST WRITES A POEM

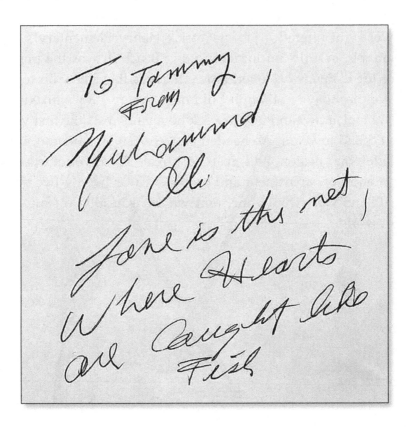

LIFE AS A NEWLYWED WAS GREAT. I was making $127 a week at the paper, and Elaine was on her way to becoming the most popular and beloved teacher at Patrick Henry Elementary. The new Mrs. Lopez taught kindergarten, the perfect classroom for her. It was a bit strange to leave the only home I could remember, though for the past several years, it had been mainly the place I changed clothes, slept, and got fed and fussed over by my mom as I raced out the door to cover the next game or story.

Now I was also part of a new family, and I could not have asked for better. Glen, my new father-in-law, was a good man who loved the Cornhuskers. Elaine adored him; married or not, she still affectionately called him Daddy and doted on him. Shortly after our wedding, Elaine's mom suffered a complete nervous breakdown. When the timing was appropriate, I had to joke, "You know why she had this breakdown after the wedding? Because that's when she finally found out that I'm Mexican!"

Jokes aside, she had had an acute mental and physical crisis, triggered by being dosed with the wrong medicine. Elaine's mom was never the same again. She could no longer work; she could barely take care of herself. Glen didn't blame the doctor; they were longtime friends. Their doctor had done his best for years on a difficult case; he too was devastated. Though I advised him to look into his legal options, Glen took on his wife's care uncomplainingly. Elaine and I did our best to help. We visited our parents most Sundays, right after church at Redeemer.

"How are you doing, Mom?" I'd ask my own mother, and she'd be off on the latest family tale or bit of gossip. Tilly was too much. One afternoon, she started telling me all about their new neighbor. "That lady, Dave, who moved in three doors down. She has five kids. Who in the world would have five kids in this day and age?"

I almost choked on my sweet roll. "MOM!" I said. "You had eight—there are still six here right now!"

She reconsidered. "Oh, well, I guess that's not so bad then. More coffee, *mijito*?"

At some point, Dad would usually say, "Hey, you doing anything right now? I told this lady that I would deliver her sofa whenever I could get some help . . ." So we'd hop in the truck and off we'd go delivering furniture, just the two of us.

By this time, Dad had mellowed somewhat. "David," he used to say, "I have learned some things. I made all my mistakes with you." He was different with the younger kids—far more tolerant of the noise, the back talk, the minor infractions. The three youngest kids, particularly, had an entirely different Dad experience than the one I lived through. I could only shake my head at what they were allowed to get away with.

Driving home from work one day in September 1970, I saw a sign: LONG BEACH CABLE, a Times-Mirror Company. I walked right in to the small, utilitarian office and introduced myself. I told the man holding down the fort that I was an experienced reporter who worked for a newspaper.

He said, "You know, we're thinking about putting a broadcast together."

LBC was a real old-time local cable station, not like we envision "cable" today. Long Beach Cable covered the Long Beach and Palos Verdes areas and was largely funded by a wealthy Palos Verdes dad whose kid loved soccer. A car dealership sponsored a block of time so his kid's games could be televised.

"We're going to start covering local high school games. Also, we have a deal signed with Long Beach State to cover men's basketball . . . so, do you do sports?" the staffer asked me.

"You bet, been covering local sports games for years," I replied. I called a couple of football games as an informal audition and did OK. I was soon hired. I don't know about being a natural, but I absolutely jumped at this opportunity be in front of the camera. I was a bit concerned about how I looked, sure. But nervous, never. This was all I wanted to do!

Long Beach Cable might have had a grand total of maybe thirty people watching our programming at any one given time, but I didn't care. I looked at it as my start in the Los Angeles market. Kids' soccer quickly became the bane of my existence; I hated it. But I also got to cover Long Beach State basketball, which was on fire under its new coach, Jerry Tarkanian. Men's football was pretty good too. Apart from soccer, I was having a ball.

I used to leave work at the newspaper every afternoon, hustle over to the cable station, and be on the air at 5:30 pm reading the straight news. I would take that day's *Press Telegram* and retype stories out of that to read on air. I was able to just ad-lib my sports segments. Whatever minimum wage was at the time, that's what I made as a TV reporter at Long Beach Cable, so I kept my day job. Appearing on cable was not good for my pocketbook, but it was invaluable experience.

My schedule was hectic, but Elaine and I enjoyed going out to dinner whenever we could. We had "date nights" well before that became a trend; our first year of marriage was charmed. Then Elaine came home from school day and said, "So, Dave, I've been looking, and I found some neighborhoods with really nice houses."

I was surprised. "We're kind of young to be getting into that whole house mode, aren't we?" I was content in our cozy apartment.

But Elaine kept insisting. "No, Dave. We need to invest. I don't want to live in an apartment forever."

That's how we found ourselves signing the papers on our first house on a date very close to our first anniversary. In July 1971, we moved into 17938 Santa Valera Street in Fountain Valley. The purchase price was $36,100; our monthly payment came to $214.31 a month. I was freaking out. What were we taking on? How would I ever afford this? Home was now a big two-story, four-bedroom house. We were both anxious for some kids to come along to fill it up. But it had already been more than a year, and Elaine had not yet become pregnant. The waiting was hard on her; she was disappointed month after month. So, we made an appointment for a checkup.

We discovered that Elaine had high blood pressure, which we hadn't known. She also suffered from a liver condition called non-alcoholic steatohepatitis (NASH)—a big phrase for a fatty liver that causes inflammation and damage. Elaine was only twenty-three years old and didn't drink or smoke, so this came out of left field. She would forever after be on medication for both conditions, and we were advised that pregnancy might not be as easy as we thought. We adjusted to her medication schedule and restrictions and hoped for the best.

Another day Elaine called me up and said, "I was in a pet store and found the perfect dog for us. A doxy beagle."

"Okay, fine. What's a doxy beagle, anyway?"

"Oh, Dave, he's just as cute as can be. So friendly, so lovable . . ." On and on.

"Okay, Elaine, how much?"

"Well . . ." Elaine hesitated. "Twenty-five dollars."

I exploded. "You're not going to pay twenty-five dollars for a damn dog! We can pay like two bucks and get one from the pound! You're out of your mind. That is just crazy; forget it."

"Too late, Dave, I already paid it. Knocky is home with me and can't wait to meet you!"

Knocky quickly won me over. He was a wonderful little dog who would share our lives for the next seventeen years. We installed a little doggy door, and housetraining was a breeze. Perfect behavior; no problem whatsoever. I'm embarrassed to admit it, but to this day, I have a portrait of our doxy beagle hanging in our garage.

One Tuesday I had a rare afternoon off work. I was sitting at home in my living room with Knocky watching a news show called TEMPO on Channel 9. Two male anchors were discussing the death of a local celebrity: Frasier of Lion Country Safari in Irvine. This was a big attraction in our area, a spot off the freeway where you could take a "safari" and see real lions. Frasier was an old, decrepit lion from England who revived at his new home in California and started siring all kinds of cubs. He had a harem of devoted female lionesses and adorable cubs everywhere trailing him. The passing of Frasier the lion was big local news.

The anchor said, "And now, Fernando's got a bulletin for us from Lion Country Safari . . ."

Their reporter, Fernando del Rio, breezed in and started reading a statement. "Frasier the lion succumbed to . . ." but he stumbled over the pronunciation of "succumbed." He said, "suck um," and the anchormen immediately cracked some jokes. "Suck 'em to death, huh?"

Big laugh on the set, but I was annoyed. I could do that; I could do *better* than that. I could get through an entire newscast and say all the words properly. I called the station when the show was over and asked for Fernando del Rio. He came right on the line.

"Mr. del Rio, my name is Dave Lopez. I work at a cable station. I am also a reporter for the *Huntington Park Signal*. I would really like to break into broadcast news. I watch you regularly and admire your work . . ." I tactfully left out any mention of "succumb" on that day's broadcast, though I did share this story with him eventually. "I'd love to be able to speak with you about the business. Do you have any time to see me?"

"Sure," he said. "I'm free tomorrow. Come in after I get off the air."

I took the next day off work and had a personal meeting with Fernando, who could not have been more gracious. We hit it off, and he said, "You know, we're looking for a reporter in the newsroom. Here, let me walk you down to the news director's office."

Bob Brady was six-foot-seven and a real character. He looked me over and listened to my pitch. "Dave, we'll audition you. Come in Monday, and we'll put you on, see how you do for a few days."

I worked for one week—taking vacation days from the paper—and was hired that Friday as a reporter. "We like your stuff, you're hired," Bob said, and stuck out his hand.

I've been on the air ever since. Fernando's still around, too— he went on to a long, distinguished career in the public relations business.

Being hired at Channel 9 was a huge break, and I jumped at it. I worked a double shift. I was a reporter during the day, and then I would stick around and do sports or anchor the nightly news, from 9:30 to 10 pm. Long hours, but I wasn't complaining. We didn't do a lot of on-camera live reporting because Channel 9 was a small television station with a miniscule budget, but again . . . it was Los Angeles. A major market. I didn't have to relocate to the Midwest or a small town to get a break. I was twenty-four years old and on the air in my hometown. I grabbed at this brass ring.

My first official assignment was covering a campaign stop in Los Angeles by George McGovern, who was running for president at the time. I looked around the crush of reporters and saw some really famous faces, like Connie Chung. And I was among them, yelling out questions just like they were! The story came out well, and as time passed, I was asked to do more on-camera reports. Five months into the job, I would be offered the sports reporter position. Meanwhile, I was learning everything I could.

George Putnam was a legend in the LA news world. He had worked at every major station . . . two of them gave him a Rolls-Royce while he was there, per contract. He was the "up-to-the-minute" news anchor. At this time, he was winding down a distinguished career at Channel 9. George was the only anchor I ever saw warm up his voice. You could hear him before he went on in his little booth, going up and down the scales, literally warming up his voice . . . his instrument, I suppose.

George was a character and a half. He took me to lunch one day at Nickodell's, the landmark restaurant nearby that served as our company canteen for business lunches. He insisted I order their famous Caesar salad, which I wasn't too sure about. What was a Caesar salad, anyway? That was not on Mom's extensive menu. George then sat back and enjoyed his drink as we waited for our food to arrive.

"Dave," he said, "you've got a real shot at a pretty good career. You know your stuff and you have a nice easy style. You'll do great, you just need one little correction." I was always ready to improve. "You need to trim that nose of yours down. Just a little bit. I know the perfect doctor who can take a tiny bit off. It'll make all the difference in the world."

I was a bit startled. "George, I like my nose," was all I could say.

"Oh no, don't get me wrong. Your nose is fine, but just a tweak will give you a really polished look. More of a Hollywood look. I'll pay for it."

I was flattered but politely and firmly said, "Thank you, George, but I'm not touching my nose."

Apparently, in our newsroom, tweaking things wasn't limited only to noses. One of our anchors, a lovely young woman, walked up to me one day before the newscast. "Hey, catch this!" she said, and tossed something at me. I caught it. "Dave, I'm getting a boob job this weekend. This is the implant they're going to put in. I want you, a man, to feel it. Tell me if it feels like a real breast to you."

This was a shocker. Back in the day, plastic surgery was only whispered about. I fumbled with the squishy implant. "Uh, yeah, feels pretty real to me. Here you go, good luck," I said, and tossed it back. This was LA, all right. Never a dull moment.

I was always there, ready to go the extra mile and do whatever was asked of me. My training as a journalist at the newspaper had given me the ability to ask pertinent questions and follow up. I knew I had a lot to learn about being on camera, and I was never afraid to ask for help. I studied the other reporters on TV to see what made them effective. If I ever chanced to meet them, I was never afraid to go up to and ask them questions about their jobs, the business, or anything they wanted to share. People would say, "You can't just go up to him . . ." I always said, "Why not?" And did it. What's more, they were always receptive.

Married four years and three on the air—time had flown by. Elaine and I had a beautiful home, along with a dog, a yard, and a pool. But still no children. Elaine had been talking about adoption for a couple of years now. Something in me resisted. Deep inside I felt that if we couldn't have kids, it was God's will. And if it was meant to be, it would happen. I was deep into covering a tough story when Elaine called the station as usual one night. "Dave! I'm pregnant!"

To say we were overjoyed would be an understatement. And the grandparents on both sides? Ecstatic.

Given Elaine's health issues, we took every precaution during her pregnancy. She gave up teaching at six and half months because her blood pressure was getting dangerously high. Other than that, it was smooth sailing. Everything went fine, no big problems. We expected the baby in early June, but in the middle of one May night, Elaine's water broke. We immediately called our doctor, who said, "Just stay comfortable and check into the hospital at seven a.m. I'll meet you there."

I tried to get a good night's sleep, but of course, we both stayed awake the entire night. We checked in at 7 am sharp.

It was a long day of hard labor. After hours and hours, the doctors performed a caesarian section, also not nearly as common back then. This was major surgery, but at the end of the day, on May 6, 1975, we had the most beautiful baby girl. Minutes after she was born, they wheeled her out in a tiny bassinet and showed her to me. I was standing in the hallway with my heart in my mouth. She was such a pretty little girl. She opened one eye, looked at me, and burst into tears. I knew right from the start that this was my girl!

Elaine and I both liked the name Tanya, but Patty Hearst (who had taken the name Tania after being kidnapped and conscripted by the SLA) was all over the news at the time, and we didn't want that association. We named our baby Tamira, a name Elaine had seen in a baby book and loved. We called her Tami. She was the absolute light of our lives. The day we brought her home, Knocky could not figure out this little bundle. But he quickly learned where this little bundle lived. That night as we prepared to put her down, he walked in, took a big dump right under the crib, walked to the door with great dignity, and shot us a look. He had made his point. He never did it again and was a model companion to Tami from that day forward.

Work, of course, didn't stop . . . I was racing out the door one night, late, headed to my car across the street. Old Frank, the original proprietor of Lucy's El Adobe Cafe on Melrose, waved at me. Lucy's was another landmark; everyone—from politicians to film stars to workers at the Paramount lot—ate and drank there. You never knew who you might see in an old red leather booth at Lucy's, eating the Jerry Brown Special, named after our governor's favorite dish.

"Dave, come over!" Frank called.

"Can't do it tonight!" I called back . . . I was familiar with Frank's legendary margaritas. "Headed home!"

"Dave, I insist, just one drink!" he called. "Come on, come on!"

I relented and walked inside, and Frank quickly ushered me into the secret side room. "Let me introduce you to some friends of mine," he said. "Governor Jerry Brown, Minnesota Senator Hubert Humphrey, and of course you know this man . . . Muhammad Ali."

The Greatest, just sitting there at a small table in a private room. It was just the five of us, enjoying a lively conversation; I stayed for dinner. We were eating tons of food and drinking—except for Ali, who did not drink alcohol—and having a fine time.

Finally, I stood up reluctantly. "Gentlemen, I have to go. I have a brand-new baby waiting for me at home."

Ali's face just lit up. "You do, how old?"

"Just a couple of weeks old now. Her name is Tami."

"Well, I am going to write her a poem . . . bring me a piece of paper," he said to the waiter. A sheet of paper and pen were quickly produced, and he dashed out a poem on the spot . . .

"That's T-A-M-I," I spelled out.

The verse was something whimsical about fish in a net, rhyming couplets and all, though he did spell her name with a Y. He signed the paper with a flourish and handed it over.

That was a night to remember! And, being a new dad, there were many memorable moments that first year. In fact, Tami had arrived so early that she made it to her own baby shower! In the backyard, everyone *oohed* and *aahed* over the star of the show. It was a perfect California day, the sun shining down on us. I could not have been more on top of the world.

"David," Dad pulled me aside. "I worry about you sometimes."

"Dad, why, what are you worried about?" I asked. "Everything is going so well!"

"Because you have an attitude that you can do anything, and

that nothing's going to ever stop you, which is okay. But I worry that you're setting yourself up for disappointment, because you're not invincible. You have to be aware that sometimes in this life, things will happen that you just can't control. All the work and the will in the world won't make it happen."

Dad had said things like this before once or twice as I shared my grand career plans with him. Today of all days, it seemed needlessly worrisome. I looked around the happy, laughing crowd. A beautiful yard, a big family to share our joy, our long-awaited healthy, happy baby. Work was going great, I was learning, getting better on the air every month. Elaine and I were so young; we had our whole lives spread before us. The world was our oyster.

CHAPTER EIGHT
MENTOR: PETE NOYES

I WAS THE CLASSIC BESOTTED first-time father. On my days off, I would spend hours at a time with Tami, just whiling away afternoons under the big tree on a blanket as she quickly grew strong enough to sit up on her own, then crawl.

Grandpa Glen was thrilled. In fact, he decided to retire from the brewery to enjoy every possible moment with Tami. "You never know how long you have, Dave," he said. "I don't think

I'm going to be around much longer, and I want to spend all the time I can with my grandchild." As it turned out, Glen had another good twenty-five years left on this earth, and we were happy to have him around for every one we shared with him.

To say we all doted on baby Tami, the first grandchild on both sides, would be putting it mildly.

She was especially precious to Elaine and me as we did not expect to have another child after her. She was our unexpected gift, and we did not even dream of hoping for more. Therefore, it came as a complete shock when Elaine found out she was pregnant again when Tami was thirteen months old. Talk about surprises! It was the best news . . . especially as work was starting to grate.

I'd had such big dreams when I first started. I wanted to be another Vin Scully or Chick Hearn . . . or, at the very least, the main sports guy on a network station someday. Some of my dreams did come true . . . like the time we did a thirty-minute special on the Dodgers, and I got to meet and interview Tommy Lasorda. Now that was a red-letter day. I was a twenty-six-year-old kid, Lasorda was a legend, and he was so kind to me. Throughout the years, he remained a gem and always remembered my name.

Channel 9 was a small independent station, owned by RKO, with only a half-hour news show. I worked a split shift: anchored the afternoon news in the daytime and then covered sports at night. The schedule was really tough with a baby, it was a long drive, and we didn't have many viewers . . . small aggravations were adding up. Also, after several years, I was itching for bigger arenas. The best thing about the job was the training I received and some amazing sports stories I got to cover. But, as always, I was looking ahead, working out how to get to a bigger station.

I didn't have an agent or have any idea of how to go about getting an agent. That didn't stop me from trying. I read about

Lilyan Walder—one of the top agents in New York—in an industry magazine and reached out to her.

MEMO TO DAVE LOPEZ, she replied in official blocked paragraphs of type, helpfully numbered: "When you did your live piece at the Big A you were looking at the monitor far too long before you began to speak. Use the periphery of your vision to get your cue from the monitor. Look toward the lens and be ready for the viewer. You must stand somewhere you do not have to squint. I have seen too many pieces of yours where you are squinting. Your eyes look like slits when you squint . . ." And so on.

Needless to say, she declined to represent me. Trust me when I say that news is not the business for you if your feelings are easily hurt.

Four years into my employment, management decided to do something about the ratings. Our news director had a bright idea at our regular Thursday staff meeting: every Friday I would do a camping segment on the sports section. I have no idea how those two subjects connected, but when you have no viewers, you think outside the box. Management was looking to shake things up a bit. They were looking for someone different, a little offbeat, who would not put on a straight sports segment. That was not me. I was not about to go along with this. I didn't wait to find out where I would be sent to camp out.

I walked straight from that staff meeting down the hall to the general manager's office and said without any preamble, "I want five hundred a week." At the time, I was making about $400, so this was an outrageous pay raise request. Lionel Schaen, the GM, looked at me like I was trying to pick his pocket. He didn't have to give this one a lot of thought. "That's not going to happen. I am not going to give you that raise, Dave," he said.

"Fine," I said, "tomorrow is my last day. I quit." I turned on my heel and left.

I called Elaine immediately, and she was predictably alarmed. "Dave! How could you do that? You quit without anything lined up? Do you even have any prospects?" The short answer to that was no, none. She burst into tears. "Oh, Dave, what are we going to do?"

I had a mortgage, a toddler, and a pregnant wife, who no longer worked. What I did was start making calls . . . fast . . . to all my friends and acquaintances in the industry.

Somebody told me that a station in Miami was hiring. That sounded interesting . . . I had never lived anywhere but LA; Miami might be kind of exotic and exciting. I put in a call to the news director there. I knew my tape was floating around there somewhere. He was out for the day, so I just left word.

Somebody else suggested I reach out to Pete Noyes down in San Diego. "I'm sure he knows who you are," my friend said. "Why not give him a call?"

Everybody in the business knew Pete. He was a behind-the-scenes force in the news business who worked for Channel 2, Channel 4, Channel 7, Channel 9, Channel 11, and even Channel 13 over the course of his long career. He made stops at every station in the greater SoCal area as a writer, editor, and segment producer; he'd made his bones by breaking stories on the Manson Family that led to the arrest of Charlie's whole crazy cult. Pete took zero crap. He never got fired for being inept; he quit every job in disgust at everyone else's ineptness. He was so good he could always land at another station—or return to a previous one.

The classic Pete story that had made the rounds for years concerned a top-notch anchor in LA named Jerry Dunphy. Jerry was a big star with his signature Big News, signing on with "From the desert to the sea and all of Southern California, good evening, this is Jerry Dunphy." For years, he and George Putman had been the big LA anchors, kings of the nightly news.

Stations in those days were known by their anchors, and Dunphy's ratings quadrupled any competitors.

One day, Dunphy came in complaining about the script: "Who wrote this crap?"

"I did," Pete, the producer of Big News, said. "Got a problem with it?"

"Yeah, I do, I don't like it."

Dunphy ripped up the pages right in front of Pete's face and dropped them on the floor. Pete immediately took a swing at him and missed. Big brouhaha in the newsroom. Pete was immediately sent home and told to come in the next morning at 9 am sharp. He figured he would be getting fired but showed up anyway to collect his last check.

The GM asked him what had happened, and Pete told him. The manager said, "All right, Pete. The next time you take a swing at that son of a bitch and don't hit him, I'll fire you."

This was the man I now dialed. People in the industry always keep their eye on who's on the air, so he must have known who I was. At any rate, he took my cold call. I introduced myself and explained my situation briefly.

"Huh, so you just up and quit. Got a family?" he asked in his gruff voice.

"Yes, I have a little girl and one on the way."

"You got anything lined up?"

"No."

"Pretty gutty," Pete said neutrally.

"Yes . . . but I know what I'm doing, Pete. I mean, I'm a good sports reporter. I know I could—"

Pete broke in. "I've seen you. I know who you are. I'll hire you, but not for sports."

My heart sank. "Really?"

"No. I've got a sports guy. I think you could become one hell of a newsman. I'll hire you, straight news, four hundred twenty-five a week with a raise in a year. You can start Monday if you want."

I took one week off, but nine days after the day I quit my job, I was in the downtown San Diego offices of KFMB bright and early on August 23, 1976, ready to go. And just like that, everything changed.

Everyone who becomes successful in his or her career knows you have to be lucky enough to meet someone who believes in you—a person who sees your potential, who gives you a shot. Pete Noyes did both for me. Pete was an old-school newsman, someone who appreciated my background as a print reporter. He taught everyone he worked with how to become better journalists. He refused to deal with amateurs and brooked no nonsense, but with those who had potential and grit, he was patient and generous with advice. He saw some potential in me. He took me under his wing. I would not be anywhere without him.

I needed all the help I could get, as San Diego was, and still is, a tough town for broadcasters. It's a very insular market; viewers prefer local talent and weren't especially welcoming to out-of-towners from LA. I was not a native, and far worse in this gung-ho military community, I wasn't a veteran. In 1976, at the height of the nation's bicentennial celebrations, this was not a plus. The station put me up in a little hotel room downtown, not far from the station. Elaine would bring Tami down on the weekends to visit, as we waited to see how this new job would shake out.

The lessons Pete taught were many and invaluable. First things first: always get your work done on time. He drilled that into all of us. "You don't miss a slot! I don't care if you're having a heart attack! You make sure that piece is done and ready to air on time, then you can go off and die!" I carried that with me from that day forward.

"You are on television. You are being invited into people's homes. You are in their living room. Look sharp, always. Suit and tie." Pete really reinforced this rule during the freewheeling seventies when fashions got a little outlandish. He was right, I was a guest in our viewers' homes. I always tried to look my professional best.

Pete was one of the few TV executives who would sit in the newsroom and go over every script. If he didn't like something, he'd stick the page in his typewriter and bang away with four fingers and make it better. Pete reviewed everything and always managed to make it just a bit sharper. He knew how to get right to the heart of the story. Find the hook . . . go for the jugular, as he said.

My new boss was rough around the edges, for sure. Old-school, cigarette constantly in hand, and better not try to reach him on a serious subject after 3 pm . . . because that's when the drinking really started. He'd generally get going with a couple of belts by then. In any state, Pete was a terrific writer, one of the best. I had written thousands of stories in my life, but he showed me how to find the true essence, boil it down, and then put it together for airtime.

I covered my first presidential election shortly after I was hired: Jimmy Carter against Gerald Ford. I felt fine, but apparently, I came off a bit nervous. One of the executive producers came over afterward and tried to tell me to calm down a little bit . . . but how could I? This was big stuff! I made a conscious effort to slow down and not talk quite so fast. The more excited I got, the faster I spoke . . . I made a note of it. I made many, many notes that first month.

Within weeks, I was covering some of the big stories in my new city. Pete even let me do a bit of sports, and I anchored a couple of times on the weekends. When a major tropical storm hit Baja, California, I was off to the desert to cover the mayhem. I was running around all over the place, as happy as could be. Then suddenly there was a drama at home.

Unlike Elaine's first pregnancy, this was a rough one for her. Her blood pressure shot up, and she suffered from toxemia (preeclampsia) as well. Selling our beloved house, packing it up, and moving to San Diego with a toddler was hard on Elaine, even though Tami handled it beautifully. Still, we found a lovely house in Lomas Santa Fe—a big place with a huge backyard like the one from my own childhood, not far from the Del Mar racetrack. The house was still full of boxes, and there was some work to do around the place. Piles of bricks were stacked outside for when my father could arrive to help build a garden wall.

I took the day off work one Friday to accompany Elaine to the doctor, when the due date was still seven weeks away. The wonderful Dr. Blank, a Navy veteran who didn't scare easily, was worried. He said, "You're having too much trouble here. I'm going to check you in to the hospital tonight to see what we can do. This high blood pressure is really worrisome; it's got to come down."

We checked Elaine in and an aunt and uncle of hers drove in to watch Tami. At 2 am that morning, I got a call from Elaine: "Get here, fast."

Scripps Memorial Hospital was a twenty-minute drive from our new house; I think I got there in five. The doctor said, "We have to get that baby out. Her blood pressure is skyrocketing; it's becoming too dangerous for the baby—a boy, by the way." He looked me straight in the eye. "This could get quite difficult."

What a punch to the gut. "Please tell me," I said, "is this a matter of life and death? Does this mean choosing between my wife's life and my son's?"

"No, no, no," he tried to reassure me. "We will do everything to ensure both their well-being."

The surgeon was called—emergency caesarian, it was. As they were wheeling Elaine away, the surgeon stopped. "Should we tie your tubes while you're under? Because after this, no more pregnancies. Far too dangerous."

Elaine nodded weakly, and I signed the papers on the spot. I stood there in the hallway as the gurney disappeared behind the swinging doors into the OR.

Every time they laid Elaine prone to perform surgery, her lungs filled up with fluid. She had to be operated on while sitting up. The surgeon said it was the most difficult caesarian he had ever performed. Our son weighed six pounds, one ounce and had a headful of sandy blond hair . . . apparently healthy but with slightly underdeveloped lungs. They whisked him off to NICU to monitor him carefully.

Four or five days into their recovery, there was a crowd in Elaine's room. Everyone on the medical staff was very concerned that Matt wasn't eating. "We're going to have to intubate him if he doesn't start eating on his own."

A tube down our tiny infant's throat? I swear it's like Matt heard the resident. That very afternoon, he started eating and never stopped. Two weeks after our race to the ER, we were able to return home. Elaine and I felt fortunate to be in San Diego and to have received such excellent care. On our way out, Dr. Blank pointed to his scalp and joked, "See all this? I didn't have one gray hair until your wife arrived here!" It had been an ordeal for everyone. Dr. Blank waved goodbye as a nurse wheeled Mommy and new baby out to my waiting car.

Baby Matt was so small that I could hold him in one open hand and rinse him off gently under tap at the sink for bath time. But he had no lingering health issues. We had our girl and our boy, and Elaine eventually regained her strength. There would be no more kids for us, but we were beyond thankful for our two.

Just as things were settling into a new normal at home, I got the single most important lesson of all at work: Never be afraid to go after the story with everything you've got.

San Diego was home to a huge commercial fishing industry. For decades it had been known as the Tuna Capital of the World, with canneries lining the bay. There were nearly 40,000 local workers employed in catching, selling, and processing. But the federal government and local authorities were receiving complaints about the number of dolphins killed. Dolphins that swam with schools of tuna would get swept up in fishermen's nets and rip them to get away, releasing plenty of the tuna catch as well. So fisherman were killing dolphins on the spot to preserve their hauls, which included shooting them. Activists made a huge fuss, and a review was ordered. This became known as the Tuna Hearings, and it was a major local story.

The hearings were held at a downtown hotel called Royal Inn at the Wharf. San Diego officials sat at long tables in the banquet room. Naturally the local press descended on this hearing of utmost interest to locals. I did a quick announcement about the hearings with the room in the backdrop and then I was ordered to leave. "No cameras allowed inside!" we were told.

My crew and I went outside and gave Pete a quick call.

"Dave, get back in there . . . with the camera. You have every right to be present and cover those hearings. Return at once!" he ordered.

We made our way back inside the conference room, where I announced that we absolutely intended to cover these proceedings that affected our local viewers—a right protected under California law. It turned into quite a shouting match before the main official ended the proceeding by stomping out. I chased after him, shouting questions. My crew and I were eventually escorted out of the hotel, protesting the whole way, by a U.S. Marshal.

For a change, we were the story the next day: TV CREW ACCUSED OF DISRUPTION read the headlines. You better believe KFMB covered the entire matter, including our involvement, heavily. The irate official eventually relocated the hearing to the Federal Building, where cameras were always prohibited. But I had taken it as far as I could and absorbed all the lessons my mentor had taught me. Pete's most important lesson: I would never back off a story again for any reason. Period. From that point on, I would chase every story with everything I had. I had the right to be there!

The station reaped a lot of publicity, and I received plenty of acclaim. It was my first really big story . . . and I was richly rewarded. At that year's Emmy Awards, I was just twenty-eight years old and had won an Emmy. I sat at that banquet feeling like a real big shot. The world-famous San Diego sun was truly shining on me.

CHAPTER NINE

"DID YOU KILL DAVE?"

IT HAD BEEN HARD ON US, to leave our hometown and families behind and start over in a new city. But I could not deny that relocating to San Diego had been the best move of my life. I had a shiny new Emmy on the shelf and a new house with a big backyard just awaiting a few renovations to make it more kid-friendly. Not even a year into our new life, we reveled in our good fortune.

Unfortunately, a local kid was not feeling the same way. I was soon covering the story of a shy, mousy sixteen-year-old girl named Brenda Spencer who let loose with the .22 rifle her father had recently given her as a Christmas gift. She opened fire at an elementary school near her house, killing the principal and custodian and wounding a police officer. Eight kids were hit before she was stopped.

When asked why on earth she would do such a thing, she replied that it was for the fun of it. "I just don't like Mondays," she said. "This livens up the day."

Rocker Bob Geldof would write a hit song called "Tell Me Why I Don't Like Mondays" about the incident. The Boomtown Rats song was a radio staple throughout the eighties and never failed to remind me of that story . . . back when school shootings were unheard of.

I had been in San Diego for only nine months when Pete called me into his office one afternoon. "Channel Two's interested in you."

I was speechless. He was referring, of course, to the major LA-CBS affiliate. "You're kidding."

"I think you need to go up there and talk with them."

"Pete, I don't know about that," I protested, though of course I was flattered. "I just got here, and things are going well, aren't they?" Pete had given me a raise after the Emmy, and I felt just fine: *Getting by, paying the bills,* as Dad would say.

"You're doing fine," Pete allowed. "But I gotta tell you, Dave, things aren't going real well here overall. I'll be honest with you; I don't know how much longer I'm going to be here. Things are changing," he added ominously.

There were always all kinds of behind-the-scenes drama at any news station . . . generally concerning news directors and ratings. It was a minefield that I did my best to avoid by staying out as much as possible, chasing stories.

"You'll make a lot more money in Los Angeles," he said pointedly. "I think you should go hear what they're offering."

I could have easily driven the 120 miles to LA, but the station sent me a plane ticket, so why not fly? The executive I met with told me right at the start of our talk that I came highly recommended, which put me immediately at ease. Channel 2 was looking for a street reporter. The news director was a notoriously tough manager named Bob Schaeffer. The interview seemed to go well; at the end, we smiled and shook hands. I was told I'd hear something in a few days. I flew home, and sure enough, a few days later I got the call. They wanted to hire me. An official contract arrived in the mail.

It was a fairly standard three-year employment contract, but it had thirteen-week windows built in. Meaning, after thirteen weeks, I would be evaluated and possibly terminated. After the initial thirteen weeks, there were twenty-six-week evaluation windows for the rest of the three-year contract. The starting pay was $42,000 a year, a sum that stunned me. If I made it the full three years, I'd be making $48,000 a year. As a reporter. I would be rich! I felt like I had won the lottery!

Pete looked over the contract for me. It took him less than two minutes; as usual, he knew just what to zero in on. "Ahhh, you could probably get a few more bucks out of them, but this salary's OK," he said. "I don't like these windows, but that's pretty standard. They're not gonna fire you after thirteen weeks, so that's all right. You want to make sure you get a seventh-day clause in here. Oh, and take that phrase out." He handed the papers back. "Okay. Send this back to them, and if they accept these changes, you take the job."

I returned the document with the changes, and they went right through. A final contract was returned to me for signature. I was still hesitating about quitting. Pete, my unofficial agent, pushed me, hard. "They're looking for a certain someone, and you fill the bill," he said. "Look, I know you. You're aggressive and have big ambitions. This town is not going to be enough for you for long. There is no better market than LA for a reporter. Go back, do the best you can. Learn all you can. I will always help you."

And this proved to be true. Pete knew everyone, everywhere. I was one of the countless people he helped in the news industry. I hated to leave him.

"There are lot of great reporters up there in LA," Pete said. "Pick their brains."

I said a reluctant goodbye, but our families were thrilled. We were coming home.

We had sold our LA dream house less than a year before, and suddenly we were back. Things were moving fast. We had a toddler and a two-month-old infant; we moved in with Elaine's folks while we looked for another house. She had her hands more than full.

The night before I started, I told Elaine, "I may not be home much, but I'm still going to be a good father and a good husband to you. I will do everything I can at home and with Tami and Matt, but this is my shot. I have to give it all I've got."

My wonderful wife smiled at me. "Whatever you need to do," she said.

The news director is the general of a small army. He—they were all "he's" back in the seventies—has many underlings, including an assistant news director, a managing editor, producers, and all kinds of foot soldiers . . . reporters. The news director is the one who determines, at the end of the day, what news is worth covering. He's the one who assigns his go-to reporter of choice to cover the big stories. He gets feedback from everybody, but final decisions are his. He sets the tone of a newsroom and the general types of stories the station will cover. He's the man, in a word. It's a big, important, and highly stressful job.

Bob Schaeffer was the news director at Channel 2 in June 1977. He was as tough as nails. He had to be—it's a dog-eat-dog business. Schaeffer had been part of what was known in the industry as the St. Louis Mafia, a bunch of news guys who came west from CBS's St. Louis station and took over Southern California's stations.

I personally knew a reporter who had worked—briefly—at Channel 2. He had known Schaeffer for years; they were old buddies from long-ago St. Louis days. When Schaeffer arrived in LA as news director, he fired that reporter in a hot second. I kept that in mind. Get on the bad side of a news director without a good solid contract, your life will be miserable—hell, even if you have an iron-clad contract. An executive named Jerry Jacobs had brought me in, handled my contract, and introduced me briefly to Schaeffer. I barely knew the man, but his reputation certainly preceded him.

I walked in the first day on June 13, 1977, not scared but maybe a little anxious—anxious to prove myself in this new arena. *I'm not going to blow it. I'm going to work my ass off. I'm going to do fine,* I told myself over and over on the drive to Hollywood. I walked onto the set for the very first time, where star anchorman Joseph Benti sat behind the desk. Joe was a superb anchorman, a real pro, but another tough customer. If he didn't like you, you were sunk. I took the seat next to him, and he turned to me and said, "Welcome," and put out his hand.

I was a bit nervous and didn't notice his hand. "Thank you, Mr. Benti," I replied.

"Oh, call me Joe," he said. "And, Dave, I've got my hand out? What, they don't shake hands where you come from?"

"Oh, I'm sorry, Joe. I didn't see it," I said, and shook.

"Good luck," he said.

My very first story that day was about an apartment fire

and a family who was rescued by eventually jumping off a second-story balcony . . . but rescue efforts had been greatly hampered by the fact that the trapped family only spoke Spanish and none of the firefighters could communicate with them. It cost a great deal of valuable time to eventually convince them to leap to safety. My story ended with the note that the Los Angeles Fire Department was beginning a program to actively recruit bilingual first responders. They were also thinking of offering Spanish classes at LAFD. Imagine . . . Los Angeles without any Spanish-speaking first-responders. That's the way it was in 1977!

I dived into my new job. There were definitely some bumps in the road. Channel 2, like all stations, was leaving film behind to go to videotape. This was a sea change in journalism, and it would leave many of the old-time film guys behind. They were resentful and didn't mind showing it; some were less than helpful, especially to the new kid on the block. I worked Tuesdays through Saturdays, not an ideal work schedule, but it turned out fine. I was on the job one Tuesday, ready to start a new week, when the earth just opened up and simply swallowed twenty-one homes in Bluebird Canyon. There had been torrential rainstorms all year, which brought on a massive landslide. This was a huge story, and I was right there on the scene to cover it.

Then a big story broke about one of our own—a local reporter, Joel Garcia. I knew Joel . . . a nice guy . . . and his wife, who worked for the secretary of Mayor Tom Bradley. They became embroiled in a horrendous messy divorce. When Joel dropped their daughter off one day after a weekend visit, the two started arguing. Possibly feeling threatened, his estranged wife shot him dead. This was, of course, all over the news, even down in San Diego.

Our former neighbor there, a dotty little old lady named

Mavis, called Elaine. "Elaine, this is Mavis. I just saw the news. Did you kill Dave?"

"I know what you told her," I said that night.

Elaine raised her eyebrows and waited for the punchline.

It came quickly: "No, but I wish I had!"

Lopez, Garcia, a reporter . . . I guess it was easy to confuse. And speaking of confusion: The first live shot I did for Channel 2 took place in Bell Gardens. Locals called it Billy Goat Town. The station got a call that three kids had been run over by a train while playing chicken on the tracks. I was sent to cover the story, and it turned out very well.

Roger Scott, who planned and assigned stories for all the reporters, pulled me aside the next day. "You know, you really kicked ass out there. Some people here were thinking you should only cover Hispanic stories. They thought those kids on the track were Hispanic."

They hadn't been . . . they were white.

I managed to impress enough people at the station who mattered with how I'd handled my first live shot. But this incident opened my eyes a bit. I had truly not paid attention to any sort of prejudicial treatment in my career. I wasn't really even aware of any. Nothing was ever blatant, and from that time on, I covered every kind of story. Nevertheless, I was certainly breaking some barriers in my own small way—me and those Spanish-speaking firemen.

Look, it's a tough job and only one thing matters in the end: the ratings. The numbers have to be good. CBS was going through a great deal of turmoil, and reporters came and went. That's simply how the business goes: talent comes and goes at the drop of a hat, but eventually, if the numbers don't rise, the news director gets the chop. Schaeffer was a tough taskmaster.

You did your job . . . God help you if you didn't. I did my job, eagerly, all the time, and I asked questions. I kept my eyes open. I got to know the style of each of our shows. I watched the other reporters. I talked to the writers. I made friends with the editors . . . all those things were important.

Schaeffer had a temper, and a couple of things happened. I wasn't privy to the details, but he was gone in early 1978. I hadn't even been on the job for six months. I learned this when an office-wide memo went out one day saying Schaeffer was moving on to a new opportunity.

"What does this mean?" I asked one of the other reporters.

"It means he got fired, and there's probably going to be a big shakeup."

I had just gotten there! I was well aware that every time the news director gets fired, his favorite reporters and executives don't stay long; the new guy brings in his own team.

My coworker saw my expression and shook his head. "Welcome to TV," he said.

This was not exactly a surprise; Channel 2 had a reputation for chewing up news directors and spitting them out. A coworker at the station told me one day that the CBS building where we worked was rumored to lay atop ancient sacred Native American burial grounds. The news director's executive office was situated directly atop the spot where their chiefs were purportedly laid to rest. Because we were disturbing sacred ground, no news director would ever prosper. So the story went.

In came Jay Feldman from Chicago. Jay was a young guy, cocky as hell, ready to set the news world on fire. He brought in a bunch of guys from Chicago, all good solid reporters. Jay was a real newsman, and he was good to me. I breathed a sigh of relief; it seemed this transition would go smoothly for me.

I was called out for another story at Lion Country Safari. One day, there was gigantic rainstorm, and Bubbles, a huge hippo on their grounds, had somehow escaped. Now, how there can be a runaway hippo on the loose for nineteen days, I don't know, but there you have it. This was news, and I was out there on the hunt. The staff eventually located Bubbles; the trick was getting him back home safely. They decided to shoot him with a tranquilizer gun. Bubbles was looking suspiciously at everyone from a small hillside. The vet carefully shot a tranq dart into his side; he eventually fell over. Unfortunately, he slid all the way down to the bottom of the small hill and landed at an awkward angle. All the pressure of his massive body was pushed up against his lungs, and he couldn't breathe. But they didn't realize that until he died from suffocation.

Bubbles was now dead. At the news conference, the PR guy, a big, burly bearded man, came out in tears. "Bubbles is dead. And I have other news. Bubbles was a female, and she was . . . pregnant."

Well, this was not a happy headline story. That was more or less the beginning of the end of California's Lion Country Safari (which eventually shut its doors in 1984), as animal rights people went bananas over this incident. A reporter on competing Channel 4 took an angle on this story that some managers thought maybe I should have tried—a discussion of the sale of Bubbles memorabilia.

Jay came up to me after the staff meeting and said, "Lopez, you took a lot of shit in that meeting today. You OK?"

"Fine, Jay, fine," I assured him, but I got a bit concerned. Maybe I was being watched. Maybe this wasn't such a smooth transition. I really watched my step after that. I was not about to give him any reason to let me go. I redoubled my efforts, really stepped it up. A good thing, as some big stories were brewing.

A monster was on the loose in Los Angeles. It had started

quietly, with the murder of the type of victims who often went unnoticed and unreported. The naked bodies of three prostitutes were found strangled on hillsides in LA in late 1977. The police and press really sat up and took notice when young, middle-class women from good family neighborhoods were abducted and met the same grisly fate. Three . . . four . . . five . . . the body count continued to rise, and the city was petrified.

The Hillside Strangler, as he came to be known, was terrorizing the city of angels. Then, just as suddenly as they had begun, the murders stopped. But the manhunt was on. I did some good reporting on the young victims, the investigations, and the frustration as the killer seemed to slip through the net.

It was covering this gruesome story where Pete's last and maybe most important lesson really hit home to me . . . cultivating sources. Any good reporter relies on his or her network of tipsters and sources, and building the network takes time and effort. I began to cultivate law enforcement and political sources all over the Southland. I made sure they would always consider me trustworthy—if they requested confidentiality, I would maintain it. Slowly but surely, my network was growing.

Bill Stout at Channel 2 was a wonderful, network-quality newsman and a household name. A brilliant writer and dogged reporter, he was a hard-charging, hard-drinking chain-smoker— real old school. He drank from a Dixie cup of vodka all afternoon as he pounded away on his typewriter. He had a photo of a woman, stark naked, framed on his desk. He claimed she was a stripper, but I didn't believe it. She weighed at least 350 pounds. "To Bill, My All Time Favorite," it was signed. He loved it.

Stout was known for his Turkey of the Month commentaries. He did one on singer and actor Sonny Bono once that was just brutal. Bono called the news station and asked for him; Stout wouldn't take his call, so the news director spoke with him. He came down to the newsroom saying, "Oh my god, oh my god, you've gotta get this guy off me, he's killing me."

Stout replied, "Good, wait till next week. I'll really kill him then."

Stout was tough; he would go after anybody. He could cut anyone to pieces with words alone. Still, he was full of great advice and as nice as could be if you were on his good side, which I fortunately was.

We were all flabbergasted that some guy we knew around the station was advancing to a top job in New York. We couldn't imagine why. Bill overheard us talking and said, "Come here, you sons of bitches. What's your problem?"

We told him.

He took a deep drag off his cigarette and said, "Let me tell you something. In this business, shit floats. Don't you ever forget it." He got up and walked away.

Bill was only one of the veterans I'd come to know during my early days at Channel 2. One afternoon I ran into reporter Bob Dunn in our company cafeteria. "Hey, Dave," he said, "let me buy you a cup of coffee." We sat down and he said, "I'm old enough to be your dad. So I hope you don't mind a little friendly advice."

"Of course not, I am all ears," I said, and I meant it.

"So, you've been here a little while now. I've seen your stuff; you've got talent. I think you're going to go places, but as someone who's been doing this for a long time, I want to offer you a thought." He paused. "Dave, always be a nice guy. As you rise, you can stay a nice guy, or you can become a real prick. If you're going to be a prick, you better make sure that you're so good that the station can't fire you, because you're irreplaceable. But I'm here to tell you that no one is irreplaceable." He let that sink in.

He continued, "Act like a prima donna, they'll eventually

get rid of you. I haven't heard any stories about you getting out of line, which is great . . . you'll last longer. Keep treating others respectfully and keep out of management's hair. Stay like you are right now . . . tough. By all means, stand up for yourself, but always low-key and polite. Just a thought to keep in mind."

This was excellent advice and exactly what I needed to hear. In less than a year, I had already observed several "stars" who quickly became insufferably arrogant. Bob's advice would be my Bible for the rest of my career. So many top-notch reporters lost their jobs because they couldn't keep their mouths shut or they got pissed off and lost their tempers with coworkers or just thought they were too great to be replaced. That would never be me.

Rumors were flying all over the station . . . supposedly our operation was going to expand. Our one-hour newscast would become two full hours, and a new full-time position covering Orange County was opening. A reporter named Ken Jones thought he had this new job all wrapped up. I didn't pay much attention . . . I was just happy that the station was growing and that I was approaching my first anniversary.

Nearly a year to the day I had started at Channel 2, I was summoned to a meeting with assistant news director Johnathan Rodgers. It was a Friday afternoon. "You're the new full-time Orange County reporter," he said. "You start Monday."

My mind was racing. It had been a good year, I thought. I had covered some major LA stories and was deeply involved in the Hillside Strangler hunt. Being sent to Orange County sounded like punishment, and I said so. He assured me this was not the case, that this was in fact a big break.

"I thought you were going to send Ken Jones!" I protested.

"No, no, we considered him, but you're our top choice.

You're good at live shots, and you're fast. Most importantly, we know you'll get the story done. We don't need to watch over your shoulder. You'll be fine."

Elaine and I had just bought a house in Downey, so this was not particularly convenient. But I had a much bigger concern. "If I'm down in OC, I'll never get on the air," I said.

"Not at all, we have it all worked out. We will still bring you to LA to cover major stories."

I was not happy, but I didn't have a choice. "OK, fine," I said. What else could I say?

"Dave, this is a good thing for you. Jay and I know you'll do great. Good luck!"

And just like that I was off to cover Orange County, starting on June 13, 1978.

CHAPTER TEN

MEETING THE DEVIL

HUNTINGTON PARK

DAILY SIGNAL

20 CENTS A COPY | Two Sections | TUESDAY, DECEMBER 15, 1981 | VOL. LXXVII-NO. 84

Reporter rips Bonin's defense

Broadcaster tells Bonin's confessions

By David Figura, Staff Writer.

South Gate resident Lavada Gifford won't have to pretend anymore that the body of her son, Sean Paige King, was never found – thanks to David Lopez.

Lopez, a KNXT-TV News reporter, and Downey Resident, took the stand Monday "as a citizen" in the trial of accused Freeway Killer William G. Bonin, and testified Bonin confessed to the killing of King, along with 21 other murders, during the course of seven personal interviews at the Los Angeles County jail.

The reporter also testified Bonin related how in December of 1980 he led Los Angeles Police Department officers to the location of King's remains in the San Bernardino Mountains.

"Bonin said, 'I took them to the body of Sean King . . . I talked'," testified the reporter.

Lopez mentioned the defendant also confessed to killing 21 victims and quoted him as saying he would have kept on killing if he hadn't been caught because "it was getting easier with each kid."

Lopez previously refused to divulge any specifics concerning his interviews with Bonin, citing the recently enacted Shield Law protecting reporters from being cited by a court to disclose information obtained during the course of their duties.

Lopez and another reporter, Tim Alger of the Orange County Register, were called upon on Nov. 30 to testify to reported interviews the two newsmen had with Bonin on separate occasions.

Alger, who wrote a three-part series which ran in the Register in April entitled, "I was on a Destruction Course," likewise refused to testify, citing the Shield Law. Currently, Alger has still refused to testify.

However, after a few weeks, Lopez said he decided to take the stand after weighing his duties as a

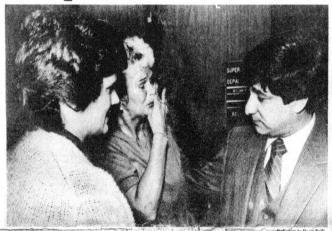

Tearful thanks — Lavada Gifford, center, of South Gate, wipes away tears after thanking KNXT-TV news reporter David Lopez, right, for testifying Monday at the trial of accused Freeway Killer William G. Bonin. Lopez, a Downey resident, said Bonin – another Downey resident – confessed to killing 21 young men and boys during a series

of personal interviews at the Los Angeles County Jail – including Gifford's 14-year-old son, Sean Paige King. Lopez had previously refused to testify, citing the Shield Law, which protects journalists from testifying to information obtained during the course of their duties. Also pictured is Gifford's daughter, Randi Mancini.

journalist and as a citizen.

"I decided I'm a citizen first," he said later outside the courtroom.

In regard to King, Lopez told the jury Bonin said he received a letter from Gifford in which she said she forgave Bonin, but wanted to bury "my little baby."

Lopez said he asked Bonin why he had led authorities to King's body and that Bonin replied, "I was dying for a hamburger, and I knew if I went with the cops I would get a

hamburger."

The remains of King's body, which were identified by dental records, were later cremated and scattered during a burial at sea last Easter.

Previously, the whereabouts of King's body was kept from the jury because the only connections between Benin and the 14-year-old South Gate boy were from Bonin's reported confession to the LAPD in December of 1980 – and the inter-

Continued on Page A-2

Newscaster's citizenship came first

The fate of a grisly multiple murder case that is receiving nationwide media attention may have been sealed Monday due to the testimony of a Downey resident.

KNXT-TV News reporter David

Cudahy poker campaigning ploy stirs angry protest

By Sue Hansen, Staff Writer

Cudahy residents awakened Monday to find fliers on their doors and fences urging the defeat of the poker ordinance by "Neighborhood Watch" – but representatives of the Neighborhood Black Watch crime prevention organization say they have nothing to do with the campaign.

Both police and black watcher spokesmen furiously denied that their black watchers have taken any stand on the card club issue.

"Black watchers takes no political stance whatsoever," declared William E. Talbott, police department coordinator for the black watcher program in Cudahy and Bell. "This could bit us in the head."

Talbott said police have no idea

hours before today's election, in which voters will decide whether or not to allow poker clubs in Cudahy.

The leaflets say "Don't let gamblers destroy our town! Save our churches. Vote no on poker!" The message is repeated in Spanish.

Continued on page A-2

Deadline for Christmas contest just 2 days off

Deadline for entering CLAS Newspapers' My Favorite Christmas Contest is fast approaching.

If you'd like a chance to win $5, $10 or $15 just for telling us about your favorite Christmas you must send your entry by Dec. 18 to:

My Favorite Christmas Contest
CLAS Newspapers

DON'T LET GAMBLER'S DESTROY OUR TOWN!

I WENT KICKING AND SCREAMING—I stomped around the house all weekend—preparing to take on my new assignment covering Orange County. How was I to know that this was the best thing that could have possibly happened to me, career-wise? My new beat was filled with all kinds of colorful local stories, and I was still on tap to report live on major breaking news out of Los Angeles. Soon after the major changes in format, length, and staffing had been adopted, Jay Feldman departed for greener pastures—a network job, I believe. Johnathan Rodgers got bumped up to the top spot as the new Channel 2 news director. He was a charismatic Black man. When Barack Obama came along years later, he reminded me of my old boss. He was just fantastic.

I jumped right in. The usual floods and fires that were the bane of Sothern California were my bread and butter. In late February, there was a particularly heavy storm; the dry Santa Ana riverbed was transformed into a rushing river. I wanted to demonstrate how dangerous it would be to fall in. The current was so powerful that it would easily bash anyone in the water against some huge pillars. How could I demonstrate this to viewers? Obviously, I wasn't about to try swimming in there myself.

On live TV, I kicked a soccer ball, and it landed squarely in the middle of the raging waters. The ball bobbed along for seven or eight seconds before it smashed up against those pillars. It was a great, vivid shot.

My cameraman said afterward, "Geez, Dave. What would have happened if you hadn't made it? What if the ball didn't land in the river? You could have really screwed everything up!"

I had no intention of screwing up on live TV in my new assignment. I had played sports, and I liked to think I still had some athletic ability!

A really big story broke my very first week on the job. Anaheim Police Chief Harold Bastrup was tired of high-speed chases through his communities. Too many of these chases had ended badly: cars were wrecked, young people killed. It was terrible publicity for the area.

The chief held a press conference and announced, "From now on, we're not going to engage in high-speed chases in our town. People want to race through here, so be it. We're not going to chase them down, but California Highway Patrol can. We're done."

This caused quite an uproar and sent the Anaheim City Council into a tizzy. I did a live shot from their late-night emergency meeting at 11 pm one night, and it got a major reaction.

Rodgers called me the next day about 9 am and said, "You were terrific last night. Jay and I watched you and we told each other, 'We made the right decision, to put you in Orange County.' So, tell you what, take the day off. It's Friday, don't come in, just take a day to yourself and have fun."

In addition to being a great boss, Rodgers was a terrific newsman, the first news director we ever had who would go out into the field and look around to see what was really happening. His wife was a network reporter; Johnathan once said, "My wife doesn't want to be on a story you're on." I took this as the highest compliment.

During this time, I also shadowed Jess Marlow, another wonderful mentor. I picked everyone's brains, constantly. I was never afraid to come right out with it: "Look, I want to learn, please help me become better." I would never stop trying to learn and grow.

I had grown all too familiar with the fairly recent phenomenon of Southern California "serial killers." Before this time, news media and the justice system generally referred to "mass murderers." With the arrest of cousins Angelo Buono and Kenneth

Bianchi, the Hillside Stranglers were finally brought to justice. It emerged that the duo had posed as undercover officers and lured the young women into their car . . . whereupon they were abducted, brutally sexually assaulted, tortured, and murdered. The trial was a sensation in Los Angeles.

There was also plenty of danger afoot in Orange County. Why did our beautiful state contain so many serial killers? Southern California, land of the freeways, featured not one, not two, but three separate Freeway Killers. Patrick Kearney had originally been dubbed the Trash Bag Murderer for his habit of dismembering his male victims and leaving the pieces in trash bags on the side of freeways. These murders were particularly gruesome given Kearney's predilection for necrophilia.

Kearney's dozen-year killing spree had started in the early sixties; he finally went down over the killing of a seventeen-year-old male when his DNA was found on the scene. Riverside police did not expect that he would confess to the murder of twenty-eight separate victims when he was arrested in 1977 . . . later, he added eight more names to the list. Kearney was safely behind bars when I arrived on the beat, but the body count in Orange County had not stopped.

Randy Kraft, an Air Force officer, enjoyed a short-lived military career. Decades before "don't ask, don't tell," he was granted a medical discharge from the Air Force in 1969. The reason? He had come out as gay to his family and his employer, the military. He found work as a bartender. Less than a year later, he committed his first sexual assault—on a thirteen-year-old boy. Soon afterward, the murders started, when a body was discovered by the Ortega Highway in 1971. Kraft killed a reported sixty-seven young men between 1971 and 1983. Mostly, he lured them to their deaths with offers of drugs and alcohol. He had a special interest in torturing and killing Marines.

Southern California was terrorized by these two killers for years, both of whom were eventually put away for life. Both were frequently referred to as The Freeway Killer. Though both Kraft and Kearney were big news, one serial killer affected my own life and livelihood like no other. That was the man I always refer to as the Real Freeway Killer, William Bonin.

Young men, mostly teenagers, many with troubled backgrounds, many gay, often hitchhiking, were still disappearing. Someone was picking these kids up right off street corners in a van—which they apparently entered willingly—and driving off with them. The news media would be called when another bound and mutilated body was found, dumped off the side of the freeway. There was naturally some confusion with Kraft's victims, but police eventually connected the dots.

Bill Bonin was a twice-paroled serial sex offender who lived in a modest apartment and worked as a delivery driver. He was well known in the complex for allowing young males to hang out and party at his place. Bonin palled around with two young neighbors, Vernon Butts and Gregory Miley. Butts was a seriously twisted dude whose idea of a good time when he wasn't working at a factory was dropping beneath the city streets and running through the sewers for hours, exploring. Miley was illiterate, intellectually challenged, and got by doing odd jobs. These guys not only partied together but also murdered together. Both young men freely admitted to being fascinated and frightened by Bonin. Both had been willing accomplices to stomach-turning abductions and murders.

Bonin's mother lived in a small house in Downey, where my family and I also lived. Along with every other member of the local media, I raced over there the day news of Bonin's arrest broke. It was a madhouse on that quiet street in Downey that afternoon. His mother was completely caught off guard and looked stricken as she was besieged by reporters. Bonin was a ruthless sociopath, but his mother was just like every other mother in the world. She couldn't believe her own child was the monster police were claiming he was.

As I was leaving that night, I saw her through the lighted kitchen window. Bonin's mother was just sitting there, all alone at the kitchen table, head in hands. I felt sorry for her. I also thought that if I returned the next day, I might get lucky. I returned to her home the next day and knocked on her door. Sure enough, she gave me an interview. I treated her respectfully, as I did with anyone I interviewed. Then I was back to the courthouse to keep chasing developments in the story.

At his bond hearing, Bonin's attorney approached me and said, "Bonin saw your story on the news. His mother said you were really nice to her, and he appreciates that. So, here's my card. Anytime you want to talk to him in the jail, he's willing."

That's how it started. Interviewing Bonin was a real scoop. It was also extremely disturbing for me as he shared gruesome details of the killings as calmly as if we were discussing baseball scores. "Oh, that one barely even put up a fight . . ." "Oh, that guy—after I had sex with him, I put his body in my mom's new refrigerator box. I drove around looking for a place to dump him. I went through a drive-thru window and got nervous because the body was starting to smell; I knew I needed to get through that line, fast."

The details horrified me, but Bonin and I had an agreement: he would speak with me exclusively, as long as I did not share any incriminating details on the news. I visited him on the third floor of the downtown jail a total of seven times.

"I could not stop killing," Bonin told me. "Could not."

It was eerie. He wanted to confess and plead guilty but be spared the death penalty. He also wanted his confession to be breaking news that would interrupt the daily soap opera lineup, which his mother never missed. He asked if I could arrange that for him . . . that was about the time I began to feel disillusioned. I had never bargained on coming across such evil.

Then I found out he was playing me; he was also granting

another reporter from a newspaper interviews. He started pitting us against each other.

My dad pointed out, "Well, you tried to make a deal with the devil . . ."

I decided to leave well enough alone. But Bonin had broken his end of our deal; I felt no obligation to uphold mine. The moment I said on the air that he had confessed to me, all hell broke loose. I did not give details due to California's shield law, which I had no intention of breaking.

The shield law was put in place to protect reporters from testifying to anything they did not broadcast and to allow them to retain their own notes. But everyone from law enforcement to attorneys on both sides now wanted my notes and for me to testify at Bonin's trial. I was never a big note-taker. If I did take notes, it would be on a scratch pad or random sheet of paper that I would later toss. The prosecutors in the case tried like hell to get me to give up my notes. The judge eventually ruled that the shield law protected me and all reporters from testifying about what they didn't put on the air. My case became quite a cause célèbre in journalism law.

Bonin's cohorts eventually confessed and agreed to testify against him. It came out in the trial that Miley's official IQ was 59. I had no idea the scale even went that low. He was so accustomed to saying, "Not guilty" that on the day he came in to enter his plea, they said, "Mr. Miley, you are entering a plea as accessory to murder. How do you plead?"

"Not guilty," he said. His attorney immediately whispered into his ear. "Guilty, your honor," he said. "I mean, guilty!"

The judge was not pleased. "Mr. Miley, are you aware of what you are pleading guilty to here? I suggest a recess while you discuss this with your attorney." This guy didn't even know what he was pleading to.

The trial was coming to a close. Bonin was in a holding cell with another guy, who beat the crap out of him after his last day of testimony. Due to his injuries, Bonin couldn't attend court that final day, a Friday, so the judge decided to try to wrap things up the following Monday. I had the weekend to really think things over. I reached out to newsman Bill Stout. "Bill, you know the situation . . . what do you think?"

He told me, "Dave, always remember one thing. You're a citizen before you're a reporter."

I felt that I had proven my point that a reporter cannot be forced to testify against his will due to the shield law. It was my decision whether to come forth as a citizen, and I decided I would. On Saturday, I called the prosecutors and said, "OK, I will testify." Maybe the Good Lord was giving me a sign. I am not the kind of guy who thinks God ever hits you over the head with a hammer and you hear a voice from the sky. But I truly believe that if you listen or pay attention, God does speak to us. Maybe he was trying to tell me something with this unexpected trial delay. I listened.

My dad showed up in the courtroom that day for moral support. I would need it; my cross-examination was harsh. Bonin's defense attorney made all kinds of insinuations that I had been paid to testify. That I had a book deal in place. That I was seeking personal publicity. That I was angling for movie rights to this story. None of that was remotely true. His client had bragged to my face about a twelve-year old kid being the easiest to kill. If I could put the final nail in his coffin, as it were, I would. During one of the breaks, Dad said to me, "Don't look at that monster. You're looking at him as you talk, don't do it."

To this day I don't feel like my testimony was any sort of major tipping point. Bonin was found guilty of ten murders in LA County and four in Orange County with overwhelming evidence of his guilt. My testimony at both trials was just the frosting on the cake. I was not prepared for the backlash. I received a great deal of criticism for testifying. Plenty of people, including some of my fellow reporters, thought I'd stepped over the line. I was suddenly inundated with my own interview requests, even from out of state.

One guy on our staff said, "Why not just quit now, go do the talk show circuit, and make a fortune?" There were some sour grapes, for sure.

I was assigned a public relations representative, Phyllis Kirk-Bush, who took good care of me. A guy I used to work with at the *Huntington Park Daily Signal* named David Shaw called me up and conducted an interview. At the end of our call he said, "Look, Dave. I need to be honest here. I'm going to come to my own conclusions in this article."

"Sure, I expect nothing less," I told him.

His article appeared in the national *TV Guide*. The first line was something like . . . "Dave Lopez got a confession from a murderer and had to make a conscience call. Dave Lopez made the wrong decision." This really stung. Shaw roughed me up pretty good.

Phyllis called me up. "David, darling," she started as she always did. "Are you OK?"

"Of course, Phyllis, why?"

"Did you see that article in *TV Guide*?"

"Yeah, he hammered me. But what can you do, how many people read that thing anyway?"

"Well, David, only about four and a half million people."

So, four and a half million Americans now thought I was a complete jerk. Nothing much I could do. I was never going to cash in on an event like this. It had come down to me deciding I would not let myself down. Bonin and his buddies left the severed genitals of a thirteen-year-old kid next to his body on the side of a desolate freeway. Yes, I did what I felt was right as a human being and citizen and testified against him. I would stand by my decision.

I did put in a request to see Bonin before he was executed; he refused. The last thing he said on the record was to a reporter from Sacramento, who asked him if he had any regrets. His answer was "Yeah, I regret that I did not become the professional bowler I always wanted to be."

I didn't make the list of witnesses to his actual execution. I remembered one of the last things Bonin had ever told me: "If I ever get executed, these family members think they'll feel relief. They'll get their revenge. But they won't feel any better. They'll get nothing."

Bonin was duly executed. Miley was imprisoned for life. Butts hanged himself in his jail cell. Revenge or justice . . . I don't know.

So many mothers had lost their sons. Bonin had told me that he killed twenty-one people and gave me all the names. He had mentioned that a kid named Eric Lundgren was one of his victims, though he was not officially convicted of that particular murder. To this day, Mrs. Lundgren calls me, asking me if I remember anything more. And I just don't. Over the years I spoke to many retired investigators, asking them if there was anything more to dig up; all came up empty-handed.

Mrs. Lundgren is eighty-eight years old now and still hopes for closure. She was excited to hear I was writing a book; she thought I might revisit this monster's crimes in some detail. I wish I could help her. The details of her son's murder will remain a mystery that I cannot solve. This is a harsh lesson that every reporter learns the hard way, sooner or later.

CHAPTER ELEVEN

EVEN MORE EVIL

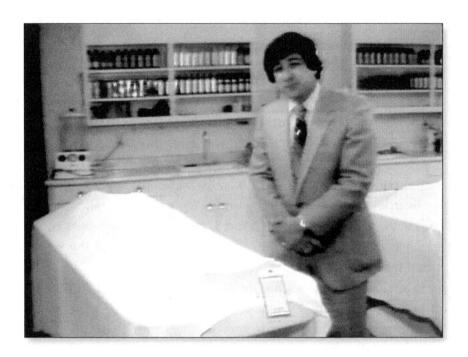

I THOUGHT I HAD SEEN THE WORST. But I hadn't, not yet. A little girl named Amy Sue Seitz was playing in her aunt's backyard in Camarillo one afternoon. The doors and windows to the house were wide open, family members close at hand. A man approached the fence and coaxed the trusting toddler to come toward him. In the blink of an eye, they were both gone. The two-year-old's naked body turned up in Topanga Canyon two days later. The details were unbearable; she had been brutally raped and tortured for hours before being dumped. The public was outraged, and law enforcement from all around and every agency stepped up to help.

A longtime pedophile named Theodore Frank was soon apprehended. He had molested more than 100 children in his life over four states. Frank had been released only six weeks before from Atascadero State Prison's sex offender's program, supposedly rehabilitated. Prosecutors from both Orange and Ventura counties brought in their top people to try the people's case. I covered the standing-room-only trial. The lead attorney carried two large photos of Amy in his briefcase, one as a happy smiling little girl, one a harsh black-and-white crime scene photo of her remains. Every time he opened his case, the stark contrast was there for all in the courtroom to see.

Frank was a monster . . . though highly intelligent. He once told a newspaper reporter: "Some people are put on this earth to become doctors or lawyers. I was put on this earth to molest children."

Amy's twenty-year-old mother stoically sat through every excruciating minute. Finally, the jury went out to deliberate . . . and got hung up, for days. One of the special circumstances prosecutors had charged Frank with was kidnapping. One of the jurors couldn't seem to wrap her mind around that charge. She thought that you couldn't be officially guilty of kidnapping unless the victim had made an effort to escape—even if the victim was only two years old.

Judge McBride finally stepped in and addressed the hung jury. He advised them to please use their common sense. The Saturday before Christmas, the jury reached a verdict: Guilty. Frank was sentenced to death, though that would eventually be overturned, and he would die decades later of a heart attack on death row.

A friend of mine had made a beautiful music box that operated on solar power. After the verdict came in, I approached Amy's mother, so very young herself, and gave her the music box. I prayed she would find some solace, somewhere.

I was still shaken over the Bonin brouhaha and resulting uproar when I covered this story; in fact, the two trials were practically simultaneous. But the trial of Amy's murderer took me to a very dark place. I too had a toddler daughter at home. For days, my eyes welled up every time I hugged my precious Tami, who was the same age as Amy. I would come home late from work, and there was my little girl, waiting up for me to read to her no matter how late it got. If I was tired and tried to skip a line or page of Dr. Seuss, Tami would immediately pipe up. "Read it right," she would say imperiously. Tami, with her ballet lessons and dolls, was safe at home. There but for the grace of God . . .

And Matt, my baby son. As soon as he could sit up, I began to play with him, gently tossing a rolled-up sock to him from a couple of feet away. He would gamely throw it back in my general direction. Who knew if he would have any athletic abilities, but I had hopes. Mainly I hoped only that he would love sports, like me. We had so much to do together.

Matt was an adorable toddler . . . short and squat. He looked like a mini Barney Rubble. And was he ever active. He was not yet two years old when he used to amuse himself by jumping up and down in his crib. When we'd rush in, he'd be jumping away, a gleeful smile on his face. One day I could hear the regular rhythm of him jumping. Up, down. Up, down . . . then suddenly . . . *THUD*. Silence. I raced into his room and couldn't believe it: he had jumped out of the crib entirely and was lying face down on the carpet, arms and legs spread wide. I turned him over; he had a shocked look on his face but didn't cry. He was physically fine, but he would never do that again. We got him a real bed that very day . . . well, we gave him Tami's old child-size bed and bought her a brand-new one.

For some reason, Elaine and I went out to the store, looked at every model, and bought a brand-new queen-size bed—headboard, new mattress, foundation, and all. After we had put it all together and made up the bed with fancy new sheets, we looked at each other and cracked up. Tami was a tiny little thing, completely lost in this huge bed. She barely made a bump! What were we thinking?

In July 1980, Disneyland threw a huge party for their official twenty-fifth anniversary. Did they ever do celebration right! The park was a riot of color, spectacle, fairy princesses come to life, and cartoon characters running around, along with new rides, fireworks, candy, and toys in the shops on Main Street. Our little kids were mesmerized all day, both out like lights on the drive home that night. Elaine and I were so thankful for our family. I could not ask for more.

If I had a buck for every letter I received when I was trying to break into the television business and while I worked at Channel 9, I'd be set for life. They came from stations all over the country, saying, "Dear Mr. Lopez, We have reviewed your tape. You are not quite ready for our market." Fortunately, these letters never discouraged me. I was becoming much better known in the business—The *TV Guide* article had certainly "helped" with that.

A young guy named Steve Lefkowitz signed me soon after the article appeared; he worked at the prestigious N.S. Bienstock talent agency in New York. Eventually another agent named Adam Leibner took over. Adam's dad had founded the business; he was well known for being Dan Rather's agent for years and years. I was fortunate to work with both of them.

One day, I had an hour to wait at the airport for a flight to San Francisco. I thought about killing time at a nearby bar called Bare Elegance, where nude women danced as you drank cokes—no liquor allowed. *What the hell,* I decided. I went in there and took one of the few empty tables in the back, sitting alone in the dim light.

I hadn't been there for five minutes when the emcee said, "Ladies and gentlemen! Let's give a warm Bare Elegance welcome to Mr. Dave Lopez, reporter for Channel 2, sitting right over there in the corner."

A huge spotlight came on, blinding me. I smiled weakly, and the guy next to me said, "Hey, man, you should have been here ten minutes ago . . . Maury Wills just left." Sure, I was disappointed that I didn't get to meet the former pro baseball player who was integral to the Dodgers' success in the mid-sixties. But, truthfully, I was more flabbergasted that my days of anonymity were over.

Famous or not, agent or not, at home, nothing had changed. I was still just Dave, oldest son of Al and Tilly. One of my younger brothers ran track in high school, a three-quarter mile event called the 1330. I'd ask him how the season was going when I saw him.

"How'd you do?" my parents would always ask him after the meets.

"Pretty good, came in third," he said more than once.

One afternoon at the shop Dad said, "Hey, why don't we head over to the high school and watch the race? Let's go see the kid run."

We headed over just in time to catch his event. My brother came in third all right, but there were only three guys running. Apparently, that was the way it had gone all season. Three competitors . . . and he always came in third.

With my newfound fame, Mom and Dad weren't shy about volunteering my services. I made all kinds of appearances for South Gate Park: Season opening games. The Azalea Festival every year. Emcee of the local pageant. When a brand-new 7/11 store opened in South Gate, I was master of ceremonies for this major event in the community. I was happy to support the local neighborhood, not always so much when accommodating all of Mom's requests. It felt like every time I saw her, she'd tell me that she'd signed me up to call Bingo or make an appearance at a local Rotary group.

"Who did you say this was for, Mom?" I'd always ask, trying to figure out who I was helping and why.

"It's Maria's mother's neighbor's nephew, Dave," she would say. "We were talking in the beauty parlor, and I said you'd be happy to help out."

Mom and her beauty parlor friends kept me busy. I reminded her that I did have a job to do . . . the stories kept on coming. I could barely keep up.

Robin Samsoe of Huntington Beach was twelve years old when she headed off for a day at the beach with her girlfriends. A man who claimed to be a fashion photographer lured her away, supposedly to take some photos. He kidnapped and killed the young girl. A man named Rodney Alcala was convicted on these charges. He was a tall, good-looking guy who went around with a camera all the time. In the course of reporting the story, I discovered that he had once appeared on *The Dating Game* and had actually been chosen for a date by the bachelorette. I was one of the first to focus on this angle and dug up the details, which immediately made worldwide news.

Robin's poor mother was just in agony . . . more so as Alcala's death penalty conviction was overturned on a technicality. It was just heartbreaking. Back in those days courtroom security was not what it is now, and one day, she sneaked a gun into the courtroom inside her purse. She was going to shoot Alcala down in cold blood; she was bound and determined. But at some point during the day, she changed her mind; it would not bring Robin back. I will never forget that interview. All those mothers haunted me.

Then along came a man named John Hutcherson—an old country guy who bought a shiny new motor home. He and his wife were going to take off on a trip, so he washed it and took it to the station to gas up and get ready for a nice getaway. On his way home, he saw a young woman sitting on the corner thumbing a ride. He invited her in, and they began talking. One thing led to another, and it turned out she was a prostitute. He had sex with her and, for whatever reason, decided not to pay her.

Afterward, as he drove along, his passenger became more and more hysterical. She refused to let the matter of payment go, so Hutcherson pulled over by the oil fields in Brea and grabbed a length of rope he had handy. He was a pretty strong guy; he easily overpowered her and tied her hands behind her back. He put his handkerchief over her mouth to muffle her screams and tossed her, half-naked, out the passenger door.

It didn't take Sherlock Holmes to catch him. The next day, the police rolled up on him as he was frantically scrubbing out his motor home on his driveway. He was arrested for rape, kidnapping, and assault. At his trial, he took the stand in his own defense.

"Mr. Hutcherson, you agreed to pay this woman for a sex act, correct?"

"Yeah."

"What was the price?"

"Twenty-five dollars."

"Twenty-five dollars for sexual intercourse?"

"Yeah."

"And did you have sexual intercourse with this woman in your motor home?"

"Yeah."

"So why did you refuse to pay her?"

"Didn't last long enough. Not worth twenty-five bucks," he said indignantly.

Needless to say, he was convicted. I really wished that story would run at the top of the news that night, just because he had been so foolish. But cooler heads prevailed. And then the judge made an announcement. Judge Fitzgerald said that Hutcherson had been so poorly represented that he vacated his conviction and ordered a new trial.

A highfalutin lawyer named Terry Giles took up his cause after reading about the case, and a retrial was set. That's when I first met Gloria Allred . . . she was there to represent the woman who had been defrauded and assaulted. I would see Gloria on many stories to come. Hutcherson eventually plea-bargained out and the case went away.

Many killers *were*, fortunately, brought to justice—for instance, Ralph Small, a brilliant MIT graduate who went on to medical school and became an internist/cardiologist. (Incidentally, there was never a shortage of doctors who made the news.) For whatever reason, Small thought he could make more money faster doing cosmetic surgery as opposed to heart surgery. Sure enough, he started doing breast implants, a booming business, and was making a fortune. Things were going so well that he decided to expand by offering tummy tucks and butt lifts, much more complicated procedures. On one terrible day, three women died in his office while he was performing surgery on them. One might conclude he was taking on a little too much.

He granted me a personal interview while the case was being investigated. As full-blown narcissists tend to like to do, he was anxious to get his point of view out there. I had my cameraman John Brazzell with me, and we walked into Dr. Small's office. He was a great big guy, a weightlifter, who sat at a huge desk in front of a wall completely covered with framed plaques and certificates.

"Goddamn, doc, got enough plaques on this wall? You could circumcise Jesus Christ!" John blurted out.

The doctor laughed. Then he explained to us that he was a world-class doctor, that the problems that day had been due to the anesthesia, and on and on. Dr. Small wound up being arrested, convicted, and going to jail . . . but the strangest part was that he took the fall for his anesthesiologist cohort . . . sobbing in the courtroom, "I love him; I can't stand that he could go to jail!" I couldn't make this stuff up.

Finally, the story I would never forget, where no one was at fault but tragic just the same: A local man named Willie Battle had converted an old bus for a cross-country trip. The plan was to drive a bunch of relatives across the country to a Fourth of July family reunion in Alabama. In the Cajon Pass, the propane stove blew up. Willie parked and ran outside to see what was happening; before his eyes, the bus exploded into a ball of fire. Five children and five adults died in this tragedy.

Willie himself was physically unharmed. He was so stoic when I interviewed him that I had to comment on it. "Mr. Battle," I said, "I can't believe how strong you are and why you're just not breaking apart."

He looked at me and said, "You have to understand, you cannot put a question mark where God has put a period."

This hit me like a ton of bricks. I would never forget Willie Battle or that moment.

Getting a DUI had historically been a minor offense, certainly not a career-ender or particularly costly, in terms of either fines or damage to a reputation. The tide was really starting to turn in terms of public opinion on drunk driving. MADD came alive during the eighties and got a lot of good work done. In 1983,

Downey Hospital did a public service feature about the dangers of alcohol abuse, especially drinking and driving. I volunteered to be their test subject . . . on the air, of course.

They gave me a couple of drinks, and I felt fine. "Give me a couple more," I said, and they went down just as easy. This was fun. I had no idea by the time I actually headed out to a closed course to drive that I had consumed ten drinks. Elaine and the kids were there to observe. I jumped behind the wheel, drove the course, and hit every orange cone. I knocked down every obstacle in my way and a few things that weren't. When I got out of the car, I grabbed the one cone I hadn't knocked over and put it on top of my head.

The reporter covering the story took it easy on me; he could have really crucified me with that footage. He didn't show me as a cone head—just some photos of me staggering, giddily drunk while exiting of the car. I got driven home, and Elaine was furious; she took the kids out and left me to sleep it off for the rest of the day. I felt so crappy the next morning that I could barely move. I was really suffering. That was a stupid stunt, and the viewers let me know it. Elaine didn't talk to me for nearly a week.

Our well-regarded news director Johnathan Rodgers left to go to the network, and along came Steve Cohen—great guy, very energetic, gung-ho, and team spirited. He was the kind of boss who, if we had a particularly good broadcast, would run into the newsroom and say, "Great show! Great show! Everybody, free ice cream on me!" Outside would be an ice cream cart.

Steve was into health and well-being way before his time. He practiced meditation, the first person I ever knew to do so. He used to go into the closet in his office and chant while hitting a block of wood with a small hammer. Sometimes you'd want to see him, and Cindy, his assistant, would say, "Sorry, he's in the closet."

One time a reporter wanted to negotiate a contract with him, and in the middle of discussions, Steve dropped to the floor and started doing pushups. "Don't stop talking, gotta get my workout in," he said to the startled reporter.

That was Steve. Quirks aside, the new boss was a great guy. He made it his business to know every staffer personally and how the operation worked from the ground up. It's not always a great idea to be buddy-buddy with the boss, but in our case, it worked out well. He was fantastic; I thought he'd be around forever, but it was not to be. As always . . . the numbers. Steve wasn't fazed; he left the news business altogether to run a television outlet that serviced truckers for a while before returning to the business, very successfully.

In came a guy named Andy Fisher. Andy had a reputation for being very tough on reporters; he demanded perfection. He had risen up through the ranks and was nicknamed Rocket Sox, because he flew so fast up the ladder. He more than lived up to his rep as a tough guy. He was only there for a year—the Rocket took off and landed somewhere else. In just a few short years at Channel 2, I had seen so many news directors come and go. As always, I kept my head down and went after the story.

My dad with his adopted parents, Socorro (left) and Santos, taken in 1939.

My favorite picture of Mom and Dad, taken just before Dad was shipped overseas in 1945.

Always loved dressing up as a cowboy, but never a Cowboy fan.

Did I really look that young in 1971?

CBS COLUMBIA SQUARE

DAVID LOPEZ

Games of the XXIIIrd Olympiad
Los Angeles 1984

Jeux de la XXIIIème Olympiade
Los Angeles 1984

E E

DAVID LOPEZ

KNXT TELEVISION

JOURNALIST   USA

∞   4

Saved all my credentials.

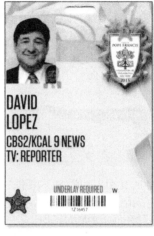

DAVID LOPEZ

CBS2/KCAL 9 NEWS

TV: REPORTER

UNDERLAY REQUIRED   W

1Z16457

WORLD SERIES 20 17

F PB IR AX BC

NATIONAL LEAGUE CITY

MEDIA TALENT/PROD./DIR.

Dave Lopez

KCAL 9/CBS2 - Los Angeles

BADGE REQUIRED FOR CLUBHOUSE ACCESS

This credential must be worn at all times. Not transferable. No autographs. Subject to conditions on reverse side. Not for use by anyone under 18.

DEPARTMENT   OF THE
SHERIFF
COUNTY OF LOS ANGELES
1970
PRESS PASS

DAVID S. LOPEZ

DAILY SIGNAL

This is to certify that the above-named person whose photograph appears hereon, is a duly accredited representative of the press.

Peter J. Pitchess

SHERIFF

Hard at work at South
Gate school paper,
The Rambler, 1966.

South Gate senior photo.
Always knew what I
wanted to do.

DAVID LOPEZ
Varsity Basketball,
Baseball, Sports
editor of Rambler
SPORTS WRITER
& ANNOUNCER

Above: Billboards high above Los Angeles, 1972. Didn't help our ratings.

Worked with the legendary Hal Fishman before he went to KTLA 5 in 1975. That's Gillian Rice, co-anchor. I did sports. Photo Courtesy of CBS

WELCOME GEORGE!

GEORGE PUTNAM

Beginning tonight a familiar face joins the Channel 9 News. At 10 O'Clock George joins Brian Kahle, Suzanne Childs, and Dave Lopez with The George Putnam Report every weeknight.

CHANNEL 9 NEWS 9:30 ⑨ KHJ-TV

Worked with the great George Putnam, 1973. Photo Courtesy of *TV Guide*

KNXT

CBS Television Stations
A Division of Columbia Broadcasting System, Inc.
6121 Sunset Boulevard
Los Angeles, California 90028
(213) 469-1212

Dear Mr. Lopez:

I appreciate knowing about your interest in KNXT and your availability. There are no openings currently, and none is anticipated in the foreseeable future.

I will keep your letter on file and contact you if that situation changes.

Sincerely,

J. ALAN SAITTA
Assistant News Director

Mr. David S. Lopez
17938 Santa Valera Street
Fountain Valley, California 92708

February 11, 1975

If at first you don't succeed . . . try, try again.

KNXT

CBS Television Stations
A Division of Columbia Broadcasting System, Inc.
6121 Sunset Boulevard
Los Angeles, California 90028
(213) 469-1212

Dear Mr. Lopez:

Thank you for sending the videotapes. I have looked at them and believe you do a competent job of sports reporting. At this point, however, we are not ready to commit ourselves to a major change in our sports department, but we shall keep you in mind.

Please let Lorraine know if you would like your tapes mailed, or whether you prefer to stop by and pick them up.

Sincerely,

AL GREENSTEIN
Assistant News Director

Mr. David Lopez
17938 Santa Valera Street
Fountain Valley, California
92708

April 24, 1973

AG:lh

First trip to Sacramento for KNXT Channel 2,
Summer 1977. Photo Courtesy of CBS

My first Emmy in Los Angeles, 1980. Photo Courtesy of CBS

An Emmy party. That is the great Bill Stout,
left of me. Photo Courtesy of CBS

CHANNEL 2 NEWS

Dave...

    You continue to
amaze me with your
skill and stamina.
I'm real glad you're
on our side.

Johnathan Rodgers

Hi David —

you were
unbelievable during
the fine Wednesday —
I don't know how
you do it — !
Congratulations —
love,
Connie

Loved receiving notes like these. It sure beats a text message.

Loved confronting politicians. Photo courtesy of CBS

An altered image... I confronted California Govenor Gavin Newsom on why he would not use his power during the height of COVID-19 to shut down beaches. He would not answer. Hours later, beaches were closed.

Could not believe the size of *Endeavour.* Photo courtesy of CBS

It's not all glamorous being on TV. Photo Courtesy of CBS

Never enjoyed covering fires. Photo by Anna DeVencenty

I love Dodger Stadium. Always considered it a second home. Photo by Anna DeVencenty

Kept a record
of every story
I covered
since 1977.
Who needs a
computer?

WELCOME
HOME DAD!
WE MISSED
YOU!

LOVE,
TAMI, MATT
& MOM

Nice to know
you are missed.

Proud member since 1972.

Nice to be recognized, but my proudest achievements are my children, Tami and Matt. Photo courtesy of Golden Mike Awards

Love bein[g]
a grandpa!
Here's Abiga[il]

My favorite
photo of Henry.

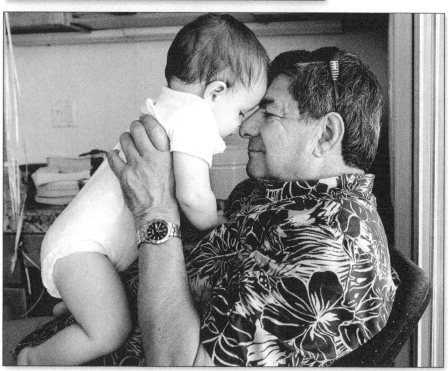

Special moment
with Hallie.

ELAINE'S LEGACY LIVES ON...

8ᵗʰ *Annual Elaine Lopez*
Memorial Scholarship
Dr. Richard A. Vladovic
Harbor Teacher Preparation Academy

ANDREA GONZALEZ-GARCIA $12,000 WINNER

"It's no secret that teachers, especially the most caring and attentive ones, like Elaine Lopez, have a lasting effect on our lives. I want to add to the effect that teachers have on their students' lives by being a school psychologist."

**-ANDREA GONZALEZ-GARCIA
LONG BEACH STATE UNIVERSITY**

A special way to honor Elaine.

A memorial garden at the church she loved,
Messiah Lutheran in Downey.

DAVE LOPEZ
SPORTS DEPARTMENT

HUNTINGTON PARK
DAILY SIGNAL

587-3412
6414 RUGBY AVENUE
HUNTINGTON PARK, CALIFORNIA

First business
card I ever had
(top). My Dad
had one, too.

COURTESY   RELIABILITY   SATISFACTION

GARFIELD
UPHOLSTERY & DRAPERIES

NEW FURNITURE MADE TO ORDER
WE SPECIALIZE IN NAUGAHYDE

4570 FIRESTONE BLVD.   SOUTH GATE

FREE ESTIMATES   AL LOPEZ

DAY OR EVE. PHONE 569-0608

Alleged Confession of Bonin Detailed

TV Newsman Ends Silence on Interviews

By GENE BLAKE,
Times Staff Writer

Television newsman David Lopez reversed himself Monday and testified to previously undisclosed details of accused Freeway Killer William G. Bonin's alleged confession that he murdered 21 young men and boys.

Lopez, a reporter for KNXT Channel 2 news, had refused Nov. 30 to testify about anything not mentioned in his newscasts. He relied then on the reporter's "shield" provision of the state Constitution, and was upheld by Los Angeles Superior Court Judge William B. Keene.

But Lopez had a change of heart over the weekend, telling reporters that he had been feeling "miserable." He said the decisions to test the validity of the "shield" law, and later to testify as a "citizen," were his own.

"I'm a citizen first," Lopez told reporters. "I feel as though a 100-pound weight has been taken off me."

Case Had Been Rested

The prosecution had rested its case against Bonin last week, shortly before he suffered injuries in a holding cell that twice delayed the trial. He wore a piece of white tape over his broken nose and dark glasses over his blackened eyes when he was ushered into court Monday.

Deputy Dist. Atty. Sterling E. Norris obtained permission to reopen his case to present Lopez's testimony, over the objections of defense attorney William Charvet.

Charvet, characterizing Lopez's testimony as "damaging" to his client, then obtained a recess until this morning to prepare for cross-examination of the reporter.

Lopez testified he had seven conversations with Bonin beginning in December, 1980, and continuing into early this year. It was on Jan. 9,

David Lopez, a TV reporter, testifying at the trial of Freeway Killer suspect William Bonin.

1981, that Bonin confessed to him in the attorney's room of the Los Angeles County Jail that he had killed 21 young men and boys, Lopez testified.

Bonin told him he had led police to the remains of Sean King, 14, whose body until then had not been found, Lopez related. He quoted Bonin as saying he did so in response to a letter from the boy's mother that pleaded:

"I forgive you for what you did. I'm a born-again Christian, but I want my baby buried for Christmas."

Mother Weeps in Court

The mother, Lavada Gifford, sat in the front row of the courtroom and wept as Lopez related the story.

It was the first time the jury heard that the King boy's remains had been found, because Bonin had furnished information to authorities on the promise that it would not used against him.

Another reason given by Bonin for his confession, Lopez testified, was that Eric Wijnaendts, 21, had been falsely accused of the murder of another victim, Harry Todd Turner, 14.

Lopez testified that on Jan. 9, Bonin showed him a "love letter" from Wijnaendts and said, "Eric didn't do it. He's innocent." Wijnaendts later was released as a suspect.

Bonin related he had picked up the King boy at a bus stop in Downey, Lopez testified. He quoted Bonin as saying, "I got the kid in the van and I killed him the way I did the others."

Lopez recalled details that he said were given by Bonin on the murders of Darin Kendrick, 19; Steven Wood, 16; Stephen Wells, 18, and James Macabe, 12.

He testified the killing described by Bonin as the "easiest one" was that of the Macabe boy, who was

picked up on his way to Disneyland.

Bonin told him he always had a knife with him and had an ability to tie up his victims quickly, Lopez testified. Although most of the victims were strangled, Lopez quoted Bonin as saying he had stabbed his second victim.

But Bonin steadfastly denied he had killed Thomas Lundgren, 13, whose penis and testes were severed, the reporter related.

16 Murder Charges

Nevertheless, the Lundgren boy is one of the 12 victims Bonin is charged with murdering in the case now on trial. He is charged with four other murders in Orange County.

Lopez said Bonin put the blame on Vernon Butts, initially a co-defendant with him in six of the murders, for thrusting an icepick into the right ear of the Kendrick boy,

Please see BONIN, Page 9

My testimony made headlines. Credit: *Los Angeles Times*

TV reporter David Lopez: criticized, defended for his testimony.

Newsmen Generally Criticize Lopez Decision to Testify in Bonin Case

By DAVID SHAW, *Times Staff Writer*

Television newsman David Lopez says his civic and parental responsibilities—and what he interpreted as a sign from God—persuaded him to testify this week in the trial of accused Freeway Killer William G. Bonin.

But several prominent newsmen say Lopez's decision could ultimately undermine both the confidence that news sources have in reporters' promises of confidentiality and the independence the press has traditionally had from the prosecutorial process.

Although two newsmen defended Lopez, most editors and reporters around the country interviewed by The Times voiced criticism of him, for a variety of reasons.

One editor said Lopez should never have agreed to listen to Bonin's confession to 21 murders on an off-the-record basis. Another editor said that, having done so, Lopez should never have violated that pledge of confidentiality, neither by reporting Bonin's confession on television nor by testifying on it in court.

Timing Questioned

Yet another editor said that if Lopez felt compelled to testify, he should have done so before the judge in the Bonin trial ruled that Lopez and another reporter did not have to testify because they are protected by the newsman's privilege contained in a state constitutional amendment approved by voters in 1980.

"I'm troubled by the somewhat twisted logic of the reporter," said Thomas Winship, editor of the Boston Globe and immediate past president of the American Society of Newspaper Editors.

"It seems to me that the judge went to bat for him and gave him protection and then, in a way, he (Lopez) ignored the protection and sang. He undercut the shield law (the newsman's constitutional privilege to maintain the confidentiality of his sources). I find it very disturbing."

A spokesman for the Los Angeles Police Department called Lopez a hero for having testified in the case, though, and Lopez himself con-

ceded that Alger's stories, which contained some allegedly self-incriminating statements by Bonin, did not contain most of the details and the case-by-case confession that Bonin had given the television newsman. But Lopez said he still saw Bonin's disclosures to Alger as violating their agreement, thus freeing Lopez from his pledge of confidentiality.

"I went to him (Bonin) in jail and said, 'You son of a bitch. You bastard. You broke our agreement. I'm going on the air' (with Bonin's confession)," Lopez said.

Bonin denied having abrogated their agreement, Lopez said.

"He said, 'I told you I wouldn't confess, not that I wouldn't talk (about the case at all),'" Lopez said.

"Station authorities" at KNXT, Channel 2, would not let Lopez go on the air with the Bonin story then anyway, Lopez said, for fear of jeopardizing Bonin's right to a fair trial. They were also concerned that the story might result in Lopez being subpoenaed, he said.

Lopez was disgruntled over losing what he had thought of as an exclusive story, but he was even

more upset in late June, he said, when he heard reports that Bonin was negotiating for a movie deal on his story.

"That did it," Lopez said.

He again asked to go on the air with his story, and on June 29, he did so.

"I believe very strongly in protecting sources," Lopez said. "But I also believe it's a two-way street. If he (Bonin) tells me something off the record and then . . . I find he's telling everyone . . . One (police) investigator even said to me, 'I don't see why you're being so secretive about this whole thing. He (Bonin) is telling everyone in the whole world.'"

But Lopez said station authorities were still concerned about the legal implications of his story, and that concern—combined with time limitations on the newscast—prevented him from going into great detail in his broadcast on Bonin's confession.

Good thing I have always had a thick skin. Credit *Los Angeles Times*

By Paul McAfee, Night City Editor

Bulls-eye!

Three cheers for Lopez

Southland television reporter David Lopez will undoubtedly earn more than his fair share of criticism for deciding to testify against William G. Bonin in the Freeway Killer case.

But around this newsroom, the comments I've heard reveal that Lopez is a bigger hero this week than Lou Grant. The reporter made a judgment call – a conscientious, moral decision – and it wasn't an easy one.

Let's face it, he could have hidden behind the newly enacted Shield Law. It worked the first time, when Lopez was called to the stand on Nov. 30. On that date, he and another reporter refused to testify on the basis of the Shield Law, which protects reporters from divulging information in the courtroom that they obtained in the course of their duties.

In effect, Lopez won a two-pronged battle. The judge complied with his refusal to testify. Therefore, a precedent was established – the first ever in the Shield Law's brief history, and one that will undoubtedly come up in many courtroom sessions to come.

But beyond that, the fact that Lopez didn't blindly hide behind the new law is laudable. He carefully considered the case, realizing that his testimony could put the icing on the prosecution's cake. After all, Lopez' testimony substantiated most of the major prosecution testimony given to that date – and it was straight from the horse's mouth through the vehicle of the media.

Lopez himself said that after weighing his duties as a journalist and as a citizen, "I decided I'm a citizen first."

But I feel his decision to testify established him not only as a conscientious citizen, but as a thoughtful newsman as well. Instead of proclaiming "First Amendment" and "Shield Law" rights in a do-or-die fashion, he sat down and sweated out a decision, a sticky judgment call. When it would have been easy to say nothing, he risked the criticism – even ostracism – of his colleagues to do something he felt was right. And I feel that kind of moral strength goes along with a journalist's job, too.

Some may say that Lopez' testifying will increase public distrust of the media's cloak of confidentiality. After all, trust is the one of the biggest aids journalists have in the quest for truth.

Yet, Lopez himself pointed out that confidentiality is a two-way street. Whatever promises he may have made to Bonin, the defendant did go back on his own word to Lopez by talking to other reporters.

Whatever verdict is finally reached in the Bonin trial, I think David Lopez can look himself in the mirror each day and hold his head high. I'd like to say, "Three cheers for Dave." It was a hard decision – and I think history will prove it to be a good one.

At least someone thought I did the right thing. Credit: *Southeast News*

At CBS Studios, my last night on the air, June 30, 2020

And they lived happily every after. . . . The End

CHAPTER TWELVE

REPORTER/DAD

OUR NEWEST NEWS DIRECTOR WAS ERIC SORENSEN . . . he was there for a couple of years in the mid-eighties. Eric and I got along famously—he was a reporter's dream boss. He left to work for Channel 11, and we floated along without a news director for quite some time. A guy named Don Dunkel essentially ran things, though he was never formally granted the title. He had come to us from the network, where he worked on *Nightline*.

Don was brilliant; he could converse on any subject in the business. Just like Pete, he made me a far better reporter just by his quick, incisive comments on my stories each day. The way he handled everything wasn't hard to understand: you did things his way or you were out. Very simple. His way was fine by me.

One day, there was a pretty big earthquake in Palm Springs. Highway 111 was literally split in half. I was perched on one side, and reporter Steve Kmetko was across the divide on the other side. Oh, how our female viewers loved this guy; he was a very good-looking, Hollywood kind of reporter. Steve was gay, but the general public had no idea back then. As usual that day in Palm Springs a bunch of girls were fawning all over him, giggling and trying to catch his attention on the sidelines. Our cameraman, who had seen this a hundred times before, couldn't take it anymore and called out to them. "Ladies! Don't waste your time. Trust me on this!"

The two of us were throwing it back and forth easily, and I thought the segment was fine. Dunkel called me on the phone later that afternoon and said, "Lopez, pretty good work out there. You're a good, solid reporter. You can out-report Kmetko, you can out-hustle him . . ." Pause. "But you'll never out-thin him."

Message received . . . lose a few pounds. I didn't take it personally. I hated when Dunkel left; I was sure he was the guy who could hold us together.

During this time in my family life, I walked Tami to kindergarten every day, at the little elementary school just around the corner from our house. She did not want to hold my hand; that was for babies.

"How about this, you just hold one finger?"

That was an acceptable deal for both sides.

On bring-your-dad-to-school day, Tami stood at the front of the class to introduce me. "Hi, this is my dad. His name is Dave. He doesn't work. He just goes on TV and talks."

I would never fail to use that story at awards shows in the future, though Tami claimed I left the real story out. "Father," she would say, "you brought autographed photos for kindergarteners. Yes, you did. Don't even try to deny it." Now, I don't think that's true, but I suppose it's possible.

Tami could be quite dramatic as she grew up; I used to call her Sarah Bernhardt after the old-time legendary stage actress. One Sunday afternoon, when Tami was about eleven years old, we were getting ready to head over to my mom's house for Sunday dinner, as usual. Tami was out in the backyard, flipping all over the place, also as usual; she was an excellent dancer and gymnast. She somersaulted and landed on a sprinkler head. She came racing in, shouting, "My wrist, my wrist, it's killing me!"

After taking a look, I concluded that it was OK and chalked it up to her usual theatrics. Elaine concurred, rounded up Matt, and the four of us headed out to my mom's. As soon as we walked in the door, Tami cried, "My arm! My arm!"

My mom rushed to put a cold wet rag around the wrist, bind it, and fuss over Tami. That night, I got up in the middle of the night to check on her. Her arm was puffed up and swollen to twice its usual size. I immediately drove her to the emergency room, where doctors determined she had a broken wrist. She came out in a special flexible wrap cast and said, "I told you! I had a broken wrist, and you didn't believe me! Grandma thought a cold rag would make it better! Child neglect!"

Outspoken though she was, Tami was a great kid; I never

had reason to discipline her. Until the day I had enough. I had told my daughter ten times that afternoon, "Do not change that channel," as I was trying to watch something for work. We had a brand-new remote, and she would not stop playing with it. I finally got aggravated, took the remote from her hand, and swatted her once, gently, across the behind. She was shocked.

"You ruined it, Father! I was going to go my whole life without ever being spanked . . . and YOU ruined it!"

There was lots of boo-hooing and drama. That was the one and only time there was any sort of corporal punishment in our house.

Tami and Matt were both just really nice kids. They attended services at Elaine's home church every week followed by Sunday school. In addition to their school friends, they were friendly with a bunch of kids from the church youth group and participated in the choir and the Christmas pageant every year. Both attended Downey public schools, and right from the start, I rewarded them for good grades. I sat them both down in first grade and said, "If you get straight As until you are sixteen and stay out of trouble, for your sixteenth birthday, you get a brand-new car."

Teacher Elaine really didn't like the idea of bribery . . .

"Honey, bribery goes a long way. Don't knock it," I told her. Worked for me. The kids were thriving, and the years were flying by.

Elaine returned to teaching school when Matt was in the second grade. She missed the rewards that came from teaching, but she also still had plenty of drive and ambition. If she had any fault, it was that she would take on too much. In addition to being supermom, she wanted her career back too. But kids came first. As busy as I was with my own job, I never missed a single dance recital. I would go kicking and screaming sometimes, but I was always there. I'd watch Tami perform and leave. The minute she exited the stage, I was gone.

"That's not very nice," Elaine would hiss as I made my way out, brushing past the seated parents in our row.

"Don't care!" I told her. I missed two Super Bowls because our daughter performed on that sacred day!

Sports was still my true love, and I got some amazing bene-fits from my job. When the Summer Olympics were held in LA in 1984, I had access to all kinds of tickets through the station. Grandpa Glen had a ball taking the kids to the events at the Olympic Arts Festival, which ran all summer long. We watched legendary decathlete Rafer Johnson carry the torch up the Cali-fornia Incline on the way to the opening ceremony. Along with the rest of America, Tami cheered as Mary Lou Retton won the gold for the U.S. in gymnastics. Our hometown really shined on the world stage; it was widely considered one of the most successful Games ever . . . and the U.S. won a record number of medals to boot.

I got to cover some great sports stories in the mid-eighties. Our regular sports guy, Keith Olbermann, refused to fly. Abso-lutely would not do it. When the Angels won the pennant in 1986, he would not fly to Boston as they faced the Red Sox in their bid to advance to the World Series. So I flew there to cover the games, a nail-biting series that went back and forth as they battled it out. Sadly, the Angels lost, but it was hard-fought. That was some amazing baseball.

That winter I flew to Chicago to cover the Rams playing the Bears for the 1986 NFC title game. It looked like they really had a chance after an up-and-down season, with the legendary Eric Dickerson on the team. I headed for Chicago, having no idea what Midwest weather was really like. No clue. I had never braved Chicago in the winter. I wore sweatpants and a light shirt so that I'd be comfortable on the plane. We landed in a distant terminal. I walked down the ramp and carried my bag several hundred yards outside and then into the terminal. That wind tore through me; it was sixteen degrees that night. I thought I was going to pass out right there on the tarmac.

The next day, I put on my suit and grabbed the California coat I'd brought with me. I walked around the corner of my hotel, and I seriously felt like I was naked. I was literally freezing on the street; I had to go buy a real winter overcoat. I was a true Angeleno, totally caught unawares. The Rams got shut out, and I flew back to LA, very happy to get home and warm up.

At that time in my life, I could easily reel off the names of the teams that played every World Series, how many games it lasted, plus the starting rotation on both sides and the managers. Same for Super Bowls and NBA finals. I could recite statistics from the 1930s until present day. I was totally, utterly sports mad. Naturally, I passed this obsession on to my son.

I realized early on that Matt was a lefty and thought briefly about trying to switch him for his own good, thinking his life would overall just be easier as a right-hander. Then I read an article that said when you try to switch kids from being left-handed to right, they often develop a stuttering problem. I remembered my own kindergarten days and dropped that idea fast.

When Matt was in the first grade, he became eligible to play basketball . . . his favorite sport. I took him to the local high school gym to teach him a few moves. Unbeknownst to me, Elaine had bought him a Michael Jordan videotape that he watched all the time. At our first practice, I was astounded as he raced down the court dribbling between his legs, making all kinds of moves. I hadn't taught him any of that!

"I watched a video, Dad!" he told me.

Matt was a natural shooter, but a big kid and not superfast. "Why don't you find five or six buddies, and we'll all sign up at the Y and form a team?" I proposed on the way home.

Matt found some friends and we all signed up, with me as the coach. I will freely admit that as a youth coach I was more aggressive than I should have been. You could go so far as to say that I gained something of a reputation as a hothead. My own hothead dad, Al, came out of retirement to help me coach the first couple of years, so this was only to be expected. The first year, we coached the boys through our local Y; the second year, we switched over to the Downey Junior Athletic Association.

We were full-service coaches; we covered every sport: football, basketball, and baseball . . . and Matt played on every team. He was in second grade the first time I coached football; I told him he was going to be the quarterback.

"What if I'm no good, Dad?"

"Doesn't matter, I'm the coach!" I reassured him. "And you're going to be fine."

This wasn't sheer nepotism on my part; Matt was a smart kid with a good grasp of the game and a strong arm. He did great! We coached some pretty decent football teams and won league championships a couple of times. It was fun for both of us.

We returned from family vacation late on the Saturday night of Labor Day weekend. Sunday morning, I told my boy, "Hey, let's go play catch."

Nine-year-old Matt and I headed to the park. My pager went off; I ignored it. It was Sunday, and I was still officially on vacation. We played some more, and the pager buzzed again. And again. After the fifth time, I said, "I'd better call in." I returned to the car and got on the two-way radio. "What's going on, guys?"

"Jesus, Dave, where've you been?" It was our news director. "There has been a horrendous plane crash, it's a huge deal."

"It's Sunday, I'm still on vacation," I protested.

"I need you, Dave. I really need you. Here's the desk with the information."

I jotted down the address, a suburban street in Cerritos, and Matt and I went home. I changed clothes and took off.

As I got closer, I could see the fire and the smoke in the sky. A small private plane had crashed into an Aeromexico jet. The father with his family on board was flying his personal small aircraft. He'd had a heart attack—whether that caused the crash or was a result of panic just before the crash could never be determined. Anyway, on this most beautiful clear day, he had flown too close under the jet and clipped its wing. This took out the hydraulics, and both aircrafts soon came plummeting down. The passengers on the full Aeromexico jet had thirty long seconds in the air to contemplate the crash ahead. The idea of that was horrifying.

Everyone on board the planes died upon impact. A dozen homes were wiped out, with nearly twenty people on the ground dead. The smoking fuselage was still lying in the middle of the street. The smell of death was everywhere; panicked residents ran around everywhere, trying to get home. Chaos.

I located our crew. A young female reporter was doing the initial report. "The plane crashed on this Mapbook page," she said, and held up a *Thomas Guide*. (That's how people navigated LA back then.)

After she finished, I approached her. "Hey, call the desk. They want me to do some reports here, so call in and see what's happening."

There was a reason my news director wouldn't let me be; I had been sent to replace her. After she left, my cameraman looked around carefully to be sure she was gone. Then he called me over and said, "Dave! Can I give you a hug? Thank God you're here!"

This particular employee was not the strongest hard-news reporter . . . though she would eventually go quite far and make a big name for herself on the national stage.

I did fifteen live shots that day and eight more the next day. I stayed on the scene for a week; it was an enormous story. Thirty years later, I would do the anniversary story; the reverberations of that crash on the community would last for decades to come. The human drama was incredible . . . and unbearably sad. A family in the neighborhood had gone out to church that morning, but the mom stayed home because she wasn't feeling well. In the middle of the service, the family heard the plane crash. They raced home but could not get into their own street. They lived in one of the dozen homes that had been completely wiped out, and the mom's body was eventually located, buried under the rubble. Once again, I headed home very late that second night, into our house with the lights on for me, so thankful for my family.

To be a reporter means seeing the very darkest side of human nature. Some were enormous in scope, like serial killers and plane crashes. But there was no end to the smaller personal dramas that never stopped coming in.

In 1987 a man named Michael Redding lost his job, went to a bar, and got exceedingly drunk. He stumbled out, drove off in his car, and ran a red light. He hit a mom and her three kids making a left turn onto their street. The father was home alone, waiting for his family to arrive. Eventually he heard all the sirens nearby and walked outside to see what was happening. He ran to the accident scene and recognized his own mangled car. He raced up to the police, who told him that the woman and two of the children were dead.

"What about the baby?"

"Still alive. Headed to the hospital right now, go!"

The father jumped into the back of the ambulance with his baby and prayed the entire way there aloud: "Please let my baby live, give me a reason to keep living."

The baby died. His entire family, wiped out in a single minute.

Michael Redding was the first person in Orange County to be charged with murder for a drunk driving case. He was sentenced to fifteen years. Cameras were still allowed in the courtroom at that time; I approached him for comment. He looked at me with dead eyes and said, "They might as well just shoot me right here." He was taken away by the bailiffs. The father of the victims eventually remarried; I hope he found some peace.

Also in 1987, a kid from the barrio in La Habra earned a scholarship to Harvard University. The odds were very much against him as his family members were in and out of jails and prison the entire time he grew up. His was an uplifting inspirational story of local kid from the school of hard knocks making good. That first summer home after completing his freshman year, he started knocking over liquor stores. When he got arrested and was asked how he could jeopardize such an opportunity, he said, "I just couldn't stand the idea that I was now this straight and narrow Harvard kid. I felt so out of place." He went to jail, bleak future assured.

And here's yet another grim story from 1987 to haunt my dreams for years to come. Six-year-old David Rothenberger's parents were in the middle of a horrible divorce and separated in their hometown in New Jersey. The mom soon moved on and began dating someone new. The dad promised his son a dream trip to Disneyland and Knott's Berry Farm; they flew out and rented a hotel room in Buena Park, where the dad specifically asked for a waterbed. When his little boy was asleep, his dad set him on fire. This was an act of pure vengeance. If his wife was going to remarry, he wasn't going to let them have their boy. David survived . . . but died young, in his early forties, of natural causes.

After doing the story, I stayed friendly for years with both David and his mom. I arranged for him to go to a toy warehouse and get anything he wanted. His dad only served thirteen years for this horrible crime. The judge actually cried as he handed down the punishment, saying he wished he could apply a harsher sentence, but this was the limit of the law.

I had my own son, safe and sound and nearly as crazy about sports as I was. I reported on horrible stories about boys at work all the time. I wanted to do my small part to help some kids and spend more time with my own boy. I jumped into kids' sports with a vengeance. Coach Dave Lopez was now on the scene!

CHAPTER THIRTEEN

No Lifetime Contracts

I WALKED INTO THE UPHOLSTERY SHOP one afternoon to see Dad on the phone, stabbing his finger into each hole as he dialed. He was not in the best of moods; he'd just realized that a longtime vendor was overcharging him. Their salesman was taking a bigger-than-agreed upon cut on every sale . . . until Dad found out.

"You son of a bitch," he raged to the guy on the other end of the line. "I have given you so much goddamn business. I want the invoices on every transaction with me, for the past six months through today. I want two percent off every single purchase. Get that check to me or you will never see my business again. Two percent, by the end of the week," he emphasized, and slammed down the phone. He turned to me. "And what do you want?"

Ah, Dad. In some ways he was mellowing with age; mostly he was not. He still ruled that shop with an iron fist. Backing down was not in his vocabulary. I only heard his side of that dispute, but I am sure he got his money—by the end of the week. As always, Santos, my Tata, was a silent, supportive figure in the background, calmly tying springs while Dad yelled.

Santos still loved the horses. For many years after work, he frequented the racetrack and a bar at a neighborhood restaurant where he was a regular. A young waitress who worked there had two babies in quick succession, both out of wedlock. She was poor, zero family support, in desperate straits. So my grandmother Socorro, still hungry for kids, took the two babies in. A couple of years later, she picked up another one somewhere along the way. She finally had her own three kids to raise and was busy and happy, though Tata got a little ticked off after the third kid because there was no longer any place in the small house for him to go and just sit. They were out of room. Tata spent a lot of time at the shop.

One day, he and Socorro went to the doctor for a checkup. The doctor said to my eighty-year-old grandfather, "Any particular problems, anything going on that I should know about?"

"Can't think of any, I'm fine," Tata said.

Then Socorro chimed in, "Well, except that every time he goes to the bathroom he bleeds."

"Really?" the doctor asked. "And how long has this been going on?"

"Oh, about a year."

"A year," the doctor echoed.

He performed a full examination on my grandfather on the spot and ordered tests. Tata had cancer—the worst kind, colon cancer. He was told that he needed surgery, immediately. The man was already past eighty; I wasn't sure this was a good idea and told my father as much: "Dad, don't do it. Surgery will kill him. He will not be comfortable with a colostomy bag. I know Santos, he's too proud, too macho. You'd better tell him what's in store after surgery."

Dad shook his head and crossed his arms. Stubborn.

"Come on, Dad, is there any alternative . . . what did they say?"

"There's chemo and radiation."

"Well, give him the choice. Let him know what he's in for. Don't just tell him he has to have surgery."

But Dad didn't, for whatever reason. Probably because the doctor had told him that surgery was the best option and necessary to save his father's life. So Santos had the surgery and woke up with a colostomy bag hooked up to his side. Predictably, he went crazy when the nurses explained its function. Socorro, standing in the room, blurted out, "I'm not going to clean that; I'm not going to touch that bag!" loud and clear for all to hear.

Dad hired a private nurse to care for Tata, at great expense, and visited constantly. My grandfather was never the same. He was very weak, barely eating, wheelchair bound, his spirit broken. He just wasn't my grandfather anymore. Things were not going well, post-surgery. Santos was losing strength and focus and the will to live by the day. He needed more than in-house professional care.

"Dad, where are you going put him?" I asked my father one night. Something had to change. I objected, loudly, when he told me the name of the facility, right in the neighborhood, a crappy little place.

"Dad, don't send him there. Send him somewhere else. Anywhere else!"

Dad brushed aside my objections. "No, no, no; he wants to go there, he wants to be close to the house."

So, Santos became an inpatient at a tiny private seven-bed hospital. And what were the odds—there was already another patient there, also named Santos Lopez. The *other* elderly Santos Lopez was gravely diabetic, while my grandfather was fine, at least in that one area. The nurse got their medication charts mixed up one day—an easy enough mistake—and gave my grandfather a massive dose of insulin. Tata went into diabetic shock, then a coma, and very nearly died. He recovered, but barely. What was left of his mind was gone. He was either in bed or slumping in his wheelchair. Dad ultimately had to put him in a rest home, where he soon developed bedsores. Then Socorro passed away. The hits kept on coming. It was an unending nightmare that went on for nearly a year.

Throughout this year, Dad's mind was all over the place. He was working at the shop one day on an ancient shredding machine, in which you insert a special weave of cotton to produce especially fine pillows. The machine was old, but that was Dad: "It works fine; I don't need a new one." He wasn't paying attention; his mind was on his own dad's troubles. On this day, instead of using the safety stick, he used his hands. His finger got caught and went straight into the machine. Fortunately, my brother Albert was working in the shop that day. Dad started screaming at the top of his lungs over the noise: "Albert, Albert, cut the juice, cut the juice!"

Albert managed to pull the plug on the old machine, and Dad, with one mighty yank, pulled out his mangled hand. Most of his finger was gone, just vanished. As he ran to the bathroom, dripping blood all over the shop floor, he yelled at my shocked brother, "Albert, find my fucking finger . . . it's somewhere in there, find it!"

Somehow Albert found a few seconds to call home, so I got a call from my mother.

"Your father's had an accident at the shop! He cut his finger off!"

I dropped everything and rushed over to the hospital as fast as I could, where I heard the whole story from my shaken brother. Albert had gotten on his knees, sifting through the blood-soaked cotton debris on the floor, when what do you know—he found the missing digit. Albert raced into the bathroom, handed the finger to Dad, and then fainted dead away. Dad grabbed the thing, opened up the medicine chest, and started trying to patch his finger back on with tape before help arrived to take them both to the hospital.

The ER doctors determined that Dad's finger could not be saved. He had some minor surgery and was sent home with a stump of a finger on one hand. Just another day at the shop, but a few months later, he was suffering excruciating pain in the finger that was no longer there. Dad could hardly stand up. It turned out that the original surgeon had not deadened certain crucial nerves and vessels. The pain was being caused by the fingernail, still growing, trying to cut through the skin, but there was nowhere for it to go. So, they had to cut open what was left of Dad's finger again. Another operation, but this time they fixed it.

One of my brothers had a little boy at the time who was always sucking on his fingers. At a family gathering one day, Dad looked over at him with his hand in mouth as always. "Hey, look at me. You know what's going to happen if you don't stop sucking your fingers? This!" And he stuck his huge, battered hand, minus one finger, right in my nephew's face. The boy was scared out of his wits. His hand dropped to his side, and he never sucked his fingers again.

My grandfather's grave decline and missing digits aside, Eric Sorenson was the only news director to ever leave the job and come back again for another stint. After some time away at rival Channel 11, he returned "home" to KCBS-2 in the late eighties. Once again, you did things Eric's way . . . or else. No discussion, no second chances. No problem for me; for others, it wasn't so easy.

I remembered a colleague from Eric's first time around—a good, solid reporter. Eric fired him, so he headed off to Channel 11, where he was doing just fine. Then Eric left us to become news director there. I heard the story right away.

Eric called the guy in on his first day in charge. "So, we had our differences at Channel 2. When I fired you, people thought I was wrong." Pause. "I wasn't. Bye."

Fired again. Sheer bad luck. My former colleague simply wasn't his "type." The reporter was fine; he landed on his feet. I was glad—he was a good guy in a brutal business where this happened every day.

I also remembered what a sports announcer named Tom Kelly said to me once. Tom was a very cordial man, just a great guy. He said, "You know, I had a lifetime contract with CBS. Lifetime! One day the bastards called me in and declared me dead."

Around this time, the movie *Broadcast News* starring William Hurt and Holly Hunter arrived in theaters. Naturally it was very popular in my circles. It was also a big hit with general movie-going public all over the country. My personal favorite line was when they had all these layoffs and the executive comes up to the main guy who just got axed and says, "Listen, if there's anything I can do to help, please let me know." The character played by Albert Brooks tells him, "Yeah. You can have a heart attack."

After Eric left again—this time for good—a former producer was named news director. I liked Mike personally, but how he ever became news director I'll never know. It didn't really matter, as he didn't stay long. Then something truly wonderful happened: Jose Rios was named as our news director. Jose had started out as a messenger at Channel 2. He drove a golf cart and delivered mail. Later he drove reporters to stories. He worked his way up—all the way up. When he was formally appointed to news director, it was the only time in my career I ever saw an entire newsroom erupt in applause. He was popular with everyone. Just a great, great guy. Even better, he shared my commitment to helping kids and understood my need to be available to my own children.

Matt was a sensitive kid—much more so than his outgoing, outspoken sister. I had known that since he was just a little guy. I loved my own father, worshiped him really. But I never wanted my son to fear me the way I had feared my own—and still did, if the truth be told. I vowed that would never happen to us—not on the field, not at home.

Basketball was Matt's passion. By the time he was in the fifth grade, he was tall for his age and a pretty darn good player. I decided I'd like to find some tougher competition for him outside the Downey Park program and see what we could do. I brought his entire team of kids down to Orange County, where a friend of mine coached, for a friendly game. We got killed, but Matt really shined.

Coach Gary pulled me aside. "Number eleven is a player. Get yourself a couple of taller kids, recruit a little, and you could play on the AAU side." This meant playing at a significantly higher level, for instance, at the upcoming annual Valentine's Day Classic in Santa Barbara.

I took Matt up there to observe a game, knowing the kids were going to face some real players, actual strong competition, kids who played pickup games on the street every night, the kind they had never seen before. If Matt was going to play on this level, I would have to surround him with stronger teammates. No problem. I headed outdoors and looked for kids on neighborhood playgrounds, like those I played on myself in South Gate Park as a kid. We managed to pull a team together, and we weren't bad—we put on a respectable show in the new league. I was having an absolute ball.

Word spread, and kids started approaching us to join the team. A few of the older kids were starting to get in a bit of trouble here and there . . . I took them on too, immediately, as I wanted to channel their energy into something positive. I was not about to let them fall by the wayside if I could help it. For two years, I coached two separate teams. They were both made up of middle schoolers, but two different skill levels in two different divisions. I was a busy guy.

I would film my story in the late afternoon and then race off. Matt would have a sandwich ready for me as I pulled into our driveway for a minute to pick him up, and we'd head out twice a week to the familiar Pius gym. Jose was a tremendous help, making sure I wasn't on any late assignments whenever possible. I was tough on those kids. Quite honestly, looking back, if I had a kid now on a team with me as the coach, I'm not sure I would let my kid stay. But the kids learned discipline, and I certainly offered them plenty of treats, rewards, and overnights. This was truly a marvelous and highly rewarding few years of my life. The kids and I traveled all over California . . . Santa Barbara, San Diego, Riverside, San Bernardino, and even Las Vegas. Once again, my own dad pitched in to help. I was happy he had a distraction during this hard time in his own life.

One of my stronger players, a tough eighth-grader, got injured one day and I was really scrambling, so I returned to the local YMCA for a scouting session. All the kids in the gym kept telling me about someone named Moi, a very large Mexican kid. I met his sister and asked if I could call her mom and dad. I spoke with them on the phone, told them what I was doing, and offered to pick him up for that week's game. We stopped by that morning, he jumped in the van, and we were off. Moi DeLeon wound up being named player of the game! He was a great kid.

One week we were playing in Torrance against a team from Manhattan Beach. On the opposing side was the most enormous player we had ever faced. We managed to beat them . . . barely. That kid was huge, though he turned out to be only twelve. I talked with the other coach after our first game. "That's Phil Finau," he said. "His family is from Tonga. His mom and dad will be here soon."

I watched the second game and said to myself, "I need this kid." I walked over to his parents, Mr. and Mrs. Finau, native Samoans, who had come to collect him. Lovely people. It helped that they recognized me from TV.

"Would your boy like to play on my team?" I asked. "I provide the uniforms and transportation. We play every weekend, in tournaments all over SoCal. We'd love to have him."

"Well, we live in Hollywood Park . . ." his dad said, thinking I might not want to drive out to Inglewood too often.

"That's fine, I'll pick him up at the door!" I said, willing to do pretty much anything. We had a big game in a tournament the next weekend, and I needed Phil.

Mrs. Finau came outside with her son when we stopped by in the old van, ready to head out to San Diego for an overnight. "Mr. Lopez, Phil has to attend religious services tomorrow. This is the address of our church. The service is at nine-thirty every Sunday morning, and he is not allowed to miss it, for basketball or anything else."

The next morning Phil and I got up early. I drove that kid to church forty miles away, waited for him outside, and then raced back down I-5, just in time to make our noon game. We won. Phil was named player of the tournament, with a big trophy to prove it.

Both parents came outside to greet us when we returned

home late that evening. "You are a good man. You promised to take him to church, and you did. Phil can play with you anytime. Thank you!" Mr. Finau said.

I had my star recruit! And a backup—another kid from Downey, referred to me by another boy on our team. He was a big, tall kid named Jarvis Watson; I tracked him down on the playground. I talked to his mom and gave him a uniform.

Jarvis was another star. His mother did not drive, so Elaine was bringing him to a game once and, as she was inclined to do, got lost. We kept waiting around, losing badly by halftime, eyes on the gym door the whole time. Where was he? He finally showed up and swooped in, and we came back strong and won the game. It was just like a movie! Jarvis was there, being carried around the gym triumphantly by his teammates, shouting his name.

When I was coaching, I was not afraid to yell and scream. My watch would often fly off my arm because I was gesticulating so wildly . . . I can't even estimate how many watches I broke over those four years of coaching. I kicked bleachers, and I would throw down my clipboard in disgust over a bad call. I was a little too intense; Elaine and Tami were mortified, sitting up there in the bleachers pretending they did not know me. At one tournament, the referee looked at me just before the game started, as we were going over the ground rules, and said, "I am aware of your reputation, Lopez. Watch yourself today."

"Wait a minute, you've never laid eyes on me until today . . . you're warning me before the game even starts? What bullsh—"

"Technical foul!"

"You can't call a technical foul; the game hasn't even started!"

"Technical foul! One more and you're out!"

Thanks to those technicals, we were down 4–0 before the game even started. I turned and headed for the bench without another word. One move out of me and it was curtains for the coach. I was afraid to open my mouth. I barely moved off the bench . . . I didn't want to get thrown out of the game . . . which we did end up winning in spite of me.

Moi would grow up to become a teacher and school principal. Jarvis became an English instructor in Japan—a long, long way from Downey, California. Phil would go on to much bigger things than my basketball league. He was all set for a full ride at USC on an athletic scholarship after breaking high school records everywhere. Then, tragically, one day he collapsed in the locker room due to an undiagnosed blood clot in his brain. He survived, but a brilliant athletic career ended. I sat down and cried the day I received the news; Phil had been a true superstar who had saved our team many a time. Overall, I felt privileged to be able to coach such a great bunch of kids.

CHAPTER FOURTEEN

DANGEROUS ASSIGNMENTS

WHEN MY GRANDFATHER SANTOS FINALLY DIED, his wish was to be buried in the town where he grew up and lived as a humble fruit picker. Guadalupe, Mexico, was a tiny dust-blown town just across the Texas border. My grandfather had been born on All Saints Day, November 1. After he fulfilled Santos's final instructions, my dad made an annual pilgrimage to visit his gravesite on his birthday each year. I accompanied him on the second anniversary of Tata's death. I had no idea what to expect. We flew into the El Paso airport, rented a car, and crossed the border.

Tata's eternal home was inside a typical Mexican cemetery—not a manicured park like many in America. Really it was just a small, abandoned field on the edge of town, with some grass trying to poke up here and there in places. The place looked abandoned, except for my grandfather's spot. Santos's grave had an iron gate around a nice little monument engraved with his name. His small section was covered in beautiful green grass, and the monument was decorated with fresh flowers. The gravesite was impeccable, and we bowed our heads.

At a small shack on the edge of the field, Dad knocked on the keeper's door. When the man answered, Dad thanked him and handed him a wad of hundreds. It was this man who kept up the gravesite, and he was certainly doing a good job. Then we headed into to the little village of Guadalupe. Just like at home, my dad had made his presence known there, too.

We parked the big American car on the quiet main street and got out. There wasn't much to see. Then we began to walk, and it seemed like everybody in the entire town suddenly popped out to say hi. It was like the famous scene in *The Godfather Part II* where young Michael Corleone watches as the local don takes a stroll in his immaculate white suit, and everybody's bowing to him as he passes. My dad got stopped every few feet, greeting and dispensing twenty-dollar bills to all who approached. The townspeople—men, women, and children alike—were practically genuflecting at his feet.

"Antelmo, Antelmo . . . Antelmo is here!" The shout went out, and the whole town showed up.

I walked beside Dad, shaking my head in amazement. It took a couple hours to cover the main street; we ended up in small a café drinking coffee before returning to the car.

My dad was the Godfather of Guadalupe. He never explained to me what all the adulation was about, but I could see he was the king. Again, I regret not asking him to explain what, exactly, he did with and for these townspeople, or his secret family members. But I had teenage kids, financial pressures, stress at work . . . the time to press him for details came and went. Guadalupe was just another of Dad's mysteries.

It was time to live up to my end of the bargain. Our daughter had notched straight As for years running. So, for Tami's sixteenth birthday, I bought her a brand-new sports car and hid it at a neighbor's house up the street. We threw a huge family party for her, and as the day passed, she was becoming more and more anxious about her long-promised car. The presents were opened, the cake was cut, "Happy Birthday" was sung . . . no car.

Finally, I made the big announcement. "OK, Tami, it's time for your car!"

She raced outside, where a friend of mine had parked his ancient, beat-up VW in front of our house. I explained to her that the car needed a little work, but in a couple of weeks, it would be running. If looks could kill. "I'm only teasing. Come on, jump in my car, I'll take you to your real car."

Tami was furious. "I'm not going, I am not even talking to you!"

"Come on, Tami, come on."

We drove to neighbor Kitty's house where a shiny new Mustang awaited, decked out with huge ribbon that said, "Happy Birthday!" just like dad had done for me. I was forgiven, but Tami never forgot the way I teased her. I couldn't help it. I was glad for these happy family moments because work had become a nightmare.

Our popular news director Jose was so bright and innovative. He was skilled at every aspect of his tough job. He made it easy to talk to him and became a close personal friend of mine. But the numbers weren't good enough for corporate headquarters, so he was let go. He would land on his feet at Fox 11, where he would become one of the longest-running news directors in the company's history. Jose was fine; the rest of us weren't. Another news director was coming our way from a sister station.

John Lippman was his name. Word quickly spread among the station about this new hire. We started getting calls and notes from colleagues in Seattle, where this new guy was coming from. "LOOK OUT," they all said. They called him the Prince of Darkness. They said he was the worst. They sent us black roses with a condolence card. By this time, I had seen what, ten or twelve bosses come and go? No one could be *that* bad.

In came Lippman, and he was absolutely that bad and worse. At least in my humble opinion, and plenty of others agreed. We had never met a guy like this. He was mean to the bone; to this day, I don't know what made him tick. He had started his career on the air, but he wasn't some ace reporter. It was not apparent exactly what his great skill might be. But he had failed his way upward to news director—News Dictator was more like it. The complaints about my work started on day one and never stopped:

"The other day you went ten seconds too long."

"You looked to your left too much."

In no time flat, I started keeping a file of his daily written criticisms, just to protect myself. I had to. As time passed, I felt sure he was trying to antagonize me into quitting, though I had recently signed a four-year no-cut contract. If he fired me, I would still get paid, so there wasn't much he could do . . . except try to make me leave on my own.

These were dark days. My dad used to always say about any bad situation, "Look at it like it's a bucket of shit. The more you kick and scream and flail around, the more shit you get covered in. Just get out of it!"

All I could do was stay away as much as I could from the constant nitpicking. I had nowhere to go. I did know enough to let my agents handle as much as they could. A good agent does everything, including handle tricky personnel issues. Mine was worth every penny. That more than anything else saved me, that plus being out of the way. I wasn't there for the daily BS in the newsroom. Then suddenly . . . the city blew up.

In 1991, Rodney King, a Black man who lived in Los Angeles, spent an evening drinking and watching sports on TV at a friend's house. He was seen late that night by police speeding down the 210 Freeway in the Valley. He refused to pull over and led police on a high-speed chase through several residential areas before eventually being cornered. He refused to exit the car when asked, though his two passengers did so unhesitatingly.

King finally emerged but refused to lie flat on the ground after several requests. An officer eventually tasered him, whereupon all the officers converged on him and beat him with a baton more than fifty times as commanding officer Stacey Koon looked on. A man named George Holliday captured this on video from across the street . . . unbeknownst to the officers. Their official report said King had suffered "cuts and bruises of a minor nature" during the arrest.

Holliday's footage found its way to KTLA, and it sparked outrage nationwide. The officers were charged with using excessive force and assault with a deadly weapon. Public opinion grew so heated that the trial was moved from Los Angeles to the suburb of Simi Valley in neighboring Ventura County. On April 29, 1992, the jury issued its verdict: not guilty on all counts . . . and the city went off.

When the verdict came in, I was sent to the First African Methodist Episcopal Church in the West Adams district. AME was a center for the Black community, and hundreds of agitated citizens gathered. The mayor, Tom Bradley, and several other elected officials showed up to try to keep the peace. Anger smoldered in the air. The crowd would not be pacified.

All the other news stations were replacing their white reporters and cameramen with Black reporters and crew. Except for Wilson Posey and me; we had worked together for years and had an established rapport. A great cameraman is essential to any reporter; through the years, I'd been lucky to work with many who made me look better. We approached the scene, where the crowd was getting rougher and rougher; there was no containing this level of anger and frustration. Then we started smelling smoke. We walked outside, and we could see fires burning; I think it all started with a gas station. I had another cameraman with me, Marshall Sherwood, a tall redheaded guy. He told me he was going to go get some shots.

"Marshall, it is not safe right now, stay here," I told him. But he wouldn't listen and took off toward the smoke.

I was standing there with two city council members . . . both of whose cars were destroyed by rioters that night.

One of them said, "It's time to get out of here."

"Dave, we best be leaving," the other said. "The natives are getting restless." With that he turned and walked away.

Suddenly Marshall staggered back, dazed, with blood pouring down his face from a cut on the head where he'd been clobbered with a two-by-four. In my coaching years, my teams had played several teams from this area. Suddenly, a kid passing by who had played for Watts recognized me as the Downey coach. He came running up to us as I was trying to tend to Marshall.

"Hey, Mr. Lopez, remember me? I played basketball against your team? What's going on? Man, your friend got beat up!"

"Yeah, and his camera was stolen too."

"What? I'll get it back, don't you worry." He sprinted off and damned if he didn't return about twenty minutes later with

Marshall's camera. He handed it right over. *How the hell?* I had fifty bucks in my pocket and gave it to him.

Someone from the station arrived to take Marshall to the hospital, and I turned a corner to look for Wilson. As I headed to the parking lot, I saw twenty to thirty raging men standing in a group, yelling at the top of their lungs. They were rocking our news truck as hard as they could, trying to tip it over. Little did I know Wilson was inside, lying on the floor, hiding in fear that he would be seen, dragged out, and beaten mercilessly.

Then, out of nowhere, along came my colleague, debonair Black sports reporter Jim Hill, driving his massive SUV. Like a knight in shining armor, he parked next to me and jumped out. "Dave, how you doing out here, buddy? What's going on?"

"Jim, look at this!" I pointed.

He walked right over. "Hey, guys, I'm Jim Hill, what's going on?"

The group was immediately distracted by his presence, and many greeted him happily, clustering around the man they saw on TV all the time. "Hey, guys, listen, that guy over there, Lopez? He's cool, really. He's cool. This is his work truck, so leave it alone, OK?"

"OK, Jim, OK . . ." and the angry crowd magically dispersed. The door to the van opened, and a very shaken-up Wilson emerged.

"Jim," I said, "you are the answer to a prayer. What the hell are you doing here?"

"Just driving by, saw you, wanted to make sure you were OK," he said. "That's all."

We all got back in the van, and I told Wilson, "Get out of here!" I radioed the desk and said, "Things are really blowing up here, fires, furious crowds, you name it. I'm going to go home and start fresh tomorrow."

"Fine. Oh, by the way, Lopez. Your parents called . . . they're worried about you."

They had called the house looking for me from out of town, where they had seen the news. Elaine called the station to pass on the message. I found a safe phone booth and called my folks and then got on the Santa Monica Freeway to get home. All I could see was smoke and fires burning everywhere.

For the next four or five days, there were riots. We raced from one hot spot to another. Unbelievable turmoil. Jim Hill saved Wilson Posey's ass that night, plus a very valuable news truck. Why, exactly, this man showed up at exactly the right time to rescue us I'll never know, but we counted our blessings. What I remember most about that time was the rage erupting in the community. All told, sixty people would be killed, two thousand were injured, and the property damage was in the hundreds of millions. Decades of anger was boiling over. We would not see such devastation again until 2020 when a man named George Floyd was killed during his arrest.

My agent Steve Lefkowitz at N.S. Bienstock and I were talking over my current predicament one day, and he suggested that an extended international trip might be a good idea. "You're thinking about expanding, Dave," he said. "And they did offer you first crack at it. Why don't you accept and go to Somalia?"

Ten thousand miles away, a nation was collapsing. In 1991, African dictator Mohamed Siad Barre had been overthrown in a military coup, leading to an extended battle between two opposing warlords for control of the country. Somalia was on the brink of famine, with more than 4 million people literally starving to death. United Nations humanitarians doing their best to help were endlessly harassed; planes full of emergency food supplies were hijacked and looted. The streets of the capital city, Mogadishu, were deadly mayhem. President George Bush, who had just lost a reelection bid to Bill Clinton, proposed that U.S. troops be sent to protect aid workers. Every station in America was hot to cover the story and the landing of 25,000 Marines.

I could barely pronounce Mogadishu; I couldn't find Somalia on a map. Still, this was certainly an important international story, completely different from anything I had been involved with up to this point and way out of my comfort zone. I accepted the assignment and started to read up on the nation's history and present situation. Then, having gained a bit of knowledge and hearing the steady drumbeat of bad news coming into the station, I decided I might back out, but by then it was too late.

Tami was currently preparing to take the SATs. When I told her I would be going to Somalia, she didn't score very well. She promptly blamed me, because she said she was so worried about me that she couldn't concentrate. (She did much better the second time around.) My good friend, the brilliant Dr. Albert Attyah, gave me all kinds of immunizations before I left. As I sat in his office getting jabbed over and over, he chided me. "Travelers usually get these shots over a period of three or four days. Diphtheria, malaria . . . You're getting them all at once!"

By the time I left that clinic, I felt like a pincushion. Dr. Attyah had given me all kinds of tips . . . I packed light clothes and planned to leave what I didn't use behind. A well-meaning friend gave me a guidebook called *Useful Phrases to Use When Traveling in a Muslim Area.* It didn't help in Somalia.

I would take this trip with a producer named Danny Tobias. I said my goodbyes to Elaine and the kids back at home. My parents accompanied me to Los Angeles International Airport, where Danny and I were going to board a flight to London, then go on to Kenya, and then to Mogadishu. I had never been to Africa before. I was excited . . . naively excited. This Orange County reporter, heading off to a war zone, had no idea what I was getting myself into . . . none at all.

"So, are we going to be able to do any live shots, Danny, do you think?" I asked him at LAX as we waited for our flight.

He replied offhandedly, "We're not going to get out of there alive."

"WHAT?" I said.

Seeing my parents' stricken faces, he hastened to reassure us, "No, no, I said, *we're not going to be able to get any live shots!*"

"OK, OK," I replied, and my parents settled down.

Goodbyes were said and off we flew overnight to London. We landed early morning British time. It was pitch dark, like it was midnight. "What time does the sun come up here?" I asked.

"Oh, it's wintertime. The sun comes up around nine-thirty, ten o'clock."

This was my first big trip overseas. I had never been so far away from home, and it was thrilling. Danny used our layover to get everything set up so that when we arrived in Somalia we would be fed and have a crew ready. We then boarded a plane for Kenya, which was nearly a ten-hour flight. Our plane wasn't crowded. About halfway through I started getting the shakes and chills and was feeling quite ill. I fell into an uneasy sleep and woke up feeling fine. A reaction to the shots? Nerves? I'll never know, but thankfully, I was OK again when we landed.

It was immediately apparent just how far from home we were upon landing in Kenya. Danny carried a cell phone the size of a briefcase. I did a quick phoner back to the station to say that we had landed safely in Africa, while Danny made more arrangements. I also managed to film a report at a local Kenya station that we somehow transferred back to LA. How that was done, using the most primitive equipment I had ever seen, I cannot imagine. Next, we boarded a small plane with a couple of other reporters. The Mogadishu airport had been closed, so we were going to land at a place called Runway 33. Naive me, I thought that meant an actual runway number.

I had been told that all the people in this part of the country were dependent on a drug called khat. They chewed it constantly, all day long, like gum. Its effects are similar to cocaine's, and everyone I saw did it: men, women, old people, kids. The first thing I noticed about Somalia was that everyone carried a gun—again, I mean *everyone*. The second thing I noticed was that everyone had a toe or two missing. This was because they would get so high chewing khat that they would accidentally blow off a toe while toting their guns around. I did not see one single person of any age there with all five toes on both feet the entire time. I had heard some stories, but seeing it up close and in person was a whole different proposition.

We landed at Runway 33, which I quickly learned was so named because it was thirty-three miles from Mogadishu. It was not a runway; it was a dirt pit. The minute we landed, the plane was engulfed by a sea of eager, grabbing people, excited that the plane had landed. Our British pilot emerged carrying a whip, cracking it at the crowd, yelling and screaming at the mass to get back. They thought he was carrying khat onboard, but he wasn't—only some frightened newsmen. By this time, I was becoming sorry I had gotten myself into this.

How would we get into town, our final destination? I saw some ancient cattle trucks parked nearby. A guy started waving to get our attention. "Hey, CBS!" he called. "Come on, get in, to the bureau!"

Twenty of us crammed in and stood in the back of the cattle truck as the giant sun started to sink into the horizon. It took quite some time to travel thirty-three miles over a rutted path into Mogadishu. About five miles outside of Mogadishu proper—brown, dry, and deserted—Danny had arranged for a guy to pick us up in a Toyota. For whatever reason, Toyota appeared to be the brand of choice in that part of the world. We jumped off the truck and looked around. All I could see were people holding guns—and lots of feet with missing toes. It was surreal.

The five of us CBS staffers managed to find our guy; he packed us into the Toyota. He wasn't going fast, but as he took a hard turn, the steering wheel came off—right in his hands, just came off. We in the back seats managed to jump out just before the car plowed into a building.

"Jesus, Danny," I said. "What are we doing here?"

We were a bit shook but unharmed. Somehow, the driver reattached the steering wheel and backed the car up, revealing only minor damage to the front end. We eventually made it to the bureau.

The crew at the CBS bureau were outstanding—amazingly professional and helpful. The first night we arrived, they wanted me to do a broadcast, just to show that CBS-LA had arrived.

"Go to the airport," the bureau guy told me. "Dan Rather's there, and he knows you're coming. As soon as he's done, you can use his crew; things will be all set up already."

Danny and I headed out and stood to the side as Dan delivered his report. After he wrapped up, he glanced over at me, and to my surprise, he remembered me. We had met a couple of times, but nothing substantial.

"Hey, Dave," he said. "You doing OK? I'll be done here in just a few minutes, and then it's your turn."

He wrapped it up and moved away. I jumped into place, did my own report, and we were off and running. It felt pretty good to be recognized by such an industry titan!

The scene in Mogadishu was grim. I seriously had to wonder, was my horrible new boss actually trying to get me killed? It was the most desolate, poverty-stricken landscape imaginable. One day, I looked over and saw some young kids playing soccer, a rare pleasant scene. But the ball was misshapen and covered all over with dirty white tape. On closer inspection, I realized that the ball was a human head, covered over in bandages. I could see the bloody scalp and hair peeking out. I turned away, feeling nauseous.

We slept in cots with guards holding assault rifles outside the building. I had brought along a bunch of goodies for bribes, which served me well. The guards especially loved Tic Tacs, I think because of the noise the box made when they shook it. Our security was outstanding; these men protected us, got us from place to place, and we managed to put together and deliver our reports every night at the appointed time slot. I ate rattlesnake for the first time; it was mixed in with some tinned spaghetti. I didn't know I had eaten rattlesnake until the meal was over; I could have done without that knowledge.

I had been in some sticky situations before. Dangerous situations. I'd covered riots, uprisings, floods . . . But I had never been scared like this. I had a perpetual sick feeling in my stomach the entire time. Everything was just so foreign. The constant threat of violence in the air was palpable. There was simply no infrastructure, no government, no resources, no authorities or help to be found. The main food was an unidentifiable oatmeal mixture. When I did face-to-face interviews, I had to constantly swat the flies away from my face. It was so hot. It was brutal. And I knew I was living a privileged existence there, infinitely better than the local populace had it. When the Marines finally landed, I was elated. I felt like I personally had been liberated. We got the job done and never missed a broadcast during our five-day stay. That was more than enough for me.

We headed back to the Mogadishu airport, where a bunch of small planes were lined up outside. We walked by, asking who might be going to Kenya, till we found someone willing to let us hop a ride. The pilots weren't supposed to charge us, as they had to go there anyway, but of course they wanted money. Fortunately, we had some. Danny and I boarded an ancient Russian cargo plane with seats like benches and sat there. I strapped myself in and held on as our Russian pilot proceeded to make five separate stops in what seemed like complete wilderness.

At a desolate airstrip somewhere in the wilds of Somalia, we landed to find a big crowd on the ground, dancing and singing. An enormous man in the center eventually made his way onto the plane with the dignified bearing of a king and took his place on a bench. Eventually, we all made it to Kenya. We walked down the steps of the Russian cargo plane, and I instinctively fell to my knees and kissed the ground, just like Pope John Paul did every time he landed in a foreign country.

I was so happy to be back in civilization and have a decent bath and meal available. We checked into a modern hotel, where I proceeded to take the longest shower I had ever taken. I looked at the room service menu and called downstairs. "I want one of each—everything on the menu—oh, and bring me a dozen cans of Coke."

"Hey, Danny," I asked after the big meal. "How much expense money do we have left?"

"About three grand," he answered.

There was a casino on the ground floor of the hotel, so I made a proposal: "Let's split it and try our luck."

So we did. We had a fun night out with a crew from British Air. The next night, we joined forces with them to enjoy one of the most magnificent meals I ever had in my life at a place called the Rendezvous.

With no more stories required of us, we had two days of free time before our flight back to London so I did a bit of shopping. I found a beautiful carved ivory nativity set in the tiny town square market. The vendor wanted two hundred bucks for it. It was exquisite, but that was way too much money. I regretfully said no and started walking back to my hotel.

The persistent vendor followed me, insisting I buy it. He would not leave me alone. I actually began to believe that if I didn't buy it, I would not be leaving the country. So, I reluctantly handed over two hundred bucks and took the scene safely home. It was a real showpiece; everyone who saw it always commented on the beauty of its one-of-a-kind manger scene, with every piece carved out of black ivory.

The calendar was inching closer and closer to Christmas. On my last day on the streets of Somalia, I ran right into my old compadre Bob Schaeffer, who was currently working at a Houston station as a field producer. Small world. I didn't even recognize him at first. I borrowed his fancy mobile phone to call home and assure the kids I was on the way at a dollar a minute.

We were more than ready to go home. I had stacks of local paper money in my pocket. There was a portrait of someone who looked just like Idi Amin on the bills; I thought they would be a fun souvenir for my kids. I was going through airport customs when the officer asked me, "Are you carrying any currency?"

I wasn't about to lie, so I answered, "Oh, I have a few bucks in my pocket."

He held his hand out. "Let me see it. . . . Sorry," he said, shaking his head when he saw the stack. "Too much money . . . You have to go to a separate line, claim it, and fill out the forms."

I saw the long line where he was pointing and made a split-second decision. "Merry Christmas," I said. "You keep it."

The money vanished, and he waved me through. To this day, I have no idea how much I gave him, but I didn't care.

I landed in London at three in the afternoon, where it was once again pitch-black. I really had to wonder if the sun ever shone in this city at all. From what I had seen, they had zero hours of daylight. After our layover and another long flight, I was home. I had never been so happy to be home, from any-where—and just in time for Christmas.

I had some time to reflect as I told people of my adventures. It had been quite an experience to behold, but my nerves were shot. The station sent other reporters to Somalia later, but I had no desire to repeat the experience. I had been toying with the idea of expanding and entertained some romantic notions of becoming a traveling foreign correspondent . . . that dream was so over. I was a SoCal man through and through, and happy to be one. I got back on my beat, gratefully.

CHAPTER FIFTEEN

O.J.? WHO CARES

ITY is no longer only experienced directly,
e filtered, enhanced, distorted mediation of editors.

BETTER BELIEVE I WAS PLEASED to be home in America, with a newfound appreciation for my job and lifestyle, but my colleagues and I continued to struggle under Lippman's leadership. He made our daily working lives nearly unbearable. It's tough enough to do a television broadcast . . . go live on the air with the news every day . . . but to have someone on high sniping at you nonstop from all directions without warning was nerve-racking. He was so demanding; I was doing two and three stories a day, meaning there was no time to write out a script.

On my way to shoot, I was always thinking about what to say on the scene. I dictated to myself, always remembering what a previous managing editor, Karl Fleming, had said to me so many times: "Write like you talk." Be natural, pleasant, and get the information out in a conversational tone.

One day, racing to cover something, I said to my camera-man, "We don't have time . . . let's just wing it." I went live on the air, ad-libbed the story, and it went just fine. That was the beginning of the end of working with scripts for me. Oh, I'd jot down notes occasionally, but I became comfortable jumping into the van, grabbing the mike, and telling the cameraman, "OK, let's go." They all looked at me like I was crazy; they'd never seen this done before. But it worked out well, and it sure saved a lot of time. It felt natural to me; it wasn't difficult. I had spent a lifetime preparing!

Navigating our Jekyll-and-Hyde boss's moods was not fun. The chaos was constant; you never knew what was going to happen next. One busy day in the newsroom, our main anchor, Mike Tuck, was sitting at a spare desk, working away. Lippman raced in, in a manic rush as always, saying, "Tuck, get up! I need you on the air, right now. You're on the air in two."

Tuck got to his feet and said, "Hold on, what's this story about, exactly?"

"Don't worry about it, I've got some notes right here for you, just GO ON!" He shoved a page with some messy handwritten phrases at Tuck. "MOVE! You're live in ninety seconds!"

Tuck was incredulous. "I am not prepared. I am not going live on the air to report on a story I know nothing about with zero background and no time to research. My reputation means more to me than that. You can forget it. Absolutely not!"

Well, things got very heated and soon led to a pretty good physical tussle right there in front of the riveted newsroom. A staffer with a camera doing a video shoot nearby slowly silenced his subject and turned up the volume. The audio was captured for all eternity, and it was not pretty. Tuck didn't back down— nor did he get fired. Later that day, my colleague Tritia Toyota drew an outline around the desk in chalk like you'd see at a crime scene and tied it off with official yellow tape. Just another day in the newsroom.

I feared the worst when Lippman called me in for a face-to-face meeting. To be fair, his feedback wasn't entirely withering. He had sent me a couple of complimentary notes over the months, which were mailed directly to my house:

"Good job getting the tornado victim."

"Strong stories and made a big impact, thank you."

He had a pleasant side, but I was no longer taken in by it. My "Lippman fuck file" of the pettiest complaints, hundreds of them, was now several inches thick.

I was so paranoid that I had a cop buddy of mine fit me out with a wire before my meeting. Lippman had assured me I didn't need a union rep to accompany me, but there was no way I was going in alone. I thought he might pull . . . something. I got ready. I took notes. If he was going to fire me, I planned to sue him and have plenty of backup. Our big meeting didn't come to all that; he pissed and moaned about my excessive telephone bill. On and on, then I was abruptly dismissed to live another day.

It felt like forever, but his stay at our station was only around eighteen months. Lippman decided he wanted to record area earthquake movements and sent some station engineers over to the Cal Tech campus one day to hook a camera into their sophisticated system. He didn't bother to ask for any permissions.

When university officials found out, that was the end. We all received the one-line memo on April 30, 1993: "John Lippman is no longer with the company."

The reign of terror was over. A huge collective sigh went up in the newsroom. Some joker printed out a message: DING DONG, THE WITCH IS GONE. But . . . it was not quite over.

Oh, how we were rejoicing. We had no news director for a couple of months, and that was just fine with us, particularly as it happened to be an off year in the election cycle. I was assigned a freelance soundman one day to accompany Wilson Posey, my regular guy, for a story. We got to talking and the guy mentioned he was from Seattle.

"How did you wind up here?" I asked idly.

"Oh, we had this news director who was just a complete son of a bitch. I had to get out of there, fast. I would have gone any-where to escape him." He looked at me and said, "You know, if I had the chance to burn down that man's house, I would have." This was a perfectly reasonable man; he appeared quite profes-sional, and he was not kidding.

"What did he do, exactly?"

"He's cruel, he's vindictive, he plays favorites, he's unfair, he surrounds himself with toadies . . . trust me, you don't ever want anything to do with this guy. Bob Jordan," he spit out the name. "I gotta tell you, man, if you ever hear he's coming your way, head for the hills. He's vicious."

Duly noted. A few weeks later, I was out on a story and called it in. "Hey, we've got a new news director," the guy on the other end of the line at the station said.

"Oh yeah? Who is it this time?"

"Hang on, let me find that memo . . . OK, here it is . . . some guy named Bob Jordan, from Seattle."

Posey and I looked at each other. We couldn't believe what we were hearing. And, sure enough, Bob Jordan swept in. He'd had so many jobs that his nickname was Suitcase Bob . . . and now he was all ours. I tried to set a meeting with him as soon as he arrived. Nothing. Zippo. He never responded, despite my following up several times. Finally, one day I saw him in the newsroom and approached him in person. "Hi, Bob, I'm Dave Lopez. Got a few minutes?"

"Nope, no time. Call my secretary," he brushed me off, without even looking me in the face.

As bad as Lippman had been, this guy was worse. Unbelievably, we had gone from the frying pan into the fire. Our very latest news director was exactly as advertised. We'd been suffering under his reign for nearly a year when all hell broke loose.

Early on a gorgeous summer morning in June 1994, Steve Crawford was working the desk. He got a tip that a violent crime had gone down in Brentwood—a most unusual occurrence. He put two and two together and realized the address might be O.J. Simpson's ex-wife's home. Carl Stein from our station arrived on the scene first, whipped out his camera and started filming some shocking footage. There were still large pools of darkening blood from the two victims on the walkways; Carl got it. He had received confirmation that the female victim was Nicole Brown Simpson and knew this was destined to be a major story.

Back at the station, I was told by people in the editorial meeting that morning that when Jordan was told about the O.J. story he said, "O.J.? He's a washed-up has-been. Nobody will care about this." Someone—no one has ever officially fessed up—ordered Carl to leave the murder scene immediately and go to another story. Carl fought like hell, but he left.

A short time later, according to Carl, Jordan called him on the phone and asked, "Why did you leave the scene?" Carl answered, "I was told to."

"By whom?"

"The desk. Do you want me to go back?"

Jordan said, "No, I'll take care of it from here."

It's hard to overstate the role the evening news played in the O.J. Simpson murder case. O.J. was a beloved local figure, a sports god, still revered for his football days at USC. I personally would never forget being in the USC locker room after he carried the ball a remarkable fifty-five times in one game. Coach John McKay was once asked, "Are you worried about overworking him?" He replied, "Why, does he belong to a union? The ball's not heavy."

Now The Juice was a genial movie star, acting in silly comedy films like *The Naked Gun* and pitching fitness products and rental cars on TV. His former wife and her male friend had been viciously stabbed to death in one of the most peaceable, wealthy, and well-populated sections on the entire West Side. No one could wrap their heads around this crime. They tuned in to get the latest . . . all the time.

On the night of June 17, 1994, the entire nation came to a halt as O.J.'s former teammate Al Cowlings slowly drove his friend on a two-hour, low-speed drive down the LA freeways. O.J. was supposed to turn himself into police for questioning but took off instead. Now he had a gun in the back seat and was threatening suicide. LA residents lined the freeway for miles and miles, most waving supportive signs.

There was a major sporting event airing that night—an NBA finals game—but every single broadcast network plus CNN's all-news channel carried this astounding white Bronco "chase" live. The drama was riveting. More than 95 million Americans were glued to their screens—at home, in sports bars, sitting with their neighbors—as celebrity met sports met murder. The "chase" ended back at his Brentwood mansion, where The Juice surrendered. This night truly marked the beginning of tabloid TV.

What can I say about the trial of the century? It was enormous. It was a three-ring circus. It was news at its best and worst—and right there in our very own backyard. I soon got the call saying, "You are no longer in Orange County. For the duration of the trial, you're in LA covering the O.J. case."

Three of us reporters—Harvey Levin, Pat Lalama, and I—were the official Channel 2 staff. Harvey had an assigned seat in the courtroom; Pat and I did on-the-scene interviews outside. I stood there every day, in front of mobs and mobs of onlookers held back by fences and police, at the scene of an absolute zoo. For an entire year, this was my job.

My first day of duty I did what I always do: jumped right in. I called a buddy of mine who was a police detective on the case; he had retrieved the broken glass in O.J.'s hotel room in Chicago on the night of the murders. Bert Luper and I had gone to South Gate High together and stayed in touch. When I saw him on TV, filmed coming back from Chicago, I called him up, reminisced a bit, and then told him I'd been assigned to cover this story.

"Oh, you poor bastard," Bert said with feeling.

"Come on, us South Gate guys have to stick together!"

He would help me; many longtime sources did. I got the first interview with officer Mark Fuhrman in West Hollywood, long before his particular shortcomings were exposed in court for the world to see. But my main job was to stand outside, ringmaster of the circus. I always carried an extra hankie for my coworker Pat, who by her own admission was an "emotional Italian." She would burst into tears at anything. From Bruno Magli shoes, Nicole's faithful Akita, and her glamorous sisters to the enraged Goldman family and the incredible spectacle of O.J., one of my true sports heroes, on trial for his life—each day was more surreal than the last.

The competition for scoops was brutal. The public was gobbling up every scrap of gossip or hearsay, and we did our best to get newsworthy interviews, but all the big national shows were firmly planted in LA for the duration. *Good Morning America, The Today Show,* and the evening tabloid shows had all arrived, and they had big budgets. They could wine and dine people. Shows couldn't offer actual money for an interview, but a trip to New York, a stay in a luxury hotel, wardrobe, meals . . . we couldn't compete with that. As the trial ground on, it became a major coup to score an interview with a dismissed juror. Word started going around: "You can get more if you wait for a national show; don't bother with local media." Book deals were being thrown around along with limo rides, lunches at Spago, and theater tickets, all as incentives for exclusives. It was really tough for the local team . . . us.

From the guy on the ground who covered the O.J. trial for months on end, I have two words: *long hours.* Those days were just so endless. Reporters could not miss a minute of the action; every media outlet in the country was there, hungry for a scrap. The entire American press corps had turned into a tabloid pack of wolves. A few remained above the fray; the distinguished journalist Dominick Dunne had his own prime courtroom spot, and certain other veteran reporters like Jeffrey Toobin of *The New Yorker* also had preferred seats. Vendors sold "FREE O.J." paraphernalia outside to spectators. Some guy put together a video of outtakes from the madhouse that was outside the courtroom, and it sold briskly. We will never see a news event like that again in my lifetime.

The trial wrapped up after eight months. I raced to the station to pick up another reporter as the jury deliberated. We were driving back into downtown LA, planning a round-robin interview with the jurors. Suddenly we heard on the radio that the jury had reached a verdict! I thought my colleague would have a nervous breakdown, thinking we would miss the announcement . . . until we heard that the verdict would not be read until the following day. The cops needed time to prepare . . . for whatever the verdict might be.

I called a friend of mine that night who worked on the defense team. "So, what do you think?" I asked.

"Oh, not guilty, for sure," he said confidently.

"What do you mean not guilty; he's guilty as sin. DNA all over the place."

"He is absolutely not guilty, Dave!"

I wasn't sure if he really believed it, had been persuaded by Johnnie Cochran's glove trick, or was just parroting the party line. The next day, I was standing outside in my usual spot as news trucks lined every downtown street bumper to bumper for blocks. When that "Not Guilty" verdict was read, the entire courthouse and surrounding environs erupted in utter pandemonium. Mounted cops on horseback did their best to hold back the crowds—some in shock, some jubilating. I never dreamed of such a wild spectacle at the generally dull LA courthouse.

O.J. Simpson was found not guilty by the state of California of the murders of his ex-wife and her companion . . . the prosecution had not proved their case "beyond a reasonable doubt." The Goldman family then sued him for wrongful death in civil court. The bar of proof in this case was much lower: they only needed to show that Simpson's actions had led to their deaths by a preponderance of evidence, which they easily did.

Exactly a year after the shocking verdict in the murder trial downtown, court resumed in the civil trial in a Santa Monica courtroom. Once again, the circus was on. O.J. was forced to take the stand this time around, but there were, thankfully, no television cameras allowed, and the cast that had made such compelling news—Marcia Clark, Christopher Darden, Johnnie Cochran, Bob Shapiro, Judge Ito, and so many others—had all moved on to varying degrees of fame and fortune. There would be no criminal penalties for the disgraced star when he was convicted, but he was ordered to pay the families of the victims $33.5 million. Simpson immediately filed for bankruptcy.

We had all worked ourselves as hard as humanly possible during the year of the trial. And I will give Jordan credit for pulling me out of Orange County and assigning me to the biggest story of the century. And blessing of blessings, this trial led to Jordan's downfall. There was some controversy over a warrant served in the first trial, and we had a reporter there who insisted on going by the time code stamped on the camera. The camera had incorrectly recorded the time when we recorded Marcia Clark. The search warrant became a big controversy, and Jordan was out.

Along came a man named Larry Perret, who seemed okay; we got along well enough. He let me stay to cover the story until both O.J. trials were over and then I returned to my regular Orange County beat full time. I just wanted life and the news to go back to normal. Neither would ever do so again.

CHAPTER SIXTEEN

"Dave, You Have Cancer"

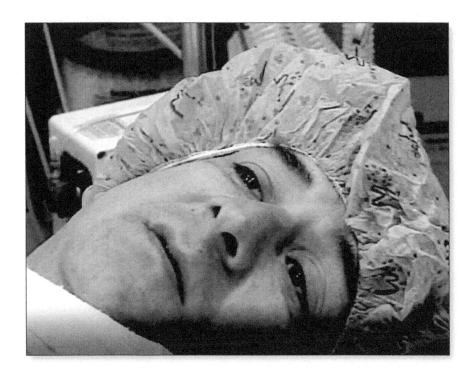

I WAS NO LONGER THE EAGER YOUNG REPORTER constantly seeking advice from more experienced mentors. I was forty-eight years old, for heaven's sake, and I'd been at the station for twenty years. News directors would come and go; I soldiered on. My buddy Jose was now news director at Channel 11. One day he called me up out of the blue. "Hey, Dave, you doing any coaching these days?"

"No, Jose, I'm done. Haven't done that in years."

Coaching Matt's teams had been a tremendous amount of work on top of the significant financial commitment. The uniforms, the balls, the insurance, van rentals . . . it all added up, not to mention I was always inconveniently out of town at a tournament for every family occasion, including my own birthday every year. I did miss the kids, though.

"Reason I ask, I have a woman sitting in my office with a major problem. Let me put her on the phone with you."

"Hi, I'm here calling on Jose about his satellite system, but we started talking about our sons and sports. My son plays on a basketball team, but they're not very good. I can't find anyone willing to coach them. If we don't get a coach by next weekend, the boys will all go into a pool, but no one will choose them because, as I said, they're not very good. We desperately need a coach!"

"How old are they?" I asked.

"Third grade."

"Oh. Little guys. I'll tell you, I haven't coached for a long time. Would you mind if my son helped me out?"

"That would be great!"

"I can't do all the legwork; I can only coach," I warned her.

Fine, fine, she was delighted to have any coach at all. It sounded interesting, so I showed up to their practice at a church in Chinatown. Matt and I walked into the gym where a bunch of little Japanese kids with hair flopping all over their faces were racing around. They were so small and skinny! What was I going to do with them? I ran them through some drills and were those kids ever smart. I'd run a drill once, and they got it—tiny, but determined. I fell in love with this bunch of scrappy kids. I could not resist the challenge. By the time we ended the season, we had won five games, lost five. Not bad!

Though Matt and I were usually the only Caucasians present at any game, the rules permitted two non-Asian players on our team. For our upcoming year, I talked to one of my players,

Sumo. "Ask your mom if I can bring a kid to play on the team who's not Asian, but Mexican."

At our next practice, Sumo said, "I talked to my mom, Mr. Lopez, and she said, 'Only one per team. We already have you. So . . . no more Mexicans!'"

I cracked up.

The second year, our team got even better; we lost only one game. The third year, better yet. I was teaching those kids all kinds of stuff, they were excelling, and we were all having a ball.

Then . . . we were getting unmercifully hammered by the ref during one game. I tried to stay calm. I had mellowed a bit, plus big displays of emotion were generally discouraged in the Asian culture. But this time I couldn't hold back. At halftime, I ran up to the ref and said, "What are you doing? You are the worst ref . . ." I went off and then returned to my bench.

A man came up to me shortly afterward with the referee at his side. Very seriously, he said, "You need to apologize to the referee."

I said, "Come on, he's a crappy ref. I'm not apologizing."

"You don't understand, he is a very big man in the community, you must apologize for impugning his integrity."

"Not apologizing, the hell with him." I did not back down, I did not apologize, and we lost the game.

Two weeks later, I got a phone call that I had to attend a special meeting with all the parents, where I was told there would soon be a change in coaches. They had voted 7–2 against me. Two parents took me out to dinner afterward.

"Guess you're the only two who voted for me," I said.

No more coaching for me, but I would miss those kids. It may have been for the best . . . coaching was about to become the very last thing on my mind.

∞

I had vowed to myself early on to always get a complete physical every year, period. I was religious about these visits once I turned forty. Every year: full tests, complete workup, like clockwork. I got a phone call out of the blue from my doctor, who also happened to be my neighbor. "Dave, we have a problem with your blood," he told me one warm fall day in September 1996.

"What kind of problem?" I asked.

"Well, your PSA is high."

"What the hell is a PSA?"

"It's a reading on the function of your prostate." The PSA test, he explained, measured levels of protein in the blood. A higher-than-normal reading was cause for concern. "Your reading is six-point-six," he said. "It's supposed to be under four, though actually we like to see under two. You need to go see a specialist, now."

He referred me to a specialist, Dr. Al Vargas. He accompanied me right over to his office, where the receptionist greeted me with, "Oh, yes, Mr. Lopez, the doctor is expecting you," and ushered me right in. I was briefly grateful for the minor perks of TV celebrity.

Dr. Vargas said, "First I'm going to take another blood test. Then I'm going to give you some really strong medication, which should make this PSA level reading go down, significantly, right away. We'll see you in a couple of weeks."

Two weeks later, after taking the medication daily, I returned for another blood test. The levels had barely budged; my new reading was 6.1. "Not good enough," said Dr. Vargas. "We need to do a biopsy."

"Sure," I said.

Little did I know what that entailed. I found myself sitting on a table, naked under a gown, as Dr. Vargas looked me right in the eye and said, "I need you to remain very still." Two nurses held me down. POP! A crack went through the room like a gunshot. I almost fell out of the chair. The pain was excruciating.

"How many more?" I gasped.

"Five more," the doctor replied calmly.

God, did that ever hurt. But it did end. I left feeling not too worried, knowing I was in good hands. Of course, I was also thinking of my father, who had suffered through his own bout of prostate cancer. There's a hereditary element to cancer, of course . . . would I draw the unlucky straw?

Around this time, I got a call asking me to come in for a meeting with the news director. We set the meeting for the next morning. I was generally prepared for anything, but was this ever a shocker.

"We're cutting your salary by ten percent," Perret said, just for openers; I had barely taken my seat. "The work you're doing doesn't justify that amount. Oh, and we're taking back your company car. Budget constraints, you know."

Discussions went downhill from there. I kept my cool . . . not that I had much choice. This was the good thing about being raised by Dad . . . there could be no bigger son of a bitch. I was well prepared for this sort of confrontation out of the blue; I didn't take it as hard as many others would have . . . and usually did. I remained polite and professional, left the office, and then immediately scribbled off a note to my agent detailing the conversation. "I have complete confidence that this will all work out. After all, no one can keep a quick-tempered Mexican down for long," I finished it.

As always, my agent Steve was on the case. He told me, "Listen, there's a new company starting up . . . Fox News. We could easily get you set up over there." I'd heard many rumors about media baron Rupert Murdoch's brand-new baby, long in the planning stages, getting ready to launch.

"Well . . . there's one more thing. I might have . . . cancer," I told him.

Silence, but just for a few seconds. "What? OK fine, well, we just won't tell them."

"Steve, what do you mean don't tell them? We can't do that! And what the hell is Fox News all about, anyway?"

"It's going to be a conservative channel, an alternative to CNN. They're looking for a guy in LA. We can get you an audition. We'll fly you to New York, have you meet with Roger Ailes . . . don't worry, Dave, we'll get you all set up."

I thought about it . . . hard. But something told me to gut it out where I was. It was only a matter of time before this news director went the way of the twelve—or was it fifteen by now?—before him. I was going to outlast him. "No, I'll take the cut."

One thing I knew I had as an AFTRA union member was top-notch health insurance . . . which had suddenly become a much bigger priority. Bosses aside, I loved my job. Channel 2 was home. I decided to make the best of it. Things would be tight, but Elaine was working. We would muddle through.

Two days later the official diagnosis arrived . . . on September 24, 1996. I had prostate cancer. I was scared and angry. I allowed myself a moment to throw a full-scale tantrum. "Why God, why?" I raged. "Of all the people, why me? For fifty years, I've done my best to live a good life. Never did anything wrong. WHY ME?" I threw rolled-up socks at the walls. Kicked the bed. Cursed at the top of my lungs, loudly and profanely. After five minutes, I was exhausted. Then I was done. That was it, out of my system. It was time to do what I needed to do.

Back in Dr. Vargas's office, I asked, "So, what now?"

"Three options," he replied. "You can do nothing, and we'll

keep you comfortable. You might live for ten years, though things will get really uncomfortable around year five or six. I'm not going to kid you, the progression will be quite painful. That's option number one."

"That's not even an option," I said. "What else?"

"Just starting there," the doctor said. "So, option number two is radiation."

Dad had had radiation and was utterly miserable throughout. The treatments were terribly painful and also left him permanently "leaky."

"If you want radiation, you will have to go to another doctor," Dr. Vargas interrupted my thoughts. "Because I don't think that's the best option. I recommend the third option—surgery. A procedure called radical prostatectomy, meaning we remove the entire prostate gland."

In 1996, this was major surgery, where they cut you wide open for a three-to-five-hour operation. The likely side effects were impotence and incontinence. Both chilling words to any man . . . the dreaded double whammy.

"I will do the best I can," Dr. Vargas said.

I knew he was a brilliant doctor with a stellar reputation; he taught at USC, where he was renowned for his work. It was an easy decision. But even at that moment, the newsman in me saw a story. "Doc, if you don't mind, I'd like to do a story about this. This could help inform a lot of families going through the same thing."

"That would be fine," he said without hesitation.

"I trust you," I said. "Let's do it."

Elaine, of course, was frightened . . . by everything coming up, but mostly by the fact that I had cancer. I had a 7.2 score on the Gleason scale, which measures how fast a cancer is growing from 1 to 10. It had to come out. "At the end, this is my decision, and I think this is the best thing to do," I told my wife. We drove to tell the kids the news in person; that was a hard day for everyone.

I had a much happier meeting with my old mentor, Pete, who was back at the station and agreed to produce a two-part special on my bout with prostate cancer. I was afraid of many things: the surgery, the side effects, and the fact that, even after surgery, we might be too late; I could still die a terrible, lingering death. But live or die, I knew Pete would have my back—as always.

I made preparations for the surgery, including donating blood for myself to use during the procedure. I went under the knife on October 21, 1996, at St. Francis Medical Center in Lynwood. "You have a fifteen to twenty percent chance of not being impotent after this, and I will do everything I can to ensure there's no incontinence." After those final assurances from Dr. Vargas, I was wheeled into surgery, camera crew following right behind.

The last thing I remember is lying on the operating table, where I was given a saddle block to ensure there would be no pain or any feeling whatsoever in the upcoming hours. When the needle went in, I became immediately woozy and then utterly paralyzed from the waist down—like a block of granite. Having no idea what I would awaken to, I went out a few moments later.

I awoke to a world of pain. I stayed in intensive care for two days immediately following surgery; it was a big deal. I had an enormous scar on my stomach and was as weak as a kitten. I stayed in the hospital for a full week, just recovering my strength. I can't say I was the best patient; I hated being cooped up in a hospital, confined to bed. But the news was good: the cancer was fully contained. It had not spread. When they removed it, my prostate gland was not walnut-sized, as a healthy one should be. It was the size of a lemon—terribly swollen and infected . . . but now it was gone.

My mother, bless her heart, said, "Come to the house." Elaine was still teaching, and they both knew I would need help around the clock. The nurses at St. Francis were happy to see me go . . . home, to my parents' house, where I'd grown up. It was just like being a kid again. Mostly, I slept a lot . . . fourteen to sixteen hours a day. I was too weak to even wash myself; I stood in the shower as my mom bathed me.

Mom also cooked and served my meals, helped me in and out of bed . . . she did everything. As always, she was there to make everything better; she waited on me hand and foot. I had been there for a week when my dad said, "I think it's about time to get your ass out of here." So I went home for the second part of my recovery.

I had lost a lot of weight . . . I got down to 189, a number I hadn't seen in quite some time. Of course, it would eventually all come back on. I was off work for three full months; it would be a full year before I felt truly well and like myself again. During that year, I did a great deal of public speaking about prostate cancer. I visited hospitals, cancer support groups, and cancer awareness foundations. I tried to turn what had turned out well for me into something that might do someone else some good. The special was well received; it got good solid ratings. After part two aired, I got a call from Perret: "Hey, Dave, can you shoot two more shows?"

"Hell no," I told him. "I'm done!"

I saved a card from a fan that I'd received in the hospital after my surgery: *Dear Dave, Wishing you a very speedy recovery. I think it's a shame that such an important part of a man's equipment should cause so much trouble.* Yes, it caused major trouble, but as always, my luck was holding. I was in the small percentage of men who were not rendered impotent. I wasn't the same, exactly, and never would be, but everything still functioned. I was also spared major incontinence. I made a full recovery, and

I knew how blessed I was. I met many fine men that year who were too late; the cancer had spread.

Cancer certainly teaches humility and straightens out one's life priorities, fast. Twenty-five years later, my PSA reading remains at 0.0. I still go to my annual physical religiously, and Dr. Vargas continued to be a legend in his field for many years to come. The cause remains dear to my heart, as I know firsthand how hard this journey is on any man. Fortunately, there have been tremendous advances in surgical procedures that minimize nerve damage since that time.

A friend of mine had the surgery recently and was simply devastated that he has to wear an incontinence pad; he can't be far from a bathroom now at any time. He leaks a bit, as we all do. "Jesus, wear a double pad, like I have for twenty years and carry on!" I said. "Come on, we're alive to fight another day! We are the lucky ones!"

CHAPTER SEVENTEEN

THE HAIDL CASE

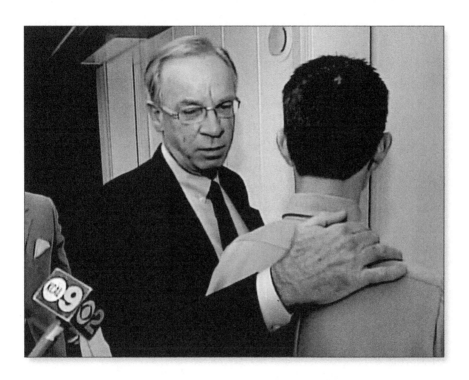

ORANGE COUNTY WAS MY HOME BEAT; the dealings at police stations and sheriff's office were my daily bread and butter. By this time, I was quite familiar with all the major players, plus I had built up a terrific network of local sources over the years. In 1998, Sheriff Mike Carona was elected as sheriff of Orange County. Carona was an interesting guy. He had served as a marshal in the court system and over the years became close with a number of law enforcement personnel. When the longtime OC

Sheriff Brad Gates, who'd been on the job forever, finally retired, Carona seized the opportunity and stepped up to run.

Carona fought a tough battle against the former police chief of Santa Ana, Paul Walters, and won. As soon as he was elected, Carona made two unexpected appointments. Don Haidl had made his fortune in the car auction business. Haidl was rich, but shady. He had a fascination with law enforcement; he badly wanted to become an assistant sheriff. Mainly what he wanted was to wear that badge and carry the gun and drive the cool cop car.

Haidl was tight with a cop named George Jaramillo and liked to keep him close. I knew Jaramillo from way back; my brother the cop knew him better. He warned me about George at the time. "Watch out with that one," he told me. In any case, Haidl and Jaramillo were given high-level positions in the reserve division; Haidl was named assistant sheriff and Jaramillo eventually became Carona's top aide. At the time, I only wondered why this guy would choose to surround himself with such characters. For a while, all was well.

Then, in the summer of 2002, a five-year-old girl was kidnapped right out of her front yard in Stanton, a small town in western Orange County. Five-year-old Samantha Runnion was playing with a friend in the front yard of their condo complex when a man approached them asking them for help finding a lost puppy. He then snatched Samantha, who started kicking and screaming. The man easily overpowered Samantha, put her into his vehicle, and drove off. It was over in an instant.

"He stole my friend," her little girlfriend told reporters.

Samantha's body was discovered the next day in Cleveland National Forest, near Lake Elsinore. She had been sexually assaulted and strangled, her tiny nude body posed in a gruesome fashion on the side of a road, hidden in some underbrush. The man who stumbled upon her body was traumatized; he had three-year-old at home. This was a nightmare story to make every parent's blood run cold. The public was in an uproar. Sherriff Carona immediately took charge. At numerous press conferences, he swore to find the person who did this. He spoke directly to the perpetrator: "You can hide, but we're going to catch you." He thanked the public for their help as tips flooded in.

The police caught the perpetrator by painstakingly matching tire tracks to a vehicle seen leaving the scene. This was really cutting-edge forensics at the time, terrific police work. It only took three days for a guy named Alejandro Avila to be located and arrested. It was a slam-dunk case; Avila had previously been acquitted of molestation charges, child porn was found on his computer, and his DNA was all over the crime scene. He was eventually put away for life. At the time of this writing, he currently resides on death row in San Quentin.

The Samantha Runnion case rocketed Carona to the national stage. He wisely used his high profile as a springboard to advance his career. He became a media darling who, for a brief shining moment, could do no wrong. Larry King called him "America's Sheriff." There were serious discussions of him running for lieutenant governor of California. Mike Carona was off and running, though truth to be told, he was in a bit over his head with his closest advisors. That very same summer, his assistant sheriff found himself in a world of hurt.

Don Haidl was a self-made man with a mansion in Newport Coast to prove it, but his teenage son, Greg Haidl, was a spoiled little punk. Greg regularly hung out with a couple of close buddies. The trio went to a party one night in San Bernardino and met a teenage girl. They made arrangements to all meet up at Haidl's house the following day, where they got the girl drunk to the point of unconsciousness and raped her. They videotaped themselves having every possible kind of sex with their victim. After they were done, they put her in a car, and as they were driving away, she vomited all over. They were furious; they dumped her in the driveway of her home and took off.

The three teens were soon arrested; an assistant sheriff's wayward son was a pretty big scandal. Of course, I covered the story. On the first day of our coverage, I approached Haidl, with whom I had a pretty solid relationship, and said, "Don, I'm sorry about this situation. I know how tough it can be, and I wish you well."

The three sixteen-year-old defendants would be tried as adults at their upcoming rape trial. Haidl's son looked much younger than his age, like a harmless kid. Naturally, he had the best defense money could buy.

Then came the night Haidl Jr was picked up for marijuana possession. According to the information I received, Greg told the cop on the scene, "Do you know who my dad is?"

The cop called his watch commander, who said, "Haidl's kid? Hold on, let me call George Jaramillo."

George could not believe it. "Where are they now?" he asked.

"Out in the field," he was told.

"And the dope?"

"We have it our possession."

"OK, listen. We've got to keep this quiet; the press will go wild. Take the kid home, confiscate the dope, don't book him or anything. I'll handle this. Don't let anyone know about this; it will just be between you and me."

The officer on the scene did as he was ordered by his watch commander.

I was sitting at my desk at the station one day working on a story when I got the call from a man Elaine called "Loose Lips." A multimillionaire with a finger in every pie in OC, this man had private numbers to every local politician and was one of my best, most highly trusted sources. He called me to say, "You're the only reporter who has the guts to do this story, so I'm going to give it to you. Here's some background . . ." and he laid out the tale of the hidden arrest. "As I said, I am only reaching out to you, Dave, because you are trustworthy. I will share everything with you, but I need you to protect me."

I promised I would, and he knew I would keep my word. For the next three months, I was fed a steady stream of audio and videotape of the buried arrest and the resultant coverup. I got tape of the phone call with Jaramillo and video footage of Haidl being stopped in the field, not the slightest bit worried, sneering, "Do you know who my dad is?"

This exclusive was an absolute blockbuster story. The trial for the son and his buddies was covered extensively and ended in a hung jury. The DA called me not two hours after the verdict was read to assure me that they planned to retry—another exclusive, which pissed off every other reporter in town once again. There was a second trial . . . and this time the three young men were found guilty.

All this coverage about Haidl's son is what led to an investigation of the sheriff's office, where some very interesting facts came to light. Investigators soon found out how deep in cahoots the sheriff had long been with Haidl and Jaramillo. In a nutshell, Haidl had financed Carona's campaign in return for his appointment. Illegal campaign contributions were just the tip of the iceberg. Below the surface? Expensing trips to Vegas with women, helicopter rides to the airport to catch a last-minute flight . . . you name it. Sex and money, major scandal.

Haidl and Jaramillo were both indicted. And was Jaramillo ever furious. He turned on his buddies in a hurry: "What about Mike Carona? He was right there! I'm not going down alone on all this!"

We went live when Jaramillo was arrested at his house. At the holding area at Santa Ana Police Department, he turned so his back was to the camera. I was on the air and said, "That is George Jaramillo, the undersheriff, or should I say the former undersheriff. His back is to us; he's the one with the large bald spot." I was honestly just trying to help the viewers identify the players.

The next day I got a call from our executive producer. "Hey, Dave. Just got off the phone with the president of the international Bald Men's Association. They don't appreciate that coverage."

I could not believe it. "That's a real, actual organization?"

"Better believe it. And they are pissed with you!"

My news reports led directly to Carona's indictment. Jaramillo went to prison. Haidl Senior was headed for prison but was persuaded to turn state's evidence against his longtime buddy Carona. The betrayal started with a phone call. As my source described it, the sheriff had received a phone call from Haidl out of the blue.

When the call ended, Carona's companion asked him, "Haidl? What the hell did he want?"

"He wants to meet for lunch," Carona told him.

"You are not going to lunch with him, that is a terrible idea," his companion warned.

"Oh come on, it's a lunch," Carona replied. "He's lonely, his kid's in prison, he's lost everything . . . no harm seeing an old friend."

The two old friends wound up having three lunches, and Haidl wore a wire at all three. And that was that. When they were putting the proverbial noose around Carona's neck, prosecutors told him, "Look, it's simple. Resign, and you won't go to prison. You pay a fine and that's it."

He said no. His arrogance infuriated the U.S. Attorney, who said, "Fine, arrest the son of a bitch. Also, arrest his wife and his girlfriend. Because they are in on it."

Sheriff Carona got arrested early one morning. They took him to the federal lockup. The sheriff was an impeccably dressed and well-groomed man, but they made him remove his belt, shoes, and tie. They handcuffed his wife on one side and his girlfriend on the other. And there the three of them sat on a hard bench together—for *six and a half hours.*

Carona was accused of six various crimes and the U.S. Attorney took it to trial. He was found "not guilty" on the first five counts. He was so elated that, by the time the jury foreman read "Guilty" on the final count, he didn't even hear it. The buzz was so loud, he completely missed it. He came out and gave a jubilant news conference. The judge was upstairs, watching the scene out the window, livid. When sentencing time came, Carona was hit with the max . . . thirty-nine months in federal prison.

Final score: Jaramillo went to prison. Former sheriff Carona also wound up in prison. The three teenage boys all did time; Greg Haidl was released after serving three years of his six-year sentence. Because he turned on his longtime buddy Carona, Don Haidl was the only one who avoided doing time. However, he was pretty much a broken man given his son's sentence and damage to his family reputation. He passed away in 2012 . . . when I heard of his death, the story came rushing back.

CHAPTER EIGHTEEN

FOREVER THE FIGHTER

ON THE HOME FRONT, it was still hard to believe that our kids were long since grown and gone . . . . Elaine and I had been rattling around our big house for a long time. We just didn't need the space anymore; it depressed me every time I walked down the halls, passing the empty bedrooms where Matt and Tami used to live. I convinced a very resistant Elaine to relocate to Long Beach, to a smaller place better suited to our needs. It was a bit of a drive, but she could still attend her beloved Stitch 'n Bitch knitting sessions at church and services every Sunday, which was her most important consideration.

There was an upside to an empty nest. For twenty-some years, we had taken family vacations together—all four of us, sometimes with friends of Tami and Matt or kids I coached accompanying us. Elaine and I didn't go anywhere on our own till both kids were safely out of college. We had the enormous relief of no more tuition payments and self-supporting kids! We started traveling, just the two of us, to see the world. But my wife's very first trip overseas was to Sweden with her cousin Alice Lynn to research their family ancestry. Both ladies loved it. Their tour guide still sends me cards to this day. That is because, quite simply, Elaine was sunshine. She made friends wherever she went . . . all over the world.

Tami graduated from law school and became a family law attorney at a young age; she wisely concentrated on her career and waited a bit to settle down and marry. Matt graduated from UCLA and entered medical sales. He was still my easygoing boy with a great temperament . . . and a hell of a golfer besides. He fell in love with a school friend of Tami's, a girl named Carrie. Happily for Elaine and me, both our kids wound up settling down with their respective spouses within five miles of our new place in Long Beach.

A red-letter day approached in the spring of 2006: our first grandchild was coming. Carrie was in labor for nearly two days, and I felt like at some point during the endless forty-eight-hour wait I should probably leave the hospital and at least attempt to cover a story or two. But who was I kidding? This was my first grandchild! I called in, everything was OK at the desk, and the baby was imminent. Elaine and I were right there outside her room when Cassie made her entrance into the world on April 20, 2006. We were both immediately transported by a happiness we could not have imagined.

As good a mother as Elaine had been, she was an even better grandmother. Cassie was bright, lively, and adored her grandma. Elaine did everything for her, including volunteering in her preschool classroom and picking her up after school most days. They liked to visit McDonald's . . . one particular location . . . the branch that doled out more ice cream in their cones than the other ("bad") McDonald's location. The two of them were so close.

Dad was still kicking up the occasional fusses. In 2004, he was seventy-eight years old, working in the shop, and calling all the shots. He was in excellent health, as he had always taken good care of himself. He could have gone on forever, but it was time to hang it up. Sadly for Dad, none of his sons took over the business; none of us had the touch, though my brother Albert showed some real skill. But Albert had become a teacher. Dad leased the space to someone else and went home to bother my mom. All was quiet, for a bit.

He called me up one day and said, "Hey, I got this letter from the LA Unified School District and the city. They're gonna buy my building, whether I like it or not." He was referring to the shop he'd purchased in 1964 for the princely sum of $16,000. "They're going to build a school where my building stands. In fact, they're going to raze the whole block. You believe that?"

I went over to see the city officials who told me, "We're going to offer your father a very fair price for this eminent domain. A ten-day escrow and we'll pay him with a cashier's check."

I explained all this to Dad and asked him if he wanted me to be present for the negotiations.

"No, no, no, don't need you there," he brushed me off. A few days later, Dad jumped right into the story: "So, it's a one-time

offer, take it or leave it. I have no choice whatsoever about selling. Can't fight it. Fair market value. Ten-day escrow. They'll
give me a cashier's check on the tenth day."

"So how much, Dad?"

"They offered 445,000 dollars."

Stunned, I said, "Well, what'd you do?"

He replied, "Well, after I shit my pants, went to the bathroom and cleaned myself up a bit, I came back out and told
them, 'OK, I guess I'll take it.'"

Dad liked to handle his own finances; he was private about
money matters and more than a bit touchy. That was just him. I
knew his old bookkeeper in Pomona had long since retired; the
man's daughter had taken over Dad's books. He continued to
pay her twenty bucks a month for years and years. I left Dad to
his windfall, until I got another outraged call, this one about the
taxes the state and feds were going to take and how he was getting ripped off. I recommended that my friend Phil, an excellent
accountant, advise him.

Phil heard me out about the matter and said, "Yeah, sure,
I'll handle this for your dad. He's going to have to buy some
property, I'm pretty sure about that, for starters."

The two of them met, and Phil worked his magic. After Dad
purchased a house and the dust had settled, that tax bill was
chopped down to less than $15,000, a fraction of where it had
started. All was well, so Phil sent Dad a bill for $1,500, a quite
reasonable fee. I'll never forget the noise when my mother called
me, frantic. Dad was absolutely screaming in the background,
"That goddamn son of a bitch!"

"Dave, Dave, please. You've got to come over here right
away. Your dad is having a fit!"

"Mom, what happened?" I asked.

"We got the bill in the mail from Phil, *your friend* Phil, today.
And Dad is going nuts!" I could hear that, all right. I drove right
over to the house.

Dad met me at the door, waving the bill. "Who in the hell does that guy think he is? Goddamn that guy, charging me fifteen hundred goddamn dollars! What a crook!"

"Dad, he is not a crook. How much money did he save you?"

"I don't give a shit! Fifteen hundred dollars!? Outrageous, I have never heard of such a thing, and I'm not paying it!"

I could see where this was going . . . nowhere, fast. I calmed Dad down and called Phil that night, from my own home. "I need a favor," I told this highly professional CPA. "Would you please send my dad another bill? Make it for $500; tell him the first one was a mistake. I'll pay the difference, of course. Okay?"

Irregular but okay with Phil. I got a call another call a couple of days later from my mother. "Your father wants to talk to you."

Dad got on the line sounding triumphant. "Yeah. Now that's more like it! That son of a bitch, I knew he overcharged me!"

Still and all, Dad liked Phil fine. So he went to him for several more years. Each year I paid the difference on every bill. That was just how things went with Dad. I spent much of my free time playing with baby Cassie . . . now that was pure family joy.

Babies were on my mind since Cassie had come along. How much the world had changed, with prospective parents now knowing whether they were having a boy or girl, gender-reveal parties, and especially the explosion of multiples. I had covered the famous Frustaci sextuplets way back in the eighties in Orange County. The mom, an English teacher from Riverside, had given birth to seven babies after being treated with the drug Pergonal. They became known as the Frustaci sextuplets, as one infant was stillborn, and three others died within a month of their birth.

The Frustaci story was a medical miracle at that time, though it took its toll on the parents involved. The children had some lingering health issues; money was tight; the parents' marriage dissolved. Four or five years after the birth, I was out having a taco; lo and behold, my server was the father of the sextuplets. The Frustacis had divorced since I had last seen the dad in a blaze of cameras flashing and worldwide press seeking interviews, surrounded by babies. He was gratefully anonymous again.

I had been on the ground floor when all the miraculous breakthroughs began to occur in the field of reproductive medicine, because it opened up a whole new branch of the law. I covered an early story about a woman who carried a baby for a couple and then changed her mind. The couple wound up keeping custody of the baby, but it was a major case because there were no laws or precedents for this kind of situation . . . yet. Another story I covered concerned a surrogate who offered to carry a baby for the couple she worked for as a housekeeper. She had a proviso written into their contract: if the couple ever divorced, she would take custody of the child.

Sure enough, the baby was born, the couple eventually divorced, and the whole matter wound up in court. The former housekeeper/birth mother really wanted that kid and had a signed contract. By this point, the husband and wife hated each other's guts; all three adults were battling each other fiercely for custody. At one point, the wife got off the stand after testifying, walked over to the husband seated in the front row, yanked off his toupee, and threw it; it sailed across the courtroom. I'd never seen that happen before. The surrogate didn't win her case; there was no case law for any of this back then. The judge simply made the best decision he could in that particular case: to split custody between the estranged parents. The birth mother lost.

This all flashed through my mind one day when I got a call. "Dave, you have to get to Kaiser in Bellflower, right away!"

"What's going on?" I asked.

"Some woman just delivered octuplets!"

"Eight babies? Wow."

This was not an Orange County story, but off I went. I never waited to be spoon-fed information. I hustled out there into the field and got it, myself. On the drive over, I called Kaiser's PR lady.

"How did you find about this?" she asked me.

"Doesn't matter how I found out. Can you give me the breakdown on the babies?"

"What do you mean?"

"Well, how many boys, how many girls? Did they all survive, are they in good health?"

"Well, they're all alive, but very tiny."

"OK, and the breakdown, boys to girls?"

"Hmmmmm . . . let me see . . . four to three. Four boys, three girls."

"That's only seven, what about number eight?"

"Uh, we don't have that information." The staff was clearly not briefed and ready for reporters yet. Fortunately, I had caught her off guard and gotten some information.

I arrived at the hospital, one of the first on the scene. Somehow, I managed to wangle an interview with the team of doctors who had delivered the octuplets. I spoke with them outside in the parking lot. I went on the air and gave my report, and just like that, the media storm erupted. Reporters descended on the scene from all over. The hospital put on a huge official press conference.

I was going to do a follow-up report for the 8 o'clock news that night, so I stuck around. I walked over to a small coffee stand on the hospital grounds and spoke to the elderly Mexican lady behind the counter. "Oooh, are you a reporter?" she asked me.

"Sure am, with Channel 2."

"That lady, the one who had eight babies? My kids go to school with one of her kids!" she said.

"One of her kids?" I wasn't sure I understood. "What, she has other kids?"

"Yeah, Nadya has six already at home!"

"Wait, are you sure?"

"Yeah, now fourteen kids, can you believe?" She shook her head and handed over my coffee.

This information had simply fallen into my lap. I called the news desk, who jumped on this tip. We were able to locate the elementary school and confirmed with the bus driver that he drove some of her older kids to school each day. It was a huge scoop!

A couple of days later, I went to a somewhat dilapidated home in La Habra to interview Nadya Suleman, who had already been christened "Octomom" by some radio guys. Much was made of her single status and slight resemblance to actress Angelina Jolie. Nadya was a difficult interview; she was not an easy woman to draw out. Nevertheless, she became a tabloid sensation. Years later, she got in some trouble for welfare fraud; I covered that as well. The kids were kept out of the limelight. Her doctor later got in some hot water for his role in treating her; it certainly ignited a discussion about fertility treatments . . . yet again.

On the subject of families and fertility, State Assemblyman Mike Duvall was a true Orange County right-to-life, family-values Christian conservative in his second term in office. He was also quite a womanizer in his not-so-secret private life. I got a call one day from one of my reliable tipsters who said, "Hey, I have an audiotape you will die for. I have video, too, you have to see this."

I went to meet my source and view the footage. The audio-tape I heard was of Duvall sitting in one of those endless sub-committee meetings, the kind that bored even the attendees. He was talking to the guy next to him, a lobbyist from Sempra, during a break and said, "I've got this girl, and you would not believe the body on her . . ." He went on from there to describe their sex life in the most graphic terms. The lobbyist responded enthusiastically with his own tales of conquest.

This was pure dynamite. The station flew cameraman Ken Koller and me up to Sacramento. I had never worked with Ken before, so I said to him, "Just follow me. Whatever you do, follow me, and keep rolling. If anyone tells you to stop, ignore them."

I showed up at Mike Duvall's office unannounced; he was not there. His secretary tried to put me off, but I said, "This is urgent, we'll try to locate him on the floor." We headed off the roped-off section where press was allowed, and Duvall immediately noticed me.

I motioned to him. "I've got to talk to you, about the tapes," I stage-whispered, loudly.

He pretended not to hear me.

When he left the floor, he immediately headed rapidly for a private area. Signs were posted everywhere: ASSEMBLY ONLY; NO PRESS ALLOWED. I ignored them. I chased him up and down the hallways, calling out, "Mr. Duvall, what about the sex tapes?! Any comment?!"

He ignored me and walked faster.

Eventually, we got stopped by security guards. Now, I had been to Sacramento so often and had been in that building hundreds of times covering countless stories. I was a familiar face in the halls. I knew very well what was and wasn't allowed. So I played dumb. "You know, I haven't been up here for so long, I didn't realize this was a restricted area," I said to the guard who stopped me.

He was in the middle of giving me a lecture when I caught sight of Duvall again, turning a corner way down the hall. The chase was on . . . again. I left the guard in the dust, cameraman following.

We didn't manage to catch him that day, but I put all the footage together and Channel 9 ran the story. Complete with the audiotape, conveniently captioned. My source had promised, "This will be huge news. Huge." I hadn't really believed it. But when we broke the story in LA and shared it with our Sacramento affiliate, it exploded. The next morning at breakfast the entire city was talking about it. "Did you see that story about Duvall? . . . Can you believe . . ."

Karen Bass, who was a vice presidential candidate and the leader of the Senate, happened to be in Sacramento that week. I walked into her offices, and she came out to greet me.

"Ms. Bass, I'm Dave Lopez, Channel 2—"

"Oh, we know who you are," she said.

I got my comment. The day after that, by the time the story had aired a second time, Duvall had resigned. Other reporters were going crazy trying to find that tape, but they couldn't. I had the only source. Finally, I gave a fellow reporter a break, and everyone else could get the story. It was two days later, but at least they now had the source material in their hands.

Mike Duvall was done with politics. He went into insurance and never spoke to me again. The good news is that his wife forgave him.

Elaine and I were heading off to China, and as we buckled ourselves into the seats for the first leg of our flight, she looked over at me and said, "Sweetheart, I know you're known for controversial stories, but I never dreamed that after one story on the air we'd have to flee to China to get away!"

CHAPTER NINETEEN

BIG CHANGES

Television

QUITE A COMBO: They'll be separate newsrooms no more. The crew from KCAL, right, will join with KCBS' news-gathering personnel Monday.

KCBS and KCAL join forces

Stations say the teaming will boost Orange County news coverage.

BY JEFF ROWE
THE ORANGE COUNTY REGISTER

GILE: She's always on the move in a live truck.

GONZALES: News director says efforts will be local.

LOPEZ: A quarter-century of Orange County coverage.

KCBS/2 and KCAL/9 make the meshing of their news teams official Monday with new sets, new logos and new music.

The change was made possible by a 1998 Federal Communications Commission rule change that allows two stations in the same market to be owned by the same entity.

In TV parlance, KCBS and KCAL formed a duopoly, a word never heard until the FCC ruling.

The change means that longtime Orange County reporters Dave Lopez and Michelle Gile will be colleagues after years of competing against each other.

Both know the county well.

This June, Lopez will mark a quarter-century covering Orange County, which he says has changed dramatically in that time.

He was assigned as the station's O.C. correspondent a year after he joined KCBS in 1977.

"Orange County is an intriguing place – it never ceases to amaze me," Lopez said. Working with KCAL rather than competing with them will expand possibilities

for coverage, he said.

Gile also is a veteran reporter; she's covered Orange County since joining KCAL in 1989.

Both Gile and Lopez work out of rolling "offices" – their live trucks. Each of the vans is crammed with tape-editing gear and transmission equipment so the reporters can report live.

KCAL's truck is 3 years old, but the 60,000 miles on the odometer translate into thousands of Orange County stories.

Until now, KCBS and KCAL typically had just the one O.C.-based reporter to call upon. But since KCBS parent Viacom bought KCAL in May, Gile and Lopez began collaborating rather than competing, in effect doubling local coverage.

The merger also gives the combined news operation two helicopters, one of which may be based in Orange County,

said Nancy Bauer Gonzales, news director.

"We're putting our effort in local, local coverage," said Gonzales, who previously was news director at KCAL and, before that, at KNBC/4. "This is the most exciting thing I have ever done," she said. "It makes my other jobs look like a vacation."

How will the stations differ?

KCAL is and will remain hyperlocal, Gonzales said. KCBS' signature is its investigative

unit, and Gonzales said she wants to maintain that. KCBS also will be a bit more conservative and perhaps not as "spunky" as KCAL.

In all, KCBS and KCAL will broadcast 11 hours of news a day.

In aspiring to boost its O.C. coverage, KCBS-KCAL will compete most directly with KABC/7, which commands the most O.C. viewers. But KCBS-KCAL clearly will have an O.C. sports advantage.

KCAL already is the home of the Angels, Ducks, Lakers and Galaxy and says it will deliver more comprehensive coverage with the combined staffs.

For the past few months, the KCBS newsroom has been a construction site as crews worked seven days a week to expand the newsroom to accommodate the KCAL staff.

The old KCAL news building, adjacent to the Paramount Pictures lot, is being converted into a soundstage for Paramount.

KCBS was originally licensed and constructed in 1931 by Don Lee Inc. as an experimental station with the call letters W6XAO.

KCAL was formerly known as KHJ-TV.

In 1996, KCAL was sold to Young Broadcasting by the Walt Disney Co., which had purchased the station in 1989.

CONTACT THE WRITER: (714) 445-6694 or jrowe@ocregister.com

228

WITH NEARLY FOUR DECADES ON THE JOB NOW, those new reporters were looking younger every year. There were plenty more shakeups to come. Perret was out, and Roger Bell, who used to work at Channel 7, took over. Channel 2 was hoping to import some ratings magic if they hired the guys who for years and years had dominated the market. For a while there was a big hiring boom for staff from Channel 7. The whole strategy didn't really pan out in terms of better ratings, but Roger was okay. He gave me a raise, so I happily chugged along.

Then Princell Hair arrived from Chicago, where he had a terrific reputation. The newsroom was thrilled; we thought everything was going to be A-OK from here on out. Like all my colleagues, I really liked this man; he ran a solid newsroom.

We had some issues with the union once, and as a union rep, he called me in. "Do me a favor, go along with us for a bit, give me some time. I will work it out," he promised, and to his credit, he did. Then Princell went on vacation. While he was gone, Channel 2 purchased Channel 9, and overnight we merged to become one big happy station. When he returned, the rumors were flying, and staff was in an uproar. He entered the newsroom and asked with a straight face, "So, anything happen while I was gone?"

It was clear we were the unwanted stepchildren muddling up this great new merger. Channel 2 had bought Channel 9, but somehow Channel 9 was running everything. They took over with a vengeance. The only thing that didn't happen was moving physical locations. We all came together under one roof in Studio City. The general manager from Channel 9 was made GM of both stations, and our GM was tossed out. At one of the initial big group meetings, the first words out of the new GM's mouth were, "CBS sucks. Your news sucks, everything about it." He told us that from now on there would be two of everything.

There was a great deal of tension, hurt feelings, and minor

indignities to bear. I couldn't get in to see anyone in charge. We had all prayed it would be a happy corporate marriage, and we were all rooting for Princell to stay, but it was not to be. In came Nancy Bauer, a woman news director for the first time. She was experienced; she had also grown up in Downey, where I lived, and we had many mutual friends and acquaintances. I tried like the devil to arrange a personal meeting with her but could not get in.

Then one of our best cameramen, Larry Greene, was killed overseas in Bahrain in a terrible helicopter accident. Larry was a real sweetheart of a man who would be greatly missed by his many friends and colleagues; he could tell a story like nobody else and top any tall tale. At Larry's funeral, I was finally able to meet Nancy. She'd been the boss for a while now. I'd been on TV as usual, but I had never spoken to her. We had a brief exchange. My contract was coming up for renewal. My agent called me and said about Nancy, "Did you do anything to piss her off?"

"No," I said, "not at all. I've only ever spoken to her once, at a funeral, and everything seemed fine."

"Well, she's not crazy about you or your work. She doesn't want to give you a raise. Quite frankly, she doesn't seem that interested in what you're doing, at all." That was a surprise. My agent said, "Tell you what, let's sign for the exact same terms, one year only. Or, of course, I could shop you around . . ."

My mind was racing. I was not too old to prove myself once again. "Let's do this, try to sign a one-year deal for me. In the upcoming year, I will do everything in my power to prove I am worthy of being on this staff and deserving of a raise and a good contract. I will do all I can do and more."

So that's what we did, and that's the year I broke the story with Sheriff Carona and followed it up with Duvall. When my contract came up, I got a big raise and a three-year contract. This was Nancy's way of telling me I had come through. My gamble paid off. Nancy and I got along fine from that point on. She lasted longer than anyone else: six years.

Then yet another general manager named Steve Mauldin swept into our station. He and Nancy clashed, and the writing was on the wall; it was just a matter of time. Nancy was soon gone, and Mauldin brought in a new guy named Scott Diener as news director. They had worked together previously, in Dallas, where they had taken their station from last place to first. Expectations were high. My agent, Adam, gave me a call to give me the lay of the land.

"Here we go again," I said. "What can you tell me about Scott Diener."

"Tough guy," he said. "I strongly suggest you set up a meeting with him right away, and whatever they say . . . whatever . . . just grin and bear it. Don't lose your temper and do not in any way give them an attitude or act like you know it all."

I set up the meeting and hoped for the best. Two days before my scheduled meeting, our helicopter guy, who had been there for twenty years, had his own meeting with the new regime. In it, he told them exactly how things should be run. He was gone a few days later. I went into my own meeting hat in hand.

"Hmmm. You've been with the station a long time now," Diener said as Mauldin looked on. "Let me see, Inland Empire reporter, right?"

"No," I said evenly, "Orange County." I was pretty sure they knew where I worked.

He asked me a few questions, and my answer to everything was, "I've been around a long time, but you're never too old to learn. No one is too big to take advice or criticism."

I left the twenty-minute meeting and reported back to Adam. "Perfect," he said.

To this day, I am convinced they were waiting for me to take offense and flare up. I held on to my cool, which turned out to be a very good thing.

Thank God for my agent's advice; later that week, Maulden went on a rampage and fired twelve people in a single day at our station. I was not one of them. In March 2010, in what became known as the March Massacre, fifteen more got canned—producers, writers, and on-air reporters, many longtime friends and colleagues. They were out, just like that. As usual, I carried on.

I managed to impress my new boss when I got a great tip: former LA police chief Daryl Gates had passed away. I called it in to the desk, and we were second on the air with the breaking news. Channel 7 beat us by a few seconds, because someone wanted to double-check the information after I called.

Diener asked me, "Who's your source?"

"Someone who was standing there at his bedside when he passed," I told him.

"You sure know a lot about LA, you have contacts everywhere," he mused.

A couple of months later, Diener called me into his office. "We're losing Mark Coogan," he told me, referring to a colleague, a splendid reporter. "He's retiring, and we don't have anyone to take his place in LA. I've looked around . . . and Steve and I decided that you're the guy."

"What? Do I have a choice here?"

"Of course," Diener said smoothly, though I knew the words meant nothing. I had one year left on my contract, and I knew what saying no to this new assignment would mean. One more year and bye-bye Dave. I was not ready to retire, though after thirty-three years there, I definitely considered Orange County my home beat.

"All this time I've been in OC, I've been on call in LA for all the big stories. Can I operate in LA the way I've been working out of OC? I don't have to attend the morning meeting every day—though, of course, I'll call in. I'll be ready for any big story you want to send me on. If we can do that, OK."

Diener considered. "We can do that."

So, as of July 2010, I was back in LA, as the main Los Angeles reporter. What a trip. My very first week, the Grim Sleeper was finally located and captured. Lonnie Franklin Jr. had been preying on women in Los Angeles since the eighties; his job as a sanitation worker helped him with the disposal of bodies—countless bodies; no one would ever know exactly how many. As my colleague Steve Crawford, God bless his soul, said, "Goddammit, Lopez. Only in Watts could you have two hundred women disappear and nobody give a shit."

I was right there when they nabbed the serial killer—it was big news as this was the first-time familial DNA was used to catch a criminal. This was really amazing new technology. Police had followed Lonnie's son to a gathering, grabbed his discarded pizza crust, taken it to the lab, and up popped a DNA match that linked him to their suspect. That night on live TV, I asked the police chief, Charlie Beck, what kind of pizza it was. "Pepperoni," he said. I covered the hell out of that story, and then others came along. Just like that, I was back in the fray. I was back home, for real, for the last part of my career.

Rival Channel 11 had covered a story about a firefighter stationed right in the middle of Skid Row downtown, and my bosses wanted me to follow up. This fireman had gotten stabbed by a woman who chased him into a grimy residential hotel and attacked. The first responder hero was in bad shape, recovering in the hospital, where Mayor Antonio Villaraigosa visited him and wished him well.

I got a tip that the whole "attack" was a scam—that this firefighter had actually been stabbed by a pimp in a dispute over one of his workers. This firefighter, along with many others in his station, regularly patronized a number of female sex workers who did business in the Skid Row area. The jig was up when the fireman's stab wound did not line up with the puncture in his uniform shirt; the whole sordid story quickly unraveled on the news. *Our news.*

My cameraman that day happened to be a part-time paramedic. When we wrapped up the live shot and prepared to go home, he said to me, "Dave, I've got a message for you from the firefighters."

"Oh yeah? What is it?"

"Better tell Lopez if he ever needs help from a paramedic down here, he'd best look elsewhere."

This was my "welcome home" to LA.

Dad was still irascible as all get-out, as he and Mom lived in their new house together. I was a devoted son who visited weekly, and it became apparent to me that my mom was starting to fail. It was not just the expected memory lapses that come with age; her mind was clearly starting to go . . . along with her formerly sweet personality.

Dad absolutely refused to hear a word about it. Every time I ventured an inquiry about getting Mom a checkup or brought up the latest disaster with lost keys or a forgotten pot left on the stove, he denied and attacked. "She's fine, absolutely fine, she's always been forgetful, you know that. Stop interfering, we're fine!"

But it was clear to me Mom wasn't. People just didn't see it the way I did. I had done a lot of stories on Alzheimer's disease and dementia. I had seen the toll it took on people, I had seen what it did to families, and I could see all too clearly what was coming for us. The truth was that Mom was in the early stages of Alzheimer's, confirmed by her doctor, but no one was willing to face it.

I had other worries, closer to home. Elaine's health had always been precarious; we both knew that. We had beaten the odds with our two healthy kids. Her liver had long been compromised due to NASH, and now she was experiencing lung issues as well. She began to tire easily and have difficulty breathing. We had just gone on a big fortieth-anniversary cruise to Eastern Europe, and the trip could not have been nicer, but this new illness was clearly sapping her strength.

It was on a small local Golden Coast cruise with friends from Stitch 'n Bitch that I faced reality. The trip was meant to be an easy weekend getaway to San Francisco, San Diego, and Santa Barbara, which of course was one of our favorite destinations. We happened to be in Santa Barbara on Good Friday, so we visited the beautiful local mission. Then we took a cab to downtown and planned to walk to the harbor, with its shops and cafes, to be taken back to the ship. And this short walk was too much for her, so I had to call another cab to go about 600 yards. An icy chill went down my spine. Until this moment, I truly hadn't realized her condition was this bad. For the first time, real fear for my wife's future struck my heart.

Our daughter, Tami, was old-fashioned; when she got pregnant, she did not want to know if she was having a boy or girl; it would be a surprise. Her daughter, Abigail, was born in the fall, once again sending the grandparents over the moon. That afternoon, Elaine was sitting in Tami's hospital room with her portable oxygen tank. One of Tami's friends had taught her how to text as we awaited the birth, and she happily texted out the news to her many, many friends. It was such a big day for Grandma! I watched her holding our daughter's brand-new daughter. She was joyous. We were so happy. No one in that room could have imagined that she had less than two years to live.

CHAPTER TWENTY

I LOSE MY FIRST LOVE

AND SO BEGAN A SLOW DESCENT straight into hell. It didn't start that way, of course; I was an eternal optimist and bullheaded to boot. Whatever was ailing my mom and especially Elaine *could* and *would* be managed. I would locate the best specialists, pay any price, and make any personal sacrifice, including donating body parts.

First things first: What to do about my parents? "Something is really wrong with Mom," I told my dad until I was blue in the face, but he simply refused to hear it. We could have gotten my mom enrolled in a USC Alzheimer's clinic program, but Dad put his foot down. He wouldn't do it because "Mom didn't need it." He was still stubborn—so, so stubborn.

Dad didn't want any help. Except, of course, that he called me whenever he needed help. One day he asked me to come by. I was standing outside the house waiting when Dad came barreling up the driveway, with my mother in the passenger seat. Dad tried to enter the garage and hit the inside wall . . . hard. He backed up, and I yelled out, "Dad! Watch it!"

He ignored me, hit the inside wall of the garage again, and backed the car up again. The third time he hit the wall, I reached in and grabbed the keys away from him. "Just stop, Dad! You're going to knock down this entire garage!"

"It's my goddamn garage if I want to hit it . . ." Same old same old.

"This is ridiculous, Dad! You shouldn't be driving!" I drove straight to his doctor's office and had a quick word with his physician privately. "Doctor, I know my brother is bringing my dad in here for an appointment later. If you don't pull his license when he comes in today, I'm going to report you. He simply cannot be out on the roads driving anymore. He is a danger to himself and others; you *must* take his license away."

When my brother and Dad showed up that afternoon, sure enough, the doctor got all over my dad and took his license away. Dad put two and two together—a nurse had mentioned seeing me earlier—and called in another rage.

I said, "Yeah, I did it! It's not safe for you to drive anymore!"

Several of my brothers and sisters called me up asking, "What did you do that for?"

Exasperated, I said, "Because he's going to kill somebody. I don't want his estate to be sued. And I don't want him to kill me or Mom or anybody else. I've covered way too many wrecks like that!"

Dad was really furious, and a couple of my siblings took his side. Elaine was sick, I was trying to work full time under a new regime, and my sister and my brother were now pissed at me. I threw up my hands and concentrated on my wife.

I would find a way to save Elaine, for sure. I had complete and utter confidence in myself and the team I would somehow put together . . . and did it ever take a long, hard time for that conviction to fade. Elaine's official diagnosis was pulmonary fibrosis of the lungs, which is an extremely rare disease. It usually strikes smokers, as it causes hardening of the lungs, but she had never smoked. She didn't drink either, yet she struggled with non-alcoholic fatty liver disease all her life. We could not wrap our minds around this dreadful diagnosis. And it was a fearsome foe. The killer disease sapped Elaine's strength more each day.

Still, I truly believed that we were going to beat this thing. Absolute worst-case scenario: she would get a lung transplant. If we couldn't find the right donor, I'd give her one of mine, so I thought at the time—naive, determined me.

Whatever it took, we would beat this. Forward, march! Physical therapy at a special gym. Rehab exercises with caregivers every day. Top specialists to consult on new treatments.

Elaine needed oxygen full time now, and it became difficult for her to even go on walks. She would gasp for air just strolling down our street. Even as her condition started to really deteriorate, I felt sure she would somehow be OK. Slowly, I adjusted my expectations. My wife might never be the same vibrant, energetic person again, but it never even crossed my mind that she would not be alive and with us for years and years to come. That was simply unthinkable.

On the night of Saturday, February 2, 2013, I had a speaking engagement at a function in Santa Barbara. The event was hosted by the LAPD, and I was to appear on a panel, which was an honor. Of course, I wanted Elaine to accompany me and asked if she felt up to a short trip to one of her favorite places, but she simply couldn't do it. Because I'd made the commitment, I thought I had to go and reluctantly headed out. We had everything covered to the very best of my ability. That night, after I gave my speech, I called the house and my daughter answered.

"Father, Mom is really having a tough time," Tami told me tearfully. "I'm taking her to the ER."

I raced home at ninety miles an hour and met them at Long Beach Memorial Hospital.

"I'm sorry," Elaine said quietly as I burst through the door to her room, and it broke my heart.

"There's nothing to be sorry about!" I said and got busy reassuring, making plans, and talking to doctors. But deep down inside, the truth was starting to dawn: Elaine was in terrible trouble. The siege was on, for the next seventy-seven excruciating days.

The next day Elaine was in a bed on the ICU, wide awake and alert, but having a hard time breathing. The Super Bowl game—Ravens vs. 49ers—was turned on in the background. Elaine was upset that we couldn't attend Tami's annual Super Bowl party and bring homemade cookies. She urged me to go, but I refused to leave her side.

Just as the game started, a doctor came in and called me outside. "I need to put your wife on a ventilator," he said abruptly. He showed me the X-rays of her chest—completely congested, all white, just tiny specks here and there of healthy tissue. "I have to put her on a ventilator today, or she won't make it through the night," he emphasized.

I almost fainted on the spot. Elaine desperately did not want to be intubated; I went in to talk to her, Matt went in to talk to her, and then I followed up again with one last plea. Matt and

I were ushered outside, the medical staff closed the blinds to Elaine's room, and when they opened them again, it was done. She was on a ventilator by 4 pm on Super Bowl Sunday. Since that terrible day, I have been unable to watch a Super Bowl game, which was usually the highlight of my sports year.

Elaine remained in the ICU for two weeks. Then she rallied, or so it seemed. For decades I had jotted a couple of lines about my day in a small yearly planner. They usually concerned a big story I covered. The daily entries now turned into terse medical reports and prayers. On February 4, I wrote, *Elaine is battling. God be with us.* Deep in my heart, I was sure he was.

February 10, my sixty-fifth birthday, was grim. On that day, I truly thought Elaine was going to die; it was that bad. She hovered on the edge but managed to pull through . . . that time. To make matters worse, the entire day passed without a call from my father. Not that it was a top concern on my list, but I hadn't heard a word from him yet, not even to check on Elaine's status. That's where we stood. It was heartbreaking.

On February 14, I brought Elaine a Valentine card, which I pinned to the wall so she would see it immediately upon awakening. The doctor had warned that if she stayed on a ventilator too long, there would be no hope. On that day of love, we had a minor miracle. I wrote: *She wakes up! Passes test, praise God.*

The signs were encouraging in the days to come, and we were able to bring her home in mid-April. Dad called that day, just as I was driving us to the house. "Hey, sorry I didn't call before," he said. "I've just been thinking of so many other things, Albert."

"Dad, I'm David, not Albert," I reminded him. It was a short call.

The station was aware of what I was going through, and both Mauldin and Diener were nothing but compassionate and understanding. Once again, my keen agent Adam handled everything for me; they only called for progress reports on how

Elaine was doing. In the topsy-turvy days of February, I missed a major news story for the first time in my life. A disgruntled former cop named Christopher Dorner, who'd been dismissed from the force, went rogue. He posted a list of forty law enforcement officers he intended to kill and started by shooting the daughter of the LAPD attorney who had represented him in his case against his former employer.

A multi-state manhunt was on . . . and eventually ended in a standoff in the San Bernardino Mountains. Dorner killed himself as police surrounded the remote cabin he was hiding in. This was as big as a news story got, but I was sitting in the ICU at the hospital. I didn't care about the Dorner story, or any story really. In fact, I was ready to quit my job for good. Retire, hang it up, and spend all my time and energies on trying to get Elaine well again. Tami talked me out of it, and she was right.

It felt strange not to be chasing the story; I hadn't missed anything big since 1972. I counted myself fortunate to have bosses who understood. I did not go back to work full time until Elaine was out of intensive care.

Elaine was home. She was not the same and would never be the same, but I was just so thankful to have her back where she belonged. I knew I could nurse her back to good health with all the care, love, and good will in the world. And for a bit, that worked. But it was not easy. I was not used to being a caregiver, and it was a challenge. We struggled with the portable toilet and my having to bring her everything she needed, from a phone to her meals to a magazine or tissue. The transition was hard on both of us. The days blended together in a roller coaster of ups and downs:

May 27: *Will she ever totally recover? I'm trying to understand, but I will never give in.*

May 28: *Best morning yet. Breathing better. I'm perplexed. Two in a row now . . . have we turned the corner?* A bit later: *Oxygen excellent, now we just have to work on her mindset.*

Elaine had lost the ability to walk, which was devastating to us both. I installed an elevator-type device on the staircase; it didn't really help. Seeing their mom like this was hard on the kids and grandkids, too. The grandbabies visited, but even they could not revive Elaine's spark. Something had gone out of her eyes; I tried everything to bring it back.

July 10: *Caregiver calls me at 2:30. Something is wrong. Doctor says we have to put her back in the hospital. Bad day, I'm confused. More confused than ever. I'm a wreck.*

On the afternoon of July 5, I went outside to do battle with an old garage door I was reluctant to replace. On that day, it finally broke. I was so angry, I just yanked it out and moved it out of the way as the caregiver watched.

"Mr. Lopez, you are so strong!" she said, surprised.

"Not strong, just pissed off," I said.

Next, doctors thought there was something wrong with Elaine's brain. More batteries of tests.

Memory slowed but improving.

One day, Elaine appeared to be getting stronger, so I went out to get her a treat, a hamburger. In the short time I was out, I came back to find everyone rushing around trying to revive her, even though she had signed a do-not-resuscitate order.

Disaster, back to the ICU at noon.

Sunday: *It's not her lungs, now it's her liver.*

The doctors had to start draining her liver on a daily basis. She was wheeled into a special treatment room for this procedure. I was sure she would die that day.

All bets are off; she's dying. Liver gone, meds aren't working.

Then the next day she got better!

Is it a miracle? Her liver is working . . .

The new meds were working. She was alert, best ever, and even sang with Tami.

Elaine left the ICU with a good attitude on July 16.

Good, good day . . . best ever . . .

That night, her sugar level rose, and she suffered a couple of anxiety attacks.

July 19: *Talking but not making any sense. Sleeping most of the day but her O2 is good. Doctor says lungs are improving. Stood up for the first time.*

Elaine was getting a little better each day; the panic attacks were receding. I returned to work on Monday, July 22, feeling hopeful. I was doing a story on, of all things, a couple who fought over the care of an elderly mother; one of her caregivers shot the other. I was reporting that story when I got a call from the hospital. "Look, your wife's ammonia level is twelve." I didn't know what that meant. "It's not good, you need to get here, now."

I raced to the hospital, where the doctor told me that a healthy person's ammonia level needs to be above 50. "And she's at twelve?" I said, incredulous.

"Yes, we must get that level back up." They gave her some injections and drained her liver once again. The next morning, I went in to see her.

Best she has looked in six months.

The next day: *She's alert and really trying. Looks like she's going to make it, rehab again. Excellent day!*

July 28: *. . . Not bad; a long way to go, but she's really improving.*

Then a minor emergency: doctors thought they detected blood clots in her legs. We got past that one.

Trying hard but getting more groggy. Ammonia level up again. Therapy is tough, but no one is giving up . . . especially her and me.

August 3: *Not again, back in the ICU.*

This roller-coaster ride of hopes rising and being dashed was exhausting; the days blurred together into one long siege. Did I mention the bills for her care were up to $1.7 million at this point? Thank God I had the insurance to cover the $800-a-bag medication when she was going through three bags a day. Of course, the insurance company started calling . . . often. "How much longer is your wife going to be in the hospital?"

"Don't know, I'm not a doctor," was my answer, and I hung up. It was now quite easy for me to really understand how people lose their minds, and all their money, in such situations.

One day in early August a nurse approached me. "Mr. Lopez, what have the doctors told you?"

"They've said this needs to run its course . . . it's going to be up and down, and up down."

"Don't be offended, but you need to hear the truth. Your wife will not be alive by Christmas."

I was shocked. I went straight into the chapel I visited twice a day, every day without fail, before I saw her and before I left. No matter what time of day or night, no matter where Elaine's room was—depending on what wing she was in it could be a good half-mile walk—but I never missed these stops. That day as usual I prayed that Elaine would get well, but my main prayer was always: *God, help us all accept what's going to happen.* That's what I wanted more than anything. *And please don't let her suffer.*

Another setback soon followed. And then another rally. *"Very very alert. Best yet, moves out of ICU, goes to the third floor.*

August 7: *God is working wonders. Things are looking much better; we might even go home. Transferred to the sixth floor.*

And, finally, a couple of weeks later: *God is good; He has blessed us. She is going to go home!*

I knew with everything I had inside me that if I could just get Elaine set up at home again, we would win. If she needed a liver transplant or lung transplant, I was ready. I had a top-notch doctor from UCLA standing by, an expert in the tricky procedure, but they could not attend her in the hospital. As soon as she was released, they would consult.

August 9: *Sleepy all day, what's happening?*

August 10: *Very alert, had a good conversation. Afternoon sleepy again, but she had a good night. I still have faith in God.*

The night of August 10 was wonderful. Elaine was sitting up in her bed, attentive and comfortable. We sang old songs and talked about when the kids were little. Their grandpa Glen used to sing "Oh What a Beautiful Morning" every time the kids woke up at his house to start their day off right. All four of us sang the old favorite. Plans were made for another round of rehab. Elaine's birthday was less than a week away; that night, I arranged for an elaborate display of 100 balloons to be delivered to her room.

Sunday night, August 12, I got the call at home, at 2 am. "Your wife has lapsed into a coma."

I raced back to the hospital and knew this was it: the death vigil. Elaine never woke up again. I sat at her side for twenty-six hours. At my request, she was taken off all those godforsaken beeping machines, given lots of morphine, and had her family around her. She was in no pain and surrounded by those she loved. Elaine died in the dawn.

Finally, August 13: *5:57 am. My beautiful bride goes home. She's in heaven.*

It was over.

CHAPTER TWENTY-ONE

READY TO QUIT

ELAINE DIED ON A TUESDAY. We buried her the following Monday, the day before what would have been her sixty-fifth birthday. Both my bosses offered sincere, compassionate support during the saddest week of my life. Elaine's funeral was held at her beloved Messiah Lutheran Church, and the station put its resources at my disposal. Two technicians stopped by and set up huge screens and speakers inside and outside the parish hall for her service. Good thing, as there was an overflow crowd; every

246

pew in the church was packed, and there were rows and rows of folding seats on every inch of the lawn. More than 500 people turned out to honor Elaine's life.

A longtime parishioner came up to me and said, "I come to all the funerals here, and a large turnout is thirty. I have never seen anything like this."

I was not at all surprised. Former students, fellow teachers, friends, neighbors, churchgoers, of course all her dear Stitch 'n Bitch ladies . . . a cliché, I know, but everyone who knew Elaine loved her. At her wake on Sunday, 300 people came by to pay their respects. She was laid to rest at beautiful Rose Hills Memorial Park, where we used to stroll on weekends as teens with her parents. Both Glen and Elinor were interred there; there was an empty plot next to Elaine's for me, someday. She was home.

My faith was greatly shaken. Elaine's death really, really, rocked me. The guilt was nearly unbearable. I felt like I hadn't done enough, starting with how I'd been out of town giving a speech when I should have been home by my ailing wife's side. That was when the nightmare had begun . . . Tami took her to the hospital, I raced to meet them, and it all became a blur from that night to this strange time.

For the first time in decades, I remembered Dad telling young me that I was heading for a fall someday, believing that nothing would ever slow me down or get in my way. Why had I been so sure I could save her? More importantly, why *didn't* I save her? I tried, I tried . . . I was truly undergoing my dark night of the soul and in my grief once again decided I was going to quit my job and retire. Tami again strenuously argued against this and convinced me to keep working. She was right. I did not need to sit home and brood. Work would keep me sane and distracted from my sorrow . . . and, at this point, life was pretty much nothing but sorrow.

One of the more dreadful side effects, as if the disease itself isn't bad enough, is how Alzheimer's disease rips apart family members. I had been sitting right there the day it happened: the day my mother no longer recognized her husband of fifty-some years. I visited my mom every Sunday of my life, before church, without fail. Elaine accompanied me until she was too weak to do so. It had been just the three of us the day my mother, the kindest, most loving soul, looked over at my dad and said, "Who's that son of a bitch sitting over there? Who's that strange man? I don't want him in this house!"

My dad was completely shattered. His decline was swift and steady from that day forward. And he continued to refuse all efforts to help . . . except for when he demanded help. When he hurt his back and would not do anything about it but complain, I picked him up to take him to see a good friend, a gifted chiropractor.

On the drive home, he said, "I don't like him or want to go back. I don't want your help. And this goddamn car of yours. The seats are too low."

I let it all just roll off my back, as always. When we pulled up to his house, he got out of the car and his pants fell down. He just stood there, in full view of the neighborhood, in his underwear.

"Well, aren't you gonna do something?" he snapped. "I can't bend down . . . help me."

I bit back a retort. I immediately pulled his pants up, and we went inside. This was a man who kept himself in great physical shape his whole life, dressed immaculately, and immediately called out a sloppy kid. This old man with his wrinkled pants around his ankles in his own driveway was miserable and no longer the man I had revered for decades. The man who had lived by certain codes of behavior all his life simply abandoned them. The towering figure of my life had finally quit; it was just too much for him. Alzheimer's disease was taking my dad along with my mom.

The day after Elaine's funeral, my sister Susie was still in town and said, "Well, let's go over to see Dad."

He'd attended her funeral service, but there had been no time to talk. I was still grief-stricken, in shock, fidgety . . . I couldn't seem to sit still. Not long into the visit, Dad looked at me and said, "Will you sit your damn ass down, stop getting up and down and wandering around. And you're talking too much, just shut it."

I blew up. I came *this close* to hitting my own father. My sister had to stop me as I walked toward him, fists clenched. I turned away and stormed outside, fuming, throwing things, trying to calm down . . . then I came back inside and let it all out. "I have had it with you. I just buried my wife! Look at Mom!"

She was sitting right there, blessedly unaware of Elaine's death and this latest storm around her.

"Really look at her, Dad. She doesn't know where she is. She doesn't know *who you are!* You've been a real bastard for a couple of years now. You don't appreciate anything I try to do. You didn't even call me when Elaine was sick. I can't believe that! I have had it with you!" and I started to walk out.

My mother's caregiver, Lahia, who had been with her since day one, raced after me, giving me the sign of the cross, urging, "Calm down, calm down, calm down."

I walked around the block twice to pull myself together and then got out of there.

I was already so stricken by Elaine's death. For the next seventy-eight days, Dad and I had no contact, the longest break of our lives. Then right around Thanksgiving, one of my brothers had had enough and set up a reconciliation meeting. We got together and talked, but it was awkward and tough. My relationship with Dad would never be the same. I had so much to grieve during these months after my wife's death.

Richard Leibner, my agent's father, called me on the phone to offer condolences. "Dave, listen . . . Please . . . don't die along with her. You still have many years left on this earth. I've known too many couples who were together as long as you and Elaine. When one dies, the other spouse is still living, but dies inside as well. Please, Dave, don't let that happen to you."

Wise words, and I took them to my broken heart.

When Elaine was very, very ill, I was sitting at her side one particularly hard day. "You know, Dave, we're going to have another grandbaby," she had said, the excitement overcoming the pain and drug haze.

"I know," I said. Matt had told us that Carrie was pregnant with their second child, and we knew it was going to be a girl.

Two and a half months after Elaine's death, Hallie Elaine was born—blond and blue-eyed, the image of her grandma. When I entered the hospital room to meet my new granddaughter, Carrie smiled at me from her bed. "I think Elaine was here with me because I had a much easier time delivering this baby," she said.

I liked to believe that was so. The pain mixed with the joy nearly brought me to my knees as I stared into that tiny, perfect face. I was here to enjoy this blessing; Elaine was not, and it broke me.

Gone but never to be forgotten—I would make sure of that. I decided that I was going to construct a memorial garden in Elaine's memory at our church. There was a large empty plot of grass just sitting outside the building. So I called the station desk. A longtime friend and terrific worker answered.

"Hey, remember that story we did a couple of weeks ago about memorial gardens? It mentioned a company who specializes in monuments and so forth—do you have their contact information?"

The highly efficient Terry Doyle gave me what I needed, and I called the company immediately. The monument company was located in Long Beach, not too far from where I lived. The church pastor, his wife, and I all met with their representatives for an entire day in their gorgeous building. I explained my idea for a memorial, and then said, "You know what, let's elaborate a little bit. How about a garden, a plaque, a fountain, a monument . . . oh, and maybe a small playground for the kids?"

The staff put in all the measurements and printed out stacks of fancy graphics. The estimate was a bit much, and the pastor was a bit deflated.

As we were walking back to our cars, I said, "Look, pastor. I'm not a filthy-rich guy, but I can handle this; I will handle this; it means that much to me. You give me the okay to build, I will cover the cost."

I appeared in front of the congregation to make my pitch and got the go-ahead. The company assigned me a really talented designer to work with, and we spoke frequently. I wanted everything to be perfect.

Meanwhile, back at the office, our news director Scott Diener had paid his respects at Elaine's funeral. We got along well, and I considered him a friend. I was unhappy when he got canned, but he was a pro and took it in stride. "Well, I just didn't hit those numbers, you know how it is in this business," he said, and headed back to St. Louis. On top of the world one day, gone the next. Enter Bill Dallman, who I would put in the top three of news directors I've ever worked with. Bill was a newsman's dream. He had worked as a reporter, and he treated people fairly. I prayed he would somehow, against all odds, be the last man standing.

Work was the best thing in the world for me. It kept me

occupied and distracted me from my grief over Elaine and my worries about my parents. At this point in my career, I rarely covered board of supervisors' meetings, but one day, I was assigned to a story in Los Angeles. While I was standing around waiting, I saw a young woman named Diandra, a former photographer for the *Long Beach Press-Telegram,* who now worked for LA County Public Works. I'd seen her around at news stories for years but had lost track of her. I was happy to run into her outside the boardroom. I gave her my number and said, "Give me a call, because I'm working on building a memorial garden for my late wife, and I need a photographer to document it all for me. You might be interested in the job."

I was lonely and antsy rattling around at home. At a certain point after Elaine's death, I told Tami that I was going to start dating again. "But I'm not going to date women my age," I told her. "I don't want anyone with kids, or step kids. I don't want anyone with an ex. I don't want a widow. Nothing." I did not want any hassle.

"Well, Father, that's certainly not leaving you much room," she pointed out. "You're going to have to find a really young woman."

Fine with me. I would give it a shot. Maybe . . . someday.

In 2010, the *LA Times* had come out with a truly scandalous exposé on the city of Bell, my beat at the time. A man named Robert Rizzo was city manager of this tiny blue-collar city where a quarter of the residents lived below the federal poverty line. Somehow, he managed to make a staggering $800,000 per year for doing this job . . . double the salary of the president of the United States—plus benefits worth another half a million . . . per year.

The sheer scale of the graft was breathtaking. Handpicked city council members in Bell were being paid a minimum of six grand a month. The chief of police in Bell was making $440,000 a year. One city councilman couldn't read or write English—he ran a little shop. It was a bombshell, but when the story broke, the station hadn't even wanted to cover it. Eventually, we did . . . and I learned far more than I ever wanted to know about Rizzo and his countless brazen schemes.

A minister was on his city council, so I asked him, "Didn't you think it was a little unusual to receive a check for six thousand dollars every month?"

"I thought it was a gift from God," he said piously.

Charges started flying. Rizzo eventually pled no contest to sixty-nine charges, everything from conspiracy to misappropriation of public funds and falsification of public records.

Now, a few years later, the huge, complicated case had finally come to trial, and I was there every day to cover it from day one. Was Rizzo ever a character. The man must have weighed 400 pounds, and he was only about five-foot-five. He was practically square.

One day, he was sitting on a bench outside the boardroom and wandered off. A reporter asked, "Hey, where's Rizzo?"

"I think he left the building," another reporter answered.

"No, come on, he didn't leave the building, he *is* the building," I joked.

One day I ran into Rizzo in the bathroom. "I remember you," he said. "I lived in Huntington Beach when you covered Orange County. I was the assistant city manager then. You know, I'd love to talk to you and give you my side of the story, but my attorney would quit on me on the spot. He can't stand you. So I gotta pretend I hate your guts. I gotta tell you, this is boring as shit. I can't stand sitting here day after day listening to all this boring crap." He waddled out.

It was true; Rizzo's attorney hated me with a passion. One day in court, Rizzo had an anxiety attack and had to be taken out of the courtroom. I was doing a live shot when, suddenly, coming out of the elevator behind me was Rizzo on a stretcher. I immediately ran after him, peppering him with questions non-stop. I swear, when they loaded defendant Rizzo into an ambulance, the whole vehicle sank. Noticeably.

In a federal case like Rizzo's, you practically had to disrobe to get inside the courtroom. I was standing in the long security line one morning with his attorney right behind me. "Do you really think you're some great reporter because you ask such insulting questions?" he asked me. "Who you gonna massacre today in your big, booming voice?" He kept needling me.

I tried to ignore him and keep my cool. Finally, I turned to him. "I'm telling you, today's not the day."

He kept it up, through the security line, onto the elevator. As we stepped into the hallway on the way to the courtroom, I said, "Listen, you son of a bitch. Today is an anniversary I don't want to remember. On this day one year ago, I brought my wife Elaine home from the hospital. I thought she was going to live. But she died. I don't need your shit, OK?"

He walked away without another word.

Rizzo wound up being sentenced to twelve years in prison for tax fraud; he was also ordered to make nearly $9 million in restitution to the city he'd almost bankrupted. Elaine was gone and nothing would never be the same, but the world kept right on turning.

CHAPTER TWENTY-TWO
LIFE DOES GO ON

FEBRUARY 2013 HAD BEEN THE SINGLE WORST month of my life. Elaine so desperately ill, my sixty-fifth birthday spent at her bedside convinced she was about to die, the silence from my father . . . all these memories were so painful. I was determined to put that misery behind me and wipe these distressing events out and dedicate Elaine's Garden in February 2014. I kept my designer busy!

Because of unusually heavy rains, we didn't quite make my self-imposed deadline, but the dedication was held in March. The groundbreaking ceremony was all that I hoped it would be. Friends and loved ones showed up in force once again to celebrate Elaine's life. The monument itself was simple and elegant: a green bowl with a constantly running fountain and plaque. I had been thinking along more elaborate lines, but Tami overruled me. "Mom would like something simple," she said, and she was right.

The garden was lush and gorgeous. The entire memorial area was enclosed by a wrought-iron fence that looked like it had always been there. I watched as my grandkids frolicked on the new playground and felt that familiar tug at my heart. So grateful to have them in my life . . . so crushed that their grandmother wasn't there to share them with me. And yet . . .

Diandra took hundreds of photographs at Elaine's dedication ceremony. That was the day a working friendship began to take a turn. A breath of fresh air, completely unexpected, blew into my life. Several months later, when I told Tami that I was dating Diandra, my daughter said, "She's quite a bit younger, isn't she, Father?"

"Yes, quite a bit," I acknowledged. "I really don't know by exactly how much."

"Oh BS," said my daughter, the lawyer. "You know precisely how old she is!"

The great thing was that my family all knew her from the dedication and gorgeous book she put together . . . and they approved.

Diandra's mother was Japanese and her father Chinese, making her an unusual combination. When I came along, I was the literal bull in their family china closet. As Diandra said, more than once, "Sometimes, Dave, they don't quite get you."

Diandra was tough, a volunteer firefighter; she kept me in line. My "fame" and being recognized every time we were out didn't impress her in the least. "You're just my boyfriend," she said.

Diandra had never married. Having emerged from a long-term, live-in relationship, she had also decided she didn't want to have children. She was perfect for me! Even I would concede that she was much too young, frankly, but we got along so well. I told her, "You screwed up my plans. You know, a babe a month, a playboy existence in LA. Then you came along!"

She just laughed.

Diandra did so much to bring my usual high spirits back. The best thing about her company was that she understood that Elaine remained a huge part of my life. She did not mind talking about my wife and my sorrow and guilt about her illness. She was entirely supportive, not at all jealous of a woman who had passed away. She allowed me to grieve on my own timetable. I was lucky, and I knew it.

Diandra fully supported my next big idea: a yearly scholarship for students who planned to become teachers in Elaine's name. Education had been her passion; I wanted to help some kids who planned to take up the profession. I established a $10,000 prize awarded at graduation to a senior headed off to become a teacher, and meeting the finalists, seeing their young, idealistic faces and passion for learning, brought me great happiness. It was a public fund; donations welcome, but I was more than happy to fund it myself, in perpetuity, even after my own death. Another way to keep Elaine's memory alive.

More happiness was on the way. Tami loved a glass of wine, and one night when we were all out to dinner, I noticed she wasn't having any. Immediately I guessed: she was pregnant again. Once again, a long, difficult pregnancy for her, and once again a surprise about whether it would be a boy or a girl.

Tami called me one afternoon as her delivery date drew near. "Father," she said, "the caesarian is scheduled for Mom's birthday. I didn't even bring up timing . . . they just chose that date," my daughter continued, nearly crying. And sure enough, Henry arrived—a boy!—on what would have been Elaine's sixty-sixth birthday. My cup runneth over.

Dad, the man who had taught me every important life lesson, was crumbling. He had shown me how to live. Now pretty much a recluse, he showed me how not to die.

Al Lopez was a giant of a man. He loved us. He was a legend in my mind . . . not to mention his community. Dad was everything that I could hope to emulate as a family man and provider. This man with a high school education and his own small shop managed to produce eight successful kids: my brother Danny, a judge; Jimmy, a cop; Susie, who owned a successful business with her husband in Oregon; Victor, a commercial painter; and Tony, the baby, who followed in my footsteps and became a newscaster in Sacramento.

Along the way, Dad saved enough money so that my mother would live in her own house until the day she died, a solemn promise he made to her over and over. But he simply couldn't handle my mother's dreadful illness. Alzheimer's took her away from him, and killed him too . . . slowly. He kept asking why. I had no answers.

Dad was quite secretive about his personal life and health; he only shared what he wanted with a very few family members. "Whaddya want?" he used to bark when anyone called to check on them. No small talk, no pleasantries, certainly no health updates.

It was obvious he was faltering in every way, but it was still a shock to get a phone call from my brother Jimmy while I was packing for a trip one afternoon. He said that it looked like our dad wasn't going to make it through the day. I hung up in shock. We had just received a doctor's note earlier that week after his checkup, and his blood pressure and heart rate were in great shape. Dad died that day in his own home . . . on New Year's Eve 2015.

I felt that my dad, like Elaine, needed some kind of memorial. A school now stood where his shop had been for so many years, surrounded by a fence and a brick wall. I approached the city of South Gate and the school to ask permission to post a plaque commemorating his business. The city did me one better: they designated the spot a South Gate historical landmark.

That winter we held a big celebration of my dad's life and posted his official plaque on the exact spot his shop had stood for decades. The speech I gave was straight from the heart. I would always, always miss Dad . . . the man he had been, not the shadow he became the last few years of his life. Maybe that was his final lesson for me.

Those bosses of mine kept getting younger. It's hard to think of yourself as a grizzled veteran, but there I was: the longest-running reporter at Channel 2—by decades. It was me who was last man standing!

We came in to work one day to hear that stellar boss Bill was no longer with us. In came a woman named Tara Finestone, promoted from her position as assistant news director. Tara forced me, reluctantly, onto social media. Diener had tried, Bill Dallman didn't care either way, but Tara refused to take no for an answer. I was going to move into the new century and have a presence on social media, period. She got me onto Facebook and Twitter, and I eventually got the hang of it, though I dragged my feet, kicking and screaming, for a long time.

But this was the new way of the world, and I got with it. *Never too old to learn something new*, I reminded myself. Now reporters were chasing stories because people tweeted out that there was a man on top of city hall with a gun, for example. Reporters with cameramen would race out, and it would turn out to be a man on top of city hall with a mop. It all seemed a bit backward and crazy to me.

And was it just me, or was chasing down a story in traffic-choked Southern California getting harder every year? The one phrase I dreaded most hearing on the job was, "But you're the closest!" One time I was in the San Fernando Valley when I got a call. "Listen, something big is happening, a woman was carjacked, we need you to get to the scene, now."

"Where is she?" I asked.

"Temecula."

"You know I am in the Valley, right?" But I made it . . . seventy miles through late-afternoon traffic, fighting every inch of the way. It would be sheer delight to never hear that phrase again, ever again in my life. Where was the "We're sending you, because we trust you to get the story right"? Nope, just "Hurry, you're closest."

I could see the business changing dramatically. I wasn't thrilled about going out to do stories about people with awesome video from their Ring camera. It also got harder and harder to get people to talk on camera. People had become reluctant to speak their minds. In the old days, people were happy to speak on the news. Minor irritations that had rolled off my back for decades were starting to grate. I had a lot on my plate.

I was the family member in charge of my mom's well-being after Dad died, and I took this charge seriously. I saw my mother all the time, and I called her every day, even when I was on a story out of town or overseas. I checked in daily, though I never knew how much my words sank in. She had marvelous caretakers, thanks to Dad's estate. She was given the very best of care in her own home, as promised. This became a problem as the years dragged on.

I felt guilty that all the excellent care my mother received had prolonged her life longer than she should have or wanted to stay on this earth. The "real" Mom was long gone. I constantly worried about whether I was doing the right thing and whether we should put her in a home. In the end, I couldn't do it. She would live out her life comfortably in her own home and die there. So, she withered away, locked in her own little world.

Some days it seemed she would go on forever, till she was 110, for all I knew. I used to joke with her caregiver Rosa: "101-year-old son visits 121-year-old Mother." I wasn't really joking. It eventually came to the point where I just couldn't take it anymore. I was only emotionally able to handle a visit with Mom in person once a week—every Sunday before going to church, as always. I couldn't stay very long; twenty minutes to a half hour or so was all I could take as the disease continued its relentless march. I found some support from wonderful people at the Alzheimer's Foundation and had yet another great cause to promote.

The years were flying by. I had my very own little player to coach in Henry . . . we worked out together every week starting when he was just a toddler. He was pure delight. Mom was still hanging on. Diandra and I had been happily together for four years. At that point, she had a talk with me: about our arrangement, my intentions, and so forth and so on . . . which she was perfectly entitled to do. I had truly never envisioned getting married again, but we were happy . . . and I loved her. A wedding was on.

I put up a bit of a fight. "Marriage does screw up my plan," I reminded her.

"What plan is that?"

"You remember . . . Joe Louis had the Bum of the Month Club; I was going to have the New Babe Every Six Months Club. Getting married will put an end to that dream."

"Oh, please, you were not." Diandra had my number. She was the one. How lucky was I, to find another "one"?

Seeing Mom was so painful. She got so skinny toward the end; she could no longer even eat. I was afraid to hug her as it might break her brittle bones. I'd sit in the car after my weekly visit before I took off for church and just cry. I always told her how much I loved her, without fail. Toward the end, after I put hospice care in place, I began to whisper in her ear, "Mom, it's okay if you want to go. We are going to be okay, go ahead. You don't need to live like this anymore."

Diandra and I planned our wedding, to be held on a Sunday afternoon. Exactly one week before the ceremony on my regular visit, I could just tell. I told her caretaker, "She's not long for this world." Gently, I held her as tight as I dared. I said to her, "Mom, I've been coming here to see you every Sunday for the last eight years. Every single Sunday. It's okay to die. It's time to go. But did you have to pick this week?"

I had to wonder how much she really heard and understood. Maybe her timing and letting go was intentional, because two brothers and a sister had flown in from out of town for the wedding. So we were all there when she passed—one last gathering for all of us. Who knows? She died on Thursday, the 28th of February . . . and Diandra and I got married three days later.

Diandra would have been happy with a service at the local community center. But I wanted to give her a celebration to remember. She made me happy; I wanted to make her happy. We had a crowded, meaningful, and most of all fun ceremony and celebration up in Silverado Canyon, above the city of Orange. We then took off on a quick little honeymoon to Monterey—just a couple of days—and came right back. In my absence, my brother

Danny had made most of the arrangements for Mom's funeral. They held a marvelous service that was simply beautiful.

Al and Tilly Lopez, my parents, married sixty-three years, seven months, and twelve days. Buried next to each other, they were finally reunited, forever.

Diandra liked to watch home improvements shows on HGTV and the like. She decided to build a picnic table, of all things; a buddy of ours lent us all the equipment we would ever need from his personal woodshop. Bob Tarlau and his wife, Barbara, were master craftsmen and happy to help. So was I, but as Dad had discovered fifty years earlier, I was not a handy guy. I made a living with my voice, not my hands. This bright idea of Diandra's . . . I tried to contribute by sanding over the weeks. It was my childhood all over again. The project turned out magnificently—no thanks to me.

One rainy day when I was pretty much just getting in the way, I said, "I've got to go." It was a drizzly day, and as soon as I pulled up to the cemetery, it began to pour buckets, just sluicing down in sheets. I raced to the gravesite and deposited my weekly flowers. This is something I have to do—every Friday and Sunday, rain or shine, no matter what. This is when I talk to Mom, Dad, and Elaine.

"Well, pin a rose on your nose!" Dad always used say if we'd done something particularly noteworthy. I buy a single perfect red rose, put it on his grave, and say, "Dad . . . here's your rose." These biweekly visits are part of my regular routine, which Diandra knew about and approved from day one.

On another day, Diandra accompanied me on my rounds and said, as we were walking back to the car, "You weren't very polite with your father; you should go back and apologize." She made me go back and say I was sorry for my tone and for not being respectful enough. I did so, sincerely.

I visited on Dad's birthday and my parents' anniversary and special times I wanted to feel his presence. My mom and Elaine get flowers twice a week, Dad gets his rose, and I visit Elaine's Garden every day. To me this isn't sad or too much . . . it's important that I show respect and honor to these people. For better and for worse, they made me.

CHAPTER TWENTY-THREE

You Want Me to . . . Tweet?

AS LEGENDARY TELEVISION PRODUCER DON HEWITT, creator of
60 Minutes once said, "I'm a twentieth-century man being taken
into the twenty-first century, kicking and screaming." I'm with
Don. I was never going to be that reporter who would shoot a
story on my handheld device, edit it, and transmit it back to
the station . . . which was clearly where my beloved business
was heading. I found the job itself hard enough—believe me, if
it was easy, everyone would jump on camera and report. And
many do, on YouTube!

Here's what I have to say: Network reporters make good money because it takes a specific talent to boil down a story into ninety seconds or two and a half minutes in a clear, concise, and engaging way. That's old-school reporting, not commentating or opining, though that has certainly changed as well. So many young reporters today think they know it all. They arrive in LA from Poughkeepsie, Illinois, and think they got a lock on it.

It's not that I begrudge progress. When I started in this business, it was still on film; reporters were accompanied by a cameraman and soundman for every single shoot. We had to be careful not to stay too long at the scene because someone had to drop off the film, return to pick up the reels once it was developed, and then take it to the station to be cut! OK, enough about what I'm sure sounds dangerously close to horse-and-buggy days.

These days, fewer and fewer people even watch the evening news; they all get their news off social media. Influencers, TikTok, streaming . . . blah blah blah. In this new media world, reporters are judged primarily on how many followers they have on social media. I was old school and couldn't make myself care about being an "influencer." I didn't want to believe that all this "progress" was getting to me, but it was. Maybe it was really, finally time to go.

I had a carefully thought-out plan . . . to retire in early 2021. I wanted to cover the All-Star game at Dodger Stadium, the political conventions, the opening of SoFi Stadium in Inglewood, and the 2020 presidential election and the inauguration. The plan was to officially retire on my seventy-third birthday in February 2021. I was going to ask my agent to put all this in writing, to be absolutely sure I would be allowed to cover these particular events . . . but he never got the chance, because of the global pandemic.

I had seen our nation in upheaval before. I had never imagined anything could top 1968 with the assassinations of Dr. Martin Luther King Jr. and Robert Kennedy. The beginning of the end of the Vietnam conflict after the Tet Offensive, with violent protests across the country. Black athletes raising their fists on the Olympic podium to protest racial discrimination in sports. And then came 2020 and a nation politically divided right down the middle.

And *then* along came COVID-19, which turned everyone's life upside down. It sure as hell affected the way media covered news. I was watching television on a Sunday during the pandemic's early days, as a government spokesperson droned on about "Anyone over the age of sixty-five is required to stay home . . ." I was still out there hustling hard at seventy-two. Still, as an older cancer survivor, I had to worry a bit about my immunity to this crazy virus that was poised to shut down California entirely.

The next day, I said to our associate news director, "Technically, I'm not even supposed to be out here, but obviously I can't stay home and do this job. From now on, I am going to work with one person exclusively, just to avoid any risk." My boss agreed; afterward, I called Anna DeVencenty, a talented young camerawoman/producer. We got along great, masked, distanced, and all. She became my full-time person throughout the pandemic.

But the ZOOM, ZAP, and ZIP of it all wore me down. The way they covered the news was becoming so foreign to me. So much is lost with this Zoom, internet, and long-distance stuff. Politicians today can hide behind these screens; reporters just can't get to them like we used to. It seemed the days of grilling politicians face to face at town halls and chasing people down corridors was over. The nation was in a crisis, and so was the news business covering it. Like everyone else, the station was bleeding money. I knew big changes were in the air.

Diandra and I had just returned from a trip overseas when COVID-19 really hit hard. I was worn out and jet lagged on the night of CBS's annual Christmas party. I had not yet met our new general manager, so I knew attendance wasn't optional. This was GM number twenty, in case you are still counting. Diandra wasn't feeling great either, but we showed up at the gala on a Saturday night at a posh country club in Toluca Lake. I met Jay Howell, the new GM, and presented him with a beautiful tie straight from Hong Kong. Then we cut the night short and went home early.

After a sleepless night, during which Diandra told me every thirty minutes she couldn't sleep, she got out of bed at 4:30 am and said, "I'm going to the cabin," referring to her previous residence, which she'd held on to. Now that's a great thing, to marry a woman with her own house! I slept in happily. At 9 am, I was far from refreshed, and I was facing a big week starting the next morning. I decided to take it very easy the rest of my last day off . . . then my phone rang. A helicopter with superstar Kobe Bryant aboard had gone down.

At noon, I got the official call confirming Kobe was on that flight and had died in the crash, along with his daughter, other parents and teammates, and the pilot. My God, was this ever a huge story. The Black Mamba, pride of the Lakers for so long, cut down in the prime of his life . . . and the unbearably tragic news of his daughter and other young players being killed on a trip to a game? All of Southern California was electrified.

But there was a problem. I didn't want to race out to Calabasas to the crash site. For once in my life, I wasn't up to it. I said to my boss, "You know, I'll work this story hard for as long as it goes, but I'm truly under the weather right now. I know if I work today, I'll wear myself out; I'd rather be fresh for this all week." I hated to beg off from such a momentous sports-related story, but I knew my limits. My boss, Paul Button, agreed and assigned me to Staples Center bright and early the next morning.

In the old days—even five years earlier—no exhaustion or illness in the world would have prevented me from racing out to that scene. Something in me had truly changed. As it turned out, I was told the next day by a colleague who was there that very little news was available in the immediate aftermath of the crash. The scene was chaos, completely disorganized, the community in shock . . . the reporters all left the initial scene highly frustrated with nothing to show.

I covered the crash, Kobe Bryant's life and career, and his moving memorial ceremony for the next week. And the whole week I kept telling myself, "You know, I keep thinking about retirement. Maybe the time is now."

Then our HR woman called me one day in early May, asking if I was available to talk with Jay later that day.

"What did I do, Maggie?" I asked.

"Why does everyone ask me that?" she responded.

"Because you're HR, he's the station manager, and that's never good!" I racked my brains, thinking about what I could possibly have done lately. I knew I hadn't groped anyone. But I had peed in paper cups that I held in my trunk on assignment. Could someone have seen me?

At 3 pm the phone rang. It was just Maggie, Jay, and me.

"Are you alone, in a private location?" Maggie started.

"I didn't mean to do it! She said I could! I thought we were friends!" I said, opening with a joke as always. "This is all a big misunderstanding!"

They both laughed. "We love you, Dave," my GM Jay said. "You're doing a great job, you're the best reporter we've ever had! But we have an offer for you to consider."

Bottom line: the station was spilling red ink. If I agreed to retire early, they would pay me through the summer plus a very attractive bonus. A significant goodbye gift, if you will.

I was surprised at the numbers I was hearing. "What's the catch?" I asked.

"There isn't one."

I was still leery—just like Dad was when the city bought his building.

"This is just for you, Dave, because of your seniority. Forty-three years."

"Let me ask you this: how long do I have to give you an answer?" I asked.

"By tomorrow, this is a one-time offer. If you say no, we'll take you off the list, and it's business as usual. You'll stay here as long as you want. Everything will be fine."

"If I say no, can you guarantee me that six or even three months from now, you won't ask me to take a pay cut?"

Silence. That was my answer. "You just answered my question. I'll get back to you by tomorrow." I called my agent and accountant; they were both happily surprised.

My agent was floored. "Damnit, Dave, I hope you said yes before they change their minds. You were going to retire in January, six months from now, and you were going to walk out of there with a handshake and maybe a gift card from Gelson's! I am on this!"

Adam jumped on the phone and started wrapping up that deal, quickly. The next morning, I called and formally accepted early retirement. Then I waited for a month, which was excruciating. During those thirty days, the station fired three anchors, four writers, three photographers, and couple of producers. It was a complete massacre, and all the fallen got was their two weeks' pay. No bonus, just a brisk goodbye and good luck.

Once again, my lifelong luck held, right through to the surprise end of my career. Though I hasten to remind those who might resent such a story during COVID-19 times that I was an exception. That final check had been paid for, time and time again, with forty-eight years of getting the story . . . period, end of story. Failure was never an option for me. I had delivered for more than half a century on the air. It was time to say goodbye.

I could not have asked for a happier ending; I wasn't even sad on my last day of work. I could look back with no regrets . . . and did so!

So, I spent a grand total of forty-eight years on television, and if you count my days as a newspaper reporter, from back when my career officially began in 1964, I chased stories for fifty-six years. It would be impossible to put between two covers, on a limited number of pages, all the funny, sad, awe-inspiring, or creepy moments I witnessed as a newsman and will always carry with me. In these pages, I tried to hit the highlights, but there were so many more . . .

Me, barely more than a Mexican kid myself, sharing a meal with a bunch of hardcore Ku Klux Klanners. They kept saying, "Just give me the white meat," as they passed chicken around. "I don't want any dark meat!" Fortunately, producer Jim Kennedy was by my side to produce an in-depth piece on this shadowy group . . . resulting in one hell of a special and awards for both Jim and me.

The PSA crash in September of 1978—the first time I ever smelled a dead body up close; it is an odor like no other. To this day, that was the most horrifying scene of carnage on a grand scale I have ever witnessed.

Another lost little boy. This one named Jeffrey Vargo—he wandered over to a fireworks stand and just like that was kidnapped. His body was found three days later, but it took nearly thirty years for authorities to find his killer. The agony his mom and dad endured for three decades will always haunt me.

The first time I saw a struggling, crying, heroin-addicted

newborn in the throes of withdrawal. No heart could remain unmoved at this sight.

My first execution. I didn't actually witness his death, but a criminal named Harris had killed a young boy in San Diego and was put to death for his crime; I covered the entire story and was outside the prison when they pulled the switch.

The trial of Richard de Hoyas, who had murdered a young girl in Santa Ana; this killer had the disquieting habit of barking like a dog when nervous. It was eerie to hear what you would swear was a loud, disturbed dog in the somber courtroom.

The riveting case of the Han sisters in San Diego: identical twins, but one was good and one was evil. The evil one was eventually put on trial for her crimes in an incredibly twisted family saga.

The van Dams in nearby Sabre Springs, whose seven-year-old daughter was kidnapped out of her bedroom one Friday night. Danielle van Dam's blood was found in engineer David Westerfield's motor home; he was an engineer who lived two doors down. The motive? Westerfield was angry that he was not invited to a swinger party at the parents' home.

The father whose teenage daughter drowned in a lake while vacationing in Mexico, but the Mexican authorities refused to release her body. He had to literally spirit her remains across the border. I interviewed him at their pleasant family home after he snuck her dead body home in the back of his station wagon.

The callousness of a young punk named Eddie Charles, who killed his mother, his father, and his brother and was put on trial for the murders. In court, they played him on tape saying to his elderly bereaved grandfather: "You're an old man. Why don't you confess to these crimes, then I can get out of here and live the rest of my life?" He was convicted and given the death penalty, though he remains imprisoned.

Of course, it wasn't always so dark. There were always the animals. I remember Beep the goose, whose beak got bitten off in a fight. Devoted doctors did their best to fix it; I did a live shot right outside the hospital during surgery. The new beak worked great . . . but then Beep ran into a coyote and shortly afterward Beep stopped beeping.

And the people I got to meet, up close and personal! I interviewed Jimmy Roosevelt, FDR's son. Babe Ruth's daughter talked to me before an All-Star game in Angel Stadium about her famous father's legacy. I spoke to Reverend Robert Schuller the day his famous Crystal Cathedral officially opened. He nudged me in the elevator on the way up to the very top and said, "What do you think of my glass shack, Dave?" How terribly nervous I was to meet and interview Billy Graham . . . just to be in the presence of someone who is so much more than a mere mortal human being. This was BILLY GRAHAM!

Seeing Tiger Woods and his dad at the dedication of the Tiger Woods Foundation and noting the visibly strong bond they shared; it was obvious Tiger adored his father.

Nelson Mandela's triumphant news conference after he was let out of prison after twenty-seven years. The legendary Bob Hope, when a ship was named after him in Long Beach Harbor. He was in his nineties at the time and still just as bright, spry, and engaging as could be.

I had hundreds of these encounters. They go on and on and on . . . with sports-related stories, of course, always nearest and dearest to my heart.

Richard Nixon laid low after he left the White House in disgrace. I got a tip that he would be attending an Angels baseball game and positioned myself so that he would have to walk right by me. "Mr. President," I called out as he walked by, "do you like baseball?" He and his entourage of bodyguards stopped for two seconds. "I love baseball," he said, then kept moving. One line, but that didn't stop the station from touting this as "Our very own Dave Lopez gets an exclusive interview with the former president . . ." all day!

Frank McCourt, right in the middle of his divorce hearing, telling me that he would not only remain the owner of the Dodgers next year but for every year to come. His ride was held up at a red light across the street and couldn't get to him. Carl Stein, my cameraman, wouldn't let McCourt out of his sight, and I kept peppering him with questions. The man was stuck . . . and furious!

The 1971 Rose Bowl game, where Jim Plunkett led Stanford to a huge upset over the Ohio State Buckeyes. I filed my story and headed to the parking lot, to discover that someone had stolen my battery right out of the car. There was no AAA roadside assistance or Uber back then. Somehow, some way, I convinced someone—at night, on New Year's Day—to drive me to a gas station, where I got a new battery and managed to have it installed. I got home around 1 am, fuming. I never covered another Rose Bowl game.

So many Super Bowl games. NBA playoffs. This hometown fan was present for the first and only time the Angels won the World Series!

But, in the end, doesn't it all just come down to . . . people? I was inside the vast movie theater the day they held Michael Jackson's funeral: the enormous audience was bereft. Later I visited Michael's elementary school, where various teachers and others remembered him as the most talented, charming little boy. So moving.

The well-off but otherwise ordinary citizens who lost their entire life savings to Bernie Madoff. Everything they'd worked for . . . gone in an instant.

Wandering around in the aftermath of Hurricane Rita, trying to figure out exactly what I was I was supposed to be doing there in Galveston, Texas. Twenty-four hours into our assignment, we were lost, starving, and firmly stuck in the mud. We got pulled out by the kindest Texans, who said simply, "Your buddy there is wearing that cap." They nodded toward my cameraman, who had on a John Deere tractor hat in this mostly agrarian community.

I remember the time I was interviewing an outstanding young track star at Fullerton. Someone tipped off the press that she was also working as an exotic dancer at a local gentlemen's club. As she said to me, "A girl's gotta make a living!"

So where do you stop? All I know is that the way I made my living was an incredible ride. I feel extremely fortunate to have witnessed these events and so many more. Clearly, I could write another book, but let me stop before I bore you too much!

So many people who knew me well predicted, "You're going to hate retirement, Dave . . ." It is true; I was never one to sit around the house, even on days off. Still, I manage to keep myself busy. I have my grandchildren and their various events. Diandra and I have beaten all the odds about marriages with large age differences and plan to live happily ever after. And I have Elaine's scholarship to administer, my weekly Facebook mini-broadcast post with producer Anna DeVecenty, and of course my rounds.

I visit the gravesites of my parents and Elaine frequently . . . as I said, some think too frequently. A fellow at the Y I attend approached me once and asked me why I went to my wife's gravesite every day. I told him, "It gives me comfort. I like to go, check in, make sure it's all tidy and clean. That all is well. And I can talk with her."

So, I sit in Elaine's Garden every day and bring flowers twice a week, every Friday and Sunday, for the graves. And I talk to those who are no longer with me . . . and to God. Not once have I ever asked, "Why, God, why did you do this?" I kept my word to accept what came, and I kept it, though it wasn't easy. It still isn't easy.

As for my parents, I know we did everything humanly possible during Mom's long, terrible decline. I kept Dad's word, something I know he would truly appreciate. It's not my position to ask God why. Instead, I offer thanks . . . for my amazing adventures and all who shared them with me, including viewers.

I still get recognized pretty regularly when I'm out . . . "You eat it up!" Diandra accused the other night at our small local diner, after a number of greetings and photos.

To which I replied, "Of course I do, I'm not going to lie! It's very nice to be recognized!"

I hope in this book I have managed to recognize those who made this such a wonderful life.

ACKNOWLEDGMENTS

THIS BOOK WOULD NOT HAVE BEEN POSSIBLE without Julie McCarron, who listened to countless hours of my stories and turned them into this manuscript. I wanted more than a rehash of anecdotes about life as a TV reporter, and she delivered; I thank her from the bottom of my heart. The Book Couple, Carol and Gary Rosenberg, put together the beautiful book you now hold in your hands. I thank all three of them for holding my hand and walking me through the entire publication process.

Writing a book is a labor of love, and many helped:

Doug Krikorian, who has been there every step of the way for 45 years; we are two peas in a pod. Thank you for a masterful foreword.

My great friend Bob Tarlau, who encouraged me throughout the writing of this book and made so many spot-on recommendations.

My old boss and news director Jose Rios . . . I'd go to work for you again in a second! I could not have done my book—or my job—without you.

Joel Fallon, who told me I should write a book. Here it is! And a special nod to mom Nina Fallon, who showed me the correct way to fill out an expense report (though I still managed to get in trouble!).

I could never list everyone who helped me along the way, but I must single out a few special people:

Alicelynn Cockrill has been a godsend to all in our family, especially me. She and Elaine were like sisters, and Alicelynn will never know just how important she is to all of us. I thank you for all the help so generously offered over the years.

Carl Stein, whom I can never repay for the solace he provided in the dark days after Elaine died. Apart from being a friend, for years he made me look so much better than I was.

I had the pleasure of working with some tremendously talented photographers over the years. There's not room enough to list them all, but a heartfelt tribute to those who are no longer with us:

Vic Nastasia, who was so helpful and caring.

Don Menzel, a top-notch pro who made me a much better reporter.

Johnny Brazell, aka Razzle Dazzle. Johnny was never without a joke and smile; he showed me how to enjoy life.

To the families of Vic, Don, and Johnny: you were blessed to have these outstanding men in your lives. I miss them every day.

My old partner Wilson Posey, who stuck by my side for more than twenty years deserves a special shout-out.

Joel Takarsh, Vic's partner in crime for many, many years. Thank you for all the good times.

The PPAGLA (Press Photographers Association of Greater Los Angeles) made me an honorary member. I could not be prouder and will carry this achievement close to my heart, always.

To the memory of Mike Daniels, a terrific writer who made a difference early on.

Lou Varella, who taught this kid reporter so much back in the early days.

Ruben Green, who retired many years ago but taught me so much.

A toast to the late, iconic Karl Fleming and all his Southern sayings. Anyone who ever had the privilege will never forget working alongside him.

Lorraine Hillman, who encouraged me when I received yet another letter saying I wasn't "quite ready" for CBS. She was always there to tell me, "Hang in there, you'll work there one day." I made it, Lorraine!

John Vincent, my cerebral better half. Our wide-ranging conversations are a delight; let's keep them going along with our friendship.

Mark Dunn, what a pro. I was there when you first started and when you beat me to retirement! I could never thank you or your dad enough for all you have done for me.

The Ray Boys: Rey Hernandez, bless his soul, and Ray Armendariz. Two guys who never met a challenge they couldn't overcome . . . thank you for everything.

Eric Leonard, up-and-coming young reporter who was a long-time fixture at KFI and now works at Channel 4. Such a bright future lies ahead!

Terry Doyle, who did a terrific job on the desk and in every other way. Never underestimate your talents, my friend.

Rod Foster, who worked the desk for so many years and along the way became a true friend.

Anselmo Perez, who helped in so many ways in that same capacity.

Marti Guerrero, a great writer and great friend.

Paul Button, erstwhile managing editor and assistant news director—A true class act, one of the finest executives I ever worked with. Same goes for Rick Brown, a true gentleman who quietly helped me in so many ways.

I must single out Van Gordon Sauter, one of the twenty-two general managers I worked for, who was and remains a treasure. I still have some of the memos you sent me . . . "all good" and I appreciate them.

Pat Harvey, who probably doesn't remember meeting my

mother one night. She made such an impression that forever after my mom would remind me, "Say hi to Pat Harvey for me!" A dream.

Dave Bryan, old buddy and one of the best reporters around. I cherish our history and our friendship.

Wyatt Hart, the most colorful public relations man I ever worked with in the sheriff's department. I could write an entire book about you!

Brad Gates, longtime OC sheriff, so kind, helpful and instrumental in me getting the story.

Speaking of PR people, Jim Amormino is the top of the top. How much fun did we have seeing our stories come to fruition? I will always cherish these memories.

Tom Martin, world-class private investigator and my dear friend. He offered insight into how to tell better stories and more gossip than I could ever use.

Mike Schroeder, I could never repay all that you have done. Hope one day the USC football program gets back on track.

Scott Bovitz, lifesaver. You taught me everything I needed to know about the Dodger bankruptcy, and I thank you.

Bill Steiner—One of the kindest, most giving people I've ever known; working with you and the Orangewood Foundation was my pleasure.

Bill DeWitt, from my old hometown of South Gate. One time Council Member and Mayor. So instrumental in assisting my family as we honored the memory of our father. We go back so far, share so many memories. A true gem.

Anna DeVencenty, who put up with so much from me, especially during the last days of the pandemic. Anna, you are the consummate professional. I appreciate all you have so cheerfully done (and do) for me.

These final four men hold a special place in my heart. The good Lord has already taken them home, and life without them will never be the same.

Cliff Gewecke, who didn't have a large family or children of his own. To his brother and nieces and nephews, please know that without Cliff, there would be no Dave Lopez, reporter.

Steve Crawford, with whom I spoke every morning for years as he worked the desk at Channel 2. Always quick with a joke or sarcastic aside, a true friend in this cutthroat business.

Pete Noyes, who played such a big role in the book, because of his outsize influence on my career and growth. All those who survive Pete, that giant of a man, will always revere him.

Raul Ramos, undersheriff of Orange County for years. To his wife, Ruth, and entire family: I cannot tell you how much I learned from Raul. It was a privilege to have him in my life.

May God rest all their souls.

If I have hurt anyone's feelings by not mentioning them, I sincerely apologize. I am one of those fortunate people who was lucky enough to have so many amazing friends and colleagues along the way; I am so grateful they all came into my life.

About the Author

DAVE LOPEZ is a retired news reporter who has won virtually every award in broadcasting and journalism over his distinguished career reporting on the air in Southern California, including nine Emmys and the Joe Quinn Award for Lifetime Achievement from the Los Angeles Press Club.

A native Angeleno, Dave and his late wife, Elaine, raised two children in Downey, where he was a noted youth coach for many years. He currently lives in Long Beach with wife, Diandra, and dotes on his four grandchildren. His mini-broadcasts can be seen on Facebook and Twitter @cbsladavelopez.